Green Asia

Economic development in Asia is associated with expanding urbanism, overconsumption, and a steep growth in living standards. At the same time, rapid urbanisation, changing class consciousness, and a new rural–urban divide in the region have led to fundamental shifts in the way ecological concerns are articulated politically and culturally. Moreover, these changes are often viewed through a Western moralistic lens, which at the same time applauds Asia's economic growth as the welcome reviver of a floundering world economy and simultaneously condemns this growth as encouraging hyperconsumerism and a rupture with more natural ways of living. This book presents an analysis of a range of practices and activities from across Asia that demonstrate that people in Asia are alert to ecological concerns, that they are taking action to implement new styles of green living, and that Asia offers interesting alternatives to narrow Anglo-American models of sustainable living. Subjects explored include eco-tourism in the Philippines, green co-operatives in Korea, the importance of "tradition" within Asian discourses of sustainability, and much more.

Tania Lewis is an Associate Professor in the School of Media and Communication at RMIT University, Melbourne, Australia.

Media, Culture and Social Change in Asia
Series Editor: Stephanie Hemelryk Donald

Editorial Board:
Gregory N. Evon, University of New South Wales
Devleena Ghosh, University of Technology, Sydney
Peter Horsfield, RMIT University, Melbourne
Chris Hudson, RMIT University, Melbourne
Michael Keane, Queensland University of Technology
Tania Lewis, RMIT University, Melbourne
Vera Mackie, University of Melbourne
Kama Maclean, University of New South Wales
Jane Mills, University of New South Wales
Laikwan Pang, Chinese University of Hong Kong
Gary Rawnsley, Aberystwyth University
Ming-yeh Rawnsley, School of Oriental and African Studies, University of London
Jo Tacchi, RMIT University, Barcelona
Adrian Vickers, University of Sydney
Jing Wang, MIT
Ying Zhu, City University of New York

The aim of this series is to publish original, high-quality work by both new and established scholars in the West and the East, on all aspects of media, culture and social change in Asia.

For a complete list of titles in this series, please visit www.routledge.com/Media-Culture-and-Social-Change-in-Asia-Series/book-series/SE0797

Recently published titles:

35 Culture, Aesthetics and Affect in Ubiquitous Media
The prosaic image
Helen Grace

36 Democracy, Media and Law in Malaysia and Singapore
A space for speech
Edited by Andrew T. Kenyon, Tim Marjoribanks and Amanda Whiting

37 **Indonesia-Malaysia Relations**
Cultural heritage, politics and labour migration
Marshall Clark and Juliet Pietsch

38 **Chinese and Japanese Films on the Second World War**
Edited by King-fai Tam, Timothy Y. Tsu and Sandra Wilson

39 **New Chinese-Language Documentaries**
Ethics, subject and place
Kuei-fen Chiu and Yingjin Zhang

40 **K-pop – The International Rise of the Korean Music Industry**
Edited by JungBong Choi and Roald Maliangkay

41 **China Online**
Locating society in online spaces
Edited by Peter Marolt and David Kurt Herold

42 **Multimedia Stardom in Hong Kong**
Image, performance and identity
Leung Wing-Fai

43 **Television Histories in Asia**
Issues and contexts
Edited by Jinna Tay and Graeme Turner

44 **Media and Communication in the Chinese Diaspora**
Rethinking transnationalism
Edited by Wanning Sun and John Sinclair

45 **Lifestyle Media in Asia**
Consumption, aspiration and identity
Edited by Fran Martin and Tania Lewis

46 **The Internet and New Social Media Formation in China**
Fandom publics in the making
Weiyu Zhang

47 **Youth Culture in Chinese Language Film**
Xuelin Zhou

48 **Green Asia**
Ecocultures, sustainable lifestyles, and ethical consumption
Edited by Tania Lewis

Green Asia

Ecocultures, sustainable lifestyles, and ethical consumption

Edited by Tania Lewis

LONDON AND NEW YORK

First published 2017
by Routledge
2 Park Square, Milton Park, Abingdon, Oxon OX14 4RN

and by Routledge
711 Third Avenue, New York, NY 10017

Routledge is an imprint of the Taylor & Francis Group, an informa business

© 2017 Tania Lewis

The right of the editor to be identified as the author of the editorial material, and of the authors for their individual chapters, has been asserted in accordance with sections 77 and 78 of the Copyright, Designs and Patents Act 1988.

All rights reserved. No part of this book may be reprinted or reproduced or utilised in any form or by any electronic, mechanical, or other means, now known or hereafter invented, including photocopying and recording, or in any information storage or retrieval system, without permission in writing from the publishers.

Trademark notice: Product or corporate names may be trademarks or registered trademarks, and are used only for identification and explanation without intent to infringe.

British Library Cataloguing in Publication Data
A catalogue record for this book is available from the British Library

Library of Congress Cataloging in Publication Data
Names: Lewis, Tania, editor.
Title: Green Asia : ecocultures, sustainable lifestyles and ethical consumption / edited by Tania Lewis.
Description: Abingdon, Oxon ; New York, NY : Routledge, 2017. | Series: Media, culture and social change in Asia | Includes bibliographical references and index.
Identifiers: LCCN 2016011641| ISBN 9781138854086 (hardback) | ISBN 9781315722351 (ebook)
Subjects: LCSH: Environmentalism--Asia--Case studies. | Green movement--Asia--Case studies. | Sustainable development--Asia--Case studies. | Consumption (Economics)--Environmental aspects--Asia--Case studies.
Classification: LCC GE199.A78 G74 2017 | DDC 304.2095–dc23
LC record available at https://lccn.loc.gov/2016011641

ISBN: 978-1-138-85408-6 (hbk)
ISBN: 978-1-315-72235-1 (ebk)

Typeset in Times New Roman
by HWA Text and Data Management, London

Contents

List of figures ix
List of tables x
List of contributors xi
Acknowledgements xv

1 Sustainability, lifestyle, and consumption in Asia 1
   TANIA LEWIS

2 From sustainable architecture to sustaining comfort
   practices: air conditioning and its alternatives in Asia 20
   TIM WINTER

3 Green marketing and green consciousness in India 37
   DEVLEENA GHOSH AND AMIT JAIN

4 "Relying on Heaven": natural farming and "Eco-tea"
   in Taiwan 51
   SCOTT WRITER

5 The Urban Wilds: ecoculture, consumption, and affect in
   Singapore 66
   CHRIS HUDSON

6 Domestic "Eco" tourism and the production of a wondrous
   nature in the Philippines 81
   SARAH WEBB

7 The greying of greenspeak? Environmental issues, media
   discourses, and consumer practices in China 99
   WANNING SUN

8 Building a green community: grassroots air quality monitoring in urban China 114
JANICE HUA XU

9 *Keitai mizu*: a mobile game reflection in a post-3/11 Tokyo, Japan 129
LARISSA HJORTH AND FUMITOSHI KATO

10 Living co-ops in Korea: sustainable living, communal labor, and social economy 142
SUN JUNG

11 Urban farming in Tokyo: toward an urban-rural hybrid city 155
TORU TERADA, MAKOTO YOKOHARI, AND MAMORU AMEMIYA

12 Farming against real estate dominance: the Ma Shi Po Community Farm in Hong Kong 169
KA-MING WU

Index 185

Figures

2.1	Thermal Modernity, Singapore	22
2.2	Airport advertisement for air sanitizer	23
2.3	Urban Greening, Singapore	25
2.4	Climate responsive furniture and fans, Melaka, Malaysia	31
5.1	Terminal 3, Changi Airport Campsite	71
5.2	Passport Control, Terminal 3	72
5.3	Terminal 3, Changi Airport	73
6.1	Map of Palawan Island	85
6.2	A sign encouraging visitors to vote in the N7WN at the entrance to the PPUR portrays an image of the cave entrance behind it	87
6.3	A billboard on the road between downtown Puerto and Sabang	87
9.1	Shibuya: underground streams	136
9.2	Keitai mizu (mobile water) game	137
9.3	Keitai mizu players	137
9.4	Co-present and ambient play examples of keitai mizu	137
9.5	Co-present and ambient play examples of keitai mizu	138
9.6	Co-present and ambient play examples of keitai mizu	138
11.1	A consequence of agro-activities found in Kashiwa City, a dormitory community in Tokyo metropolitan area	157
11.2	Urban fabrics intermixed with small farmlands in Nerima Ward, Tokyo	160
11.3	Revitalization of Jiyu-hiroba through the Kashiniwa program	164

Tables

3.1	Consumer perception about environmental degradation and perceived state of environment in the next five years	43
3.2	Consumer perception about seriousness related to various environmental concerns	43
3.3	Awareness about green initiatives taken by various government and non-government entities	44
3.4	Consumer skepticism about green practices of the organizations	46
6.1	Registered domestic and foreign visitors to the PPSRNP	84

Contributors

Mamoru Amemiya is Associate Professor at the Division of Policy and Planning Sciences, the Faculty of Engineering, Information and Systems, University of Tsukuba. After receiving a PhD degree in Policy and Planning Sciences from University of Tsukuba in 2007, he managed to develop his academic career as post-doctoral fellow at the National Research Institute of Police Science (2007–2010); assistant professor at the Center for Spatial Information Science, The University of Tokyo (2010–2014); and associate professor at University of Tsukuba (since 2014). His research interest is in social benefits of community gardening activities for social safety and security.

Devleena Ghosh is Associate Professor at the Faculty of Arts and Social Sciences at the University of Technology, Sydney. She has published widely on global and South Asian environmental issues and is currently working on a project on coal mining in Australia, Germany, and India funded by the Australian Research Council. She is the author of *Colonialism and Modernity* (with Paul Gillen; UNSW Press, 2007) and co-editor of *Water, Borders and Sovereignty in Asia and Oceania* (Routledge, 2008).

Larissa Hjorth is an Artist, Digital Ethnographer, and Professor in the School of Media and Communication, RMIT University, Melbourne. Hjorth studies the socio-cultural dimensions of mobile media and play in the Asia–Pacific as outlined in her books, *Mobile Media in the Asia-Pacific* (2009); *Games & Gaming* (2010); *Online@AsiaPacific* (with M. Arnold, 2013); *Understanding Social Media* (with S. Hinton, 2013); and *Gaming in Locative, Social and Mobile Media* (with I. Richardson, 2014).

Chris Hudson is Associate Professor of Asian media and culture in the School of Media and Communication and co-director of the Research Centre for Communication, Politics and Culture at RMIT University, Melbourne. She is the author of *Beyond the Singapore Girl: Discourses of Gender and Nation in Singapore* (NIAS Press, 2013) and co-author of *Theatre and Performance in the Asia-Pacific* (Palgrave Macmillan, 2013), which arose out of a project funded by an Australian Research Council Discovery Grant. She has published extensively on the politics of gender and nationhood in Singapore as well as cultural politics and urban development.

xii *List of contributors*

Tania Lewis is an Associate Professor at RMIT University, Melbourne. She is the author of *Smart Living: Lifestyle Media and Popular Expertise* and co-author of *Telemodernities: Television and Transforming Lives in Asia* and *Digital Ethnography: Principles and Practices*. She has edited and co-edited various collections with Routledge including *Ethical Consumption: A critical introduction*; *Lifestyle Media in Asia: Consumption, aspiration and identity*; and *TV Transformations: Revealing the Makeover Show*. She is a chief investigator on the Australian Research Council discovery project: Ethical Consumption: From the Margins to the Mainstream and on the Sustainable Urban Precincts Project.

Amit Jain is Professor at TAPMI School of Business and Director, School of Hotel Management, Manipal University Jaipur, India. He has published several articles on marketing strategy, sales management, marketing communications, and retail management. He is life member of the Indian Society for Training and Development and currently holds the position of chairman in its Jaipur chapter.

Sun Jung is a Research Fellow in the Asia Research Institute at the National University of Singapore. She has published broadly on South Korean popular cultures, lifestyles, and transnational media flows, including the monograph *Korean Masculinities and Transcultural Consumption: Yonsama, Rain, Oldboy and K-pop Idols* (HKUP, 2011). Her current projects include social media and cross-border cultural transmissions; K-pop: art of cultural capital; neoliberal capitalism, sustainable lifestyles, and media representations; participatory public space: a right to the networked city; and sexuality and gender in Asian pop cultures. Sunjung0903@gmail.com / arijs@nus.edu.sg.

Fumitoshi Kato (PhD degree in communication) is currently working as a professor at the Faculty of Environment and Information Studies, Keio University, Japan. His research interests include communication theory, media studies, socio-cultural impacts of new technologies, qualitative research methods, and experiential learning theory and practice.

Wanning Sun is Professor of media and communication studies at the Faculty of Arts and Social Sciences, UTS (University of Technology Sydney). Her research interests span a number of areas, including health and environmental communication, social change and inequality in contemporary China, and diasporic Chinese media.

Toru Terada is Project Lecturer at the Department of Urban Engineering, The University of Tokyo. He received a PhD degree in Environmental Studies, specializing in landscape and urban planning, from The University of Tokyo in 2011. After receiving his PhD degree, Dr. Terada managed to develop his academic career as Assistant Professor at the Graduate School of Frontier Sciences, The University of Tokyo (2011–2015) and project lecturer at the Department of Urban Engineering, The University of Tokyo (since 2015).

His academic interests include restoration of peri-urban landscapes, wise use of peri-urban coppice woodland (*satoyama*) through re-introduction of community-based bioenergy utilization, and evaluation of hobby farmers' agro-activities for designing urban areas with self-reliance in food.

Sarah Webb is a Sessional Lecturer in anthropology and material culture studies at the University of Queensland. Her ethnographic research in the Philippines examines how commodities are valued through everyday social practices of production, circulation, and consumption. Her doctoral research investigated the value creation of forest honey products along their trajectories. She is a recipient of the Wenner-Gren Foundation Dissertation Fieldwork Grant and a contributor to the Engagement Blog of the Anthropology and Environment Society (American Anthropological Association).

Tim Winter is Research Professor at the Alfred Deakin Institute for Citizenship and Globalisation, Deakin University, Melbourne. He currently leads two international collaborations on urban sustainability and indoor comfort, one funded by the Australian Research Council, the other by the Qatar National Research Fund. For further details see www.comfortfutures.net. tim.winter@deakin.edu.au.

Scott Writer is a Doctoral Candidate in the School of Languages, Cultures, and Linguistics at Monash University, Melbourne. His dissertation is an ethnographic study of the production, appraisal, and consumption of oolong tea in Taiwan.

Ka-ming Wu is Assistant Professor at the Department of Cultural and Religious Studies, Chinese University of Hong Kong. She is interested in questions of modernity, cultural politics, and state-society relationship in contemporary China. Her first monograph, *Reinventing Chinese Tradition: Cultural Politics of Late Socialism* (University of Illinois Press, 2015), examines the ways cultural traditions become battlegrounds where conflicts among the state, market forces, and intellectuals in search of an authentic China play out. Her second forthcoming book, *Life of Waste: Economy, Community and Space at a Scavengers' Site in Beijing* (Chinese University Press, 2016), examines the lives of a group of scavengers to analyze the many developmental contradictions of urban China. She is also interested in and has published on questions of citizenship in post-colonial Hong Kong.

Janice Hua Xu (PhD degree in communication, University of Illinois at Urbana–Champaign) is Associate Professor of communication at Holy Family University, Pennsylvania. Prior to college teaching in the United States, she worked as lecturer in international communication in Peking University in China, news assistant at the *New York Times* Beijing Bureau, and radio broadcaster at Voice of America, Washington DC. Her research interests include cultural studies, ethnography, media globalization, and grassroots activism.

Makoto Yokohari is Professor at the Department of Urban Engineering, The University of Tokyo. His professional career includes research fellow at the National Institute of Agro-Environmental Sciences (1986–1998); visiting scholar at University of Guelph, Canada (1992–1993); associate professor at University of Tsukuba (1998–2004); professor at University of Tsukuba (2004–2006); and professor at The University of Tokyo (since 2006). Dr. Yokohari has been invited to teach at more than 20 universities in North America, Europe, Asia, Oceania, and Japan. His professional career as a technical advisor in landscape-planning includes National Capital Region Planning Committee of Japan, EXPO2005 Planning Committee of Japan, and 2020 Olympic Games Planning Committee. His academic publications include more than 120 reviewed papers and 35 book articles.

Acknowledgements

This book is the product of a research project funded by a grant from the Australian Research Council (DP130100813).

I thank Tripta Chandola for her critical feedback on and input into the project in its earlier phases. I also thank: Helen Grace, Michael Keane, Fran Martin, Levi McLaughlin, Audrey Yue, Gordon Waitt, and Belinda Smaill. Thanks are also due to Jacinthe Flore for her superb editorial support; to Victor Albert, Rrishi Raote, Wokar Rigumi, and Zainil Zainuddin for their research and editing assistance; and last to Stephanie Hemelryk Donald and Peter Sowden for their support for this book project.

1 Sustainability, lifestyle, and consumption in Asia

Tania Lewis

A climate of contradictions

This edited collection is concerned with the lifestyle and consumption practices of ordinary people and their implications for environmentalism. Discussions of environmental issues in South and East Asia tend to be primarily framed as large-scale problems of state and global governance, often in turn linked to market mechanisms. In contrast, this book's concerns lie with more everyday experiences of and engagement with sustainability, including a focus on forms of everyday activism and "experiments" in sustainable living. These alternative practices and discourses are of course invariably shaped by larger state and civic structures (although in some cases grassroots interventions may have a "trickle up" impact on such structures), but they also can represent a significant critical counterpoint to state logics of environmental governance.

There are a number of reasons why everyday environmentalisms are important to examine in Asia, not least of which being the question of global environmental justice given that historically the burden of environmental impacts created by the Global North has fallen on ordinary people in so-called "developing" nations (Shiva 2008). First, while localized environmental practices in the Global North have been widely documented and debated across a range of academic scholarship, there has been much less work done in this space in South and East Asia in Asian or English-language contexts, though there has been growing media coverage across the region of the sustainability practices of ordinary people, from rooftop productive gardening in Hong Kong to China's "back-to-the-land" movement and the rise of permaculture in Malaysia (Choong 2014; *Live Curiously Magazine* 2014; Thompson 2014).

Second, while local practices may have sustainability outcomes, they may not necessarily be defined primarily in terms of environmentalism. It is important then to examine the ways in which issues of sustainability are performed and negotiated on the ground, particularly in the context of countries where civil society-state relations are only just starting to emerge. What social actors are participating in grassroots initiatives that engage with sustainability and in what ways? How do questions of class, gender, urban versus rural location, and so on frame such engagements?

Third, while many South East Asian nations have embraced elements of late industrializing capitalism, for many ordinary people their lives continue to be shaped by regimes of living that are often quite distinct from consumer-citizens of the Global North. As the chapters in this collection suggest, there is much to be learned about the potential for alternative and sustainable collective life practices from examining other pathways or modes of "modernity".

Another key reason behind this edited collection was the desire to expand the conversation on South East Asia and environmentalism beyond what are often one-dimensional depictions of the region. The political and cultural agenda of "development" in parts of Asia is often evaluated through a Western-centric moralistic critique of hyper-consumerism and imagined as a rupture with naturalistic ways of living. At the same time, key Asian cities such as Shanghai are increasingly depicted as the engine room (and future) of a floundering global economy but against the backdrop of anxieties in the Global North concerning the precarious state of the world's ecological resources. In debates around climate change, in particular, reports on Asia increasingly frame it as a space of aggressive development, rapidly growing urbanization, and dwindling natural resources. Thus, where once South East Asia was discussed in terms of a trajectory of necessary growth and development, the region is increasingly the projected site of intensifying anxieties within the Global North about population growth, over-consumption, and the increasingly visible externalized costs of capitalism. From nongovernmental organization (NGO) reports to press coverage, we are told that 60 per cent of the world's population now lives in Asia and are moving toward the urbanized, carbon-intense lifestyles that characterize the high per capita polluters of the world, such as the United States and Australia. China in particular is a source of major apprehension here, given that 800 million of its population still live in low-impact rural lifestyles. Reports suggest that if rural Chinese adopt the high consumption practices of urban dwellers, the global consequences will be catastrophic, with flooding likely to impact major cities from Shanghai to Miami and New York by 2050 (May 2011).

While these troubling predictions are underpinned by very real concerns about our global future on this planet, they gloss over the complex and uneven nature of Asian development on the ground, generalizing across a region that is extremely diverse. Furthermore, while this kind of discourse is often framed in terms of a shared collective experience or "cosmopolitan perspective" as Beck (2015) has framed it—an interconnectedness between all nation-states and peoples—there is a tendency here to project Northern anxieties regarding global environmental impacts onto the Global South. As Brand and Wissen argue, it is these same nations who have historically had the role of carrying the global environmental burden for Western consumers, as providers of resources and labor for Northern industrialism and the ecosystems able to absorb the emissions produced by Northern lifestyles (2013, p. 700).

Anxieties about a rapidly developing Asia then are underpinned by a highly uneven ecological geo-politics (Barry 2012). While notions of a global eco-consciousness or concepts such as the anthropocene position us all as belonging to a collective (carbon-emitting) species, in real terms some members of that species are much less powerfully placed than others. Such inequities are highlighted in the very calculative discourse of climate mitigation itself (May 2011). What we might see as the "biopolitics" of the anthropocene for instance positions Northerners as consumer-citizens with individualized carbon footprints. By contrast, China's 800 million rural people are depicted by that same politics of regulation and "calculative value" as eco-*masses*, as the imagined other of climate cosmopolitanism (May 2011).

This book then is a conscious and deliberate challenge to abstracted discourses of biopolitics and quantified personhood. The chapters in this collection offer instead a range of embedded socio-cultural perspectives on practices and discourses that engage with sustainable modes of living, from farming in the city to embracing cultural heritages of sustainable cooling practices. As such, this collection also represents a challenge to the notion that the future of the region is necessarily one of consumptive modernity, that is, that "developing" nations are all on the same teleological path to capitalist modes of modernization through industrialisation, post-industrialisation, and the like (Barry 2012; Shiva 2013). This book aims in a modest way to offer a counterpoint to broad brush stroke generalizations about environmentalism and Asia through offering grounded, localized examples and case studies and highlighting the way in which notions of and practices of sustainability are articulated to a variety of cultural, social, political-economic structures at a range of scales—local, regional, national, global. These are offered up not in order to deny the huge pressures and challenges the region faces but to highlight the role of ordinary citizens and communities in engaging with those challenges and attempting to develop alternative socially and ecological sustainable futures.

This introductory chapter is structured as follows.

In the first section, I offer a brief overview of environmental governance, movements, and civil society in South and East Asia, focusing on a few key examples including China. The next section moves on to a discussion of lifestyle, arguing that developmental models of Asia are often underpinned by normative conceptions of carbon-intensive lifestyles and consumption. Discussing the gap between discourses of Asian growth and the realities of Asian "middle-class" lifestyles, I question the assumption that South East Asia is necessarily marching along a path toward a Western modernity marked by globalized, middle-class modes of living and consuming. The third section introduces the concept of "multiple modernities" as a way of thinking through alternative pathways of modernization. Discussing two Chinese exemplars of "ecological urbanization," however, I discuss the limitations of technology and market-driven "innovations" that simply replicate the environmental and social costs of capitalism as usual. Finally, I suggest that case studies of transformations in lifestyle regimes might offer a more fruitful point of access into enacting and modeling the necessarily major changes in sustainability practices required on a shared, collective level and provide a summary of the chapters in this collection.

Shifting environments: From governance to civility

While this book is primarily focused on questions of lifestyle and the practices of ordinary people across a range of South and East Asian sites, clearly such activities need to be understood within the contexts of governmental politics and policies in relation to climate change recognition and mitigation, the presence (or absence) of environmental movements, and the level of civil society engagement across the region. Space prohibits mapping the specific genealogy of each and every country, but suffice it to say the region is shaped by considerable diversity in terms of political, governmental, and civic responses to environmentalism. For instance, while Japan is often assumed to be a leader in environmentalism (particularly in the post-Fukushima context), historically it has been marked by a relatively weak political response to environmental concerns such as the anti-pollution movements of the 1960s and 1970s, with much of the action in the contemporary sustainability space occurring at the level of local grassroots organizations (Ku 2011, p. 223) and lifestyle movements (Vinken 2010) such as the Sloth club, Japan's equivalent of the slow movement.

In Korea, on the other hand, the rise of the environmental movement has been closely tied to democratization and national-political structures and processes (Ku 2011). While the movement, following a period rapid industrialization, was initially driven by the victims of pollution in the 1980s, in the 1990s and 2000s it expanded its political focus and legitimacy through various environmental and civil society groups, setting its sights on larger political reform. In 2008, on South Korea's sixtieth anniversary, the president declared that the country's development over the next 60 years would be oriented toward "Low Carbon Green Growth" while the Korean Ministry of Environment (MOE) introduced a GreenCard initiative in July 2011 that rewards card holders with points and benefits for various environmentally friendly practices, including purchase of eco-certified products and conservation of household energy. The MOE announced on April 15 that the number of cardholders surpassed 2 million people on April 13 (Jungyun 2012).

In Taiwan, while the KMT (or Chinese Nationalist Party) had previously largely repressed the environmental movement, as in Korea, the 1980s was marked by a growing environmental consciousness and the emergence of environmental protests in relation to incidences of pollution (Weller 1999). After the lifting of martial law in 1987, the environmental movement developed rapidly. Though green politics have not become mainstream to anywhere near the extent they have in Korea, the country has one of the few Green parties in the region, with interest in the party boosted by anti-nuclear protests in the wake of Fukushima (although it receives a very small percentage of the national vote; Ku 2011).

Finally I spend some time discussing China, which offers one of the more complex evolving pictures of environmental politics, governance, and emerging civil and grassroots movements in the region. On the one hand, with its continued massive reliance on coal, China is one of the world's major polluters and can now lay claim to being the largest carbon emitter in the world.[1] At the same time, the Chinese government has developed a series of major policy and economic initiatives in an attempt to move toward "ecological modernization" (Dent 2014, p. 57) and has sought increasingly to brand itself as a major player in the green global economy. As Zhang puts it, "China is aggressively tying its dominance in future global politics to ambitious climate initiatives, and tactically allying its climate actions with international partners from different sectors" (2015, p. 330). However, while in 2008, when the central government boosted its environmental protection agency into a *dabui* or "super-ministry" (Li and Lang 2010), attempts to implement ecological modernization through a green gross domestic product (which includes the real cost of environmental damage and pollution) saw major pushback from many local governments fearful of the economic impact (Li and Lang 2010).

At the level of civil society, China offers a complex picture of, on the one hand, an emerging "green public sphere" (Yang and Calhoun 2007), with Geall arguing that investigative journalism and micro-blogging have brought some degree of accountability into China's environmental decision making (2013). On the other hand, Zhang and Barr note China's tendency toward "authoritarian environmentalism" (2013, p. 853). They argue, however, that a top-down conception of China's green governance doesn't quite capture the complex dynamics of Chinese social activism, where "a system of 'symbiosis' is emerging as unlicensed civil actors are tolerated so long as they refrain from calling for wholesale political reform whilst addressing social needs that help relieve pressure on the government" (Zhang and Barr 2013, p. 853). This does not mean, however, that green activists are in any way duped by government; rather, as Zhang argues in relation to the air pollution movement (discussed in chapter 8 of this book), many of these figures can be seen as "climate sceptics" who work reflexively and strategically with government:

> These sceptics [sic] do not challenge the validity of climate science per se, nor do they dismiss the necessity for collective undertaking. Rather, this discourse is highly suspicious of the social cost of climate agendas set by Western as well as Chinese state sponsored hegemonies
> (Zhang 2015, p. 333)

In terms of lifestyle and consumption, given China's large and growing urban middle class, there has also been increasing interest in "green" and "ethical" consumer markets in China. A survey of consumers conducted in 2007–2008 found that 31 per cent of Chinese consumers identify the environment as a higher priority than the economy, significantly higher than consumers in the United States (17 per cent), while the survey also found that Chinese consumers' opinions about environmentalism were tied to broader concerns about corporations and their practices rather than personally engaging in "lifestyle" practices such as recycling (*China Daily* 2008).

While such broad-brush-stroke, quantitative surveys have major limitations, these kinds of findings point to the way in which "environmental consciousness" in China, and in other parts of Asia, has a distinct flavor, situated as it is within the context of specific cultural, political, economic, and governmental trajectories. Across the region, civil society and consumer movements are emerging that are oriented toward questions of environmentalism and sustainability but are also invariably co-articulated to a range of other political, economic, and cultural concerns. As noted, this book is primarily concerned with questions of sustainability at the level of everyday living, habits, and lifestyles and, in this next section, I discuss the question of whether South East Asia might offer useful insights into alternative modes of living than those that have become normalized and naturalized in the Global North. In invoking the term *lifestyle*, however, I am by no means merely concerned with questions of individualized behaviors and motivations. Rather, as I discuss in the next section, lifestyle practices are tied to, enabled by, and in turn themselves shape *socio-technical regimes* and the larger political and governmental contexts in which they are situated. In South East Asian countries undergoing major transformations, the question of "lifestyle politics" becomes even more pressing given that questions of how to live are often shifting and contested in such settings, opening the way for potential challenges to carbon-intensive lifestyles and modes of consumption (Bennett 1998; Lewis 2015). As Beck notes, such transitional moments foreground the necessity of examining "the co-presence, and co-existence of rival lifestyles, [and] contradictory certainties in the experiential space of individuals and societies" (Beck 2006, p. 89).

Contesting lifestyles

As I've discussed, transformations in South East Asian ways of living or lifestyles over the past few decades have tended to be viewed in developmental terms, with Singapore and Japan, for instance, positioned as highly developed consumer-capitalist nations while the rest of the region is seen as playing "catch-up" with its relatively "late" modern neighbors (Berkhout et al. 2010). The assumed developmental narrative here, then, is one underpinned by a progressivist Euro-American model of modernization marked by a linear shift from agrarianism to industrialism to post-industrialism. Within an environmentalist context, much of the region is therefore seen as striving toward the taken-for-granted norms of Western lifestyles and modes of consumption that have accompanied mass industrial and, more recently, late industrializing forms of capitalism.

As social practice theorist Elizabeth Shove argues in her book *Comfort, Cleanliness and Convenience* (2004), today in much of the Global North our everyday lives are organized socially and economically to support ways of living and consuming in which a high level of everyday bodily comfort (from air-conditioned and heated cars, homes, and offices), cleanliness (for instance, an expectation of daily showering), and a lifestyle of absolute convenience (from privatized transport to access to trans-seasonal foods) have become normalized. However, she shows that, despite the fact that these lifestyle practices have become naturalized over the past few decades, there is nothing necessarily inevitable or "normal" about these highly consumptive, fossil fuel–driven practices. Indeed, for many people raised in the Global North, they can look back just two or three decades to remember a time when social and technical regimes structured and naturalized quite different practices and assumptions around lifestyle and consumption, such as weekly bathing, sharing bath water, walking and cycling, minimal meat consumption due to cost, seasonal food access and choice, and so on. Revisiting the work of classic social theorists such as Giddens and Bourdieu, social practice theorists such as Shove understand the social as being embedded in and produced through fields of embodied practices tied to shared (though contingent) norms and conventions (Schatzki, Cetina, and Von Savigny 2001; Shove, Trentmann, and Wilk 2009; Shove and Walker 2010). Thus, rather than viewing the social in terms of *a priori* power structures, relations, and institutions, then, practice theorists focus on the way in which practices are collectively organized and supported through particular socio-technical regimes.

The key point here is that while Western forms of post-industrialisation have become associated with highly carbon-intensive lifestyle practices, norms around lifestyles can potentially shift and be collectively organized in radically different ways. John Urry provides a stark illustration of this in his book *Climate Change and Society*, wherein he imagines various post-peak oil futures, from a *Mad Max* style "de-civilizing energy-starved future" to a digitized but hyper-regulated and securitized "smart" future (Urry 2011, pp. 149–53). Discussions of development in Asia, however, rarely imagine the possibility of radically different scenarios for living. Instead, these debates invariably depict the rising Asian middle classes as emerging *Western-style* consumers while presuming that the region is and/or will be subsumed by a one-size-fits-all mode of capitalist modernity or "imperial" mode of living (Brand and Wissen 2013, p. 690). For instance, Brand and Wissen argue that

> The growing middle and upper classes in industrializing "emerging markets" are adopting the lifestyles of the corresponding classes in the global North. All together, they constitute a "transnational consumer class"
> (Brand and Wissen 2013, p. 698)

But is it the case that consumerism has become the default aspirational lifestyle for all South East Asian citizens? While there is no doubt that forms of globalizing consumer-oriented capitalism *are* strongly shaping the region, with potentially dire consequences for global carbon emissions, these kinds of statements gloss over considerable complexity on the ground in relation to both so-called developing nations as well as "developed" parts of Asia. They also have a self-fulfilling quality that makes it hard to imagine any space or future outside of such processes, with critical Marxian accounts such as that offered by Brand and Wissen in certain ways ironically reinforcing rather than offering alternatives to "imperial" ways of thinking, being and living.

The assumption that South East Asia is now largely shaped by Western, middle-class lifestyles and aspirations needs to be critically scrutinized. For instance, while there has been a significant shift toward consumer-oriented modes of citizenship in many countries, the notion of a trans-national or even a trans-regional "middle class" is problematic given the diversity both within countries and across the region in terms of lifestyle and consumer practices (Lewis, Martin, and Sun 2016). While the rise of an upwardly mobile echelon across Asia has been accompanied by the expansion of a range of consumption-oriented lifestyles and consumerist aspirations, the so-called Asian middle classes often have consumption habits and lifestyles that differ significantly from their counterparts in the Global North, with the past decade offering a range of challenges to an expansionary picture of consumer middle classness.

Chua Beng Huat, for instance, presents a rather different account of what he terms "recessionary East Asia" from the usual picture of unfettered Asian growth, arguing, that, with stagnating wages and growing income inequity across the region, the middle-class dream, in "developed" nations in particular, has largely come and gone (Chua 2016). While the 1990s was a period of economic triumphalism in countries like Singapore—marked not so much by Shove's 3 Cs of "comfort, cleanliness and convenience" as by what Chua terms the 5 Cs of "cash, credit cards, car, country club and condominium"—the 2000s, he suggests, have seen a significant reframing of expectations around lifestyle and consumption. Growing precarity means that "[i]n cities like Taipei, Singapore, Hong Kong and Shanghai, there has been a re-focusing of the middle class on the necessities of housing, healthcare and social security for an aging population" (Chua 2016).

He also reminds us of the fact that these Asian "global cities" are populated less by an affluent middle class than by "a large poorly paid service class serving a thin layer of the rich" (Chua 2016). While many of these workers have jobs in services supporting consumption, with "wages are often barely sufficient to cover the necessities of everyday life," their own consumption habits are very different from the so-called "New Rich" of Asia (Chua 2016). Similarly, even in the growth economies of China and India, while there is much made of their burgeoning consumer middle classes, "[a]fter more than three decades of rapid growth, the middle class in both countries remains a thin layer, although numerically large" (Chua 2016).

Greening modernities?

> [In] Southeast Asia [...] a different vision of the future is being articulated, an alternative definition of modernity that is morally and politically differentiated from that of the West
>
> (Ong 1999, p. 29)

Chua's discussion of austerity and consumption in Asia complicates conventional accounts of Asian engagements with capitalist modernity, pointing to the limitations of one-size-fits-all developmental models. It suggests that, rather than viewing the region as moving toward one inevitable end—capitalist modernity and its associated carbon-intensive lifestyles—Asian nation-states such as China and India, for instance, might be more usefully understood as being marked by "multiple modernities" (Eisenstadt 2000). The multiple modernities paradigm assumes that countries are shaped internally by varied speeds and experiences of modernity, but it is also underpinned by the more radical concept "that modernity is not and never has been the sole preserve of the west" (Lewis, Martin, and Sun 2016). For instance, world systems scholars such Dussel (2002) argue that a narrow 200-year focus on

European modernity effaces the role of early modern formations elsewhere, such as China and India, in shaping modern processes. This foregrounds the longstanding development of Asian societies not simply as varieties of a singular modernity but as *alternative* articulations of modernization (Abu-Lughod 1989; Rofel 1999; Eisenstadt 2000; Wittrock 2000; Chakrabarty 2007; Shome 2012).

In the context of environmental debates, the multiple modernities thesis opens the way for considering how alternative forms of modernization might enable the development of potentially "green modernities." Frans Berkhout and colleagues suggest (in a special journal issue on emergent socio-technical regimes in Asia and the potential for sustainability transitions), for instance, that Asia can be seen as the site of various "sustainability experiments" that have the potential to create what they term "trajectories of change in emergent socio-technical regimes, and national and regional development pathways" (Berkhout et al. 2010, p. 262).

While still framed largely within a developmental model, Berkhout et al. put forward a kind of alternative modernity argument, suggesting that late-industrializing Asian nations might bypass the carbon-heavy industrial phase of development gone through by developed economies. Drawing upon the concept of the "socio-technical regime" (and here they overlap with the concerns of social practice theorists such as Shove and their interest in how lifestyle practices are both enabled by and shape certain socio-technical arrangements), they suggest that many South East Asian nations are marked by a relative fluidity in terms of regime formation and change and are, therefore, particularly open to innovation. The language here is rather functionalist, and there is little recognition of how existing alternative modernities might shape and enable green innovations on the ground. Nevertheless, Berkhout et al. point to the sustainability potentials of alternative and innovative articulations between various social actors and technological agents in Asian contexts—articulations that might challenge the taken-for-granted social and technical regimes that have come to support carbon-intensive 3C lifestyles.

> We claim that latecomer countries can become a source of highly novel innovations during processes of catch-up, often through novel interactions between traditional regime actors and regime outsiders, including new firms, spin-offs, environmental NGOs, farmers' cooperatives, consumer groups, etc. This is partly because sustainability experiments create new technological, actor and market configurations, models for which may not yet exist in industrialised countries
>
> (Berkhout et al. 2010, p. 262)

While the Berkhout et al. focus is largely on technology and market drivers in Asia rather than on social actors and their practices, the notion of shifting and alternative socio-technical regimes suggests the potential for "sustainability experiments" at the level of Asian everyday life practices to shape different ways of being modern, that is to model green modernities for a global "community of risk" (Beck 2015).

But what exactly might a green modernity look like? And in what ways might it challenge the normative carbon-intensive triumvirate of comfort, cleanliness, and convenience foregrounded by Shove? In recent years, China has increasingly sought to brand itself in the international community as a green modernizer, through highly visible models of eco-urbanization such as eco-cities and eco-villages (Hoffman 2011; May 2011). Hoffman, for instance, discusses the example of Dalian, the southernmost city of Northeast China, which has transformed itself from an industrialized port city with major problems of pollution into a model of green urbanism heralded across the region and globally (it was named as a Global 500 environmental city by the UN Environment Program). Hoffman asserts that cities such as Dalian, while drawing on elements of the global garden city movement, are largely situated "outside of the dominant, mainstream West and dominant planning theorizations" and as such are "important sites where regimes of urban practices are generated [...] potentially displacing the centrality of Western-generated models in urban studies" (Hoffman 2011, p. 69).

May likewise discusses "the Huangbaiyu experiment"—a United States–China co-development that sought to build an eco village of 42 houses on rural land as a sustainable model for urbanizing China's 800 million rural inhabitants. The key (if somewhat grandiose) concept for this fairly small eco-project was that "China would lead the world in solving one of the most pressing political crises for every nation in the twenty-first century: defying historical precedent by inverting the relationship between increasing quality of life and fossil fuel usage" (May 2011, p. 104). In reality, this rather top-down development saw once relatively self sufficient rural Chinese uprooted and relocated into alien urbanized contexts and socio-technical regimes, ones that, according to May, privileged a middle-class cosmopolitan eco-consciousness and related set of lifestyle practices. Hoffman similarly notes that, while the Dalian "experiment" has had global recognition, it tended to privilege middle-class "quality" (*suzhi*) citizens while marginalizing the poor and lower classes.

Both examples point to the troubling tendencies of Chinese environmental authoritarianism as well as the problem of a continued reliance on a limited conception of modernization and "quality of life" in which consumptive urban modes of living are privileged over more ruralized, productivist models of citizenship. As May puts it, the infrastructure of eco-governance "brings rural residents who were once largely self-sufficient and productive of their own needs for subsistence into complex consumptive relationships in order to receive basic services" (May 2011, p. 111).

The "green" socio-technical regimes offered up in these urban experiments, far from challenging normative "imperial" models of living, again involve relying on market and technology solutions (or "pseudo-solutions" as Shiva terms them) rather than actual transformations in ways of living and being, an approach that continues to externalize social and ecological costs (Shiva 2008; Brand and Wissen 2013). In Dalian's case this occurred quite literally—with polluting industries and non-*suzhi* citizens relocated outside of the city (Hoffman 2011)—pointing to the social inequity often underlying this kind of capital driven, high-end green urbanism. The limits of green technologies and green markets are also highlighted by the paradox of China's much-lauded production of solar panels, which have been exported widely to the

Global North but "have left behind a legacy of toxic pollution in Chinese villages, due to poor manufacturing infrastructure and illegal dumping" (Zhang 2015, p. 333).

Transforming lives

> [W]e can continue to do largely nothing to avert impending climate disaster, or we can [...reconstruct] this moment of crisis as a perceptible opening for the actualization of significant social and political transformation
> (Skillington 2015, p. 232)

While climate change is largely framed in policy and governmental discourses in terms of a crisis of contemporary fossil fuel–based ways of living, governmental and political "solutions" based on technology and market-driven approaches have had a poor track record in providing real, socially equitable alternatives to carbon-intensive collectivized life practices. As we saw with the Chinese examples above, while Asia as a "developing" region more broadly has a major opportunity to lead the way in terms of offering alternatives to "imperial" lifestyles, through drawing on a range of different social and cultural practices, and governmental, economic and political heritages, its governments are often imbricated in global marketized systems of value and relations of power that greatly limit the ability or will to change.

As noted, Ulrick Beck has argued for a refiguring of understandings of the global shared risk of climate change in terms of "a cosmopolitan perspective" in which a full recognition of the consequences of climate change involves what he terms "emancipatory catastrophism." For Beck, the era of the anthropocene is one that radically reframes our basic ethical and existential parameters:

> Climate change is not climate change; it is at once much more and something very different. It is a reformation of modes of thought, of lifestyles and consumer habits, of law, economy, science and politics
> (Beck 2015, p. 79)

There is not much evidence of Beck's emancipatory global cosmopolitanism to date at the level of nation states, and global organizational efforts likewise, it could be argued, do little more than fiddle around the edges of capitalist modernity rather than offering a radical new cosmopolitan imaginary. Craig Calhoun, discussing both the potential and the limits of Beck's conception of climate-based cosmopolitanism, argues that "destruction of the environment may be proceeding on a global scale, creating shared risks that put all humanity into a 'community of fate,' but this does not guarantee that we will find a cosmopolitan solution" (Calhoun 2010, p. 607).

Given this context, this collection is concerned with thinking through how everyday social practices and ways of living might offer a more fruitful point of access into enacting and modeling the necessary changes in sustainability practices required on a shared, collective level. While the practices examined here (from food communities to air pollution monitoring) are often highly localized, are not necessarily reflexive and/or cosmopolitan, and may be articulated to concerns that are not necessarily framed in terms of sustainability (i.e., food safety, social justice, community health, land management, and/or rural identity), many of these practices revolve around and construct communities of risk in which there are shared, strategic moments of connectivity and civic participation. As Calhoun puts it,

> Addressing risks affecting all humanity is crucial, but action is not likely to be organized simply on the scale of humanity as a whole, nor in some sort of "glocal" connection of the largest and smallest units. It will involve the forging of solidarity of a range of scales from local communities to ethnic groups, cities, countries, social movements, and religions
> (Calhoun 2010, p. 605)

The focus in this collection, then, is largely on initiatives that straddle the boundary between civic forms of engagement and ordinary, everyday practices life—what Scholsberg and Coles have termed "the new environmentalism of everyday life" (Schlosberg and Coles 2015). In some cases, such practices have developed due to a level of skepticism regarding political will and governmental action toward environmental issues. As we'll see, these kinds of practices are not necessarily just driven by middle-class consumers but often bring together eclectic communities of actors. While some of the cases discussed here may be small scale and localized, they offer examples of how we might do things differently across a range of scales of sustainability transition. Participatory, "community"-forming but often digitally and globally connected, they suggest a kind of located cosmopolitanism premised on local decision making rather than top-down modes of environmentalism that often marginalize certain actors. This is not an argument against policy-driven changes in socio-technical regimes but rather a call for policy initiatives that draw from the lessons learned from grassroots innovations, enabling democratic forms of change at the level of collectivized life practices and habits.

***

The chapters in this volume speak to a range of the broad themes touched upon in this introduction, from larger-scale discussions of urban design, discourses, practices, and lifestyles to specific, focused case studies of "green" consumption and sustainable living. While the first chapter sets the scene with a regionally focused discussion, the remaining chapters offer a mix of national, city, and locally based case studies. Chapters 3 to 6 focus on green consumption and eco-tourism; chapters 7 to 9 discuss the role of media, activism, and environmentalism; while the last three chapters examine community-based experiments in urban living, with a particular focus on food production—an arena which, as Vandana Shiva's work foregrounds, has been a key site for battles around environmental justice but also for modeling other ways of living beyond a dependence on fossil fuels (Shiva 2008).

Tim Winter's opening chapter on cooling and air-conditioning practices in Asia offers a highly generative case study of the limits of narrow developmental frameworks of modernity and urban lifestyles. Discussing the ways in which air conditioning is becoming increasingly pervasive across Asia, he highlights the pernicious effects of globalized discourses and technologies of "thermal comfort." While a number of Asian cities are attempting to develop local alternatives to energy-intensive methods of cooling through innovations such as "tropical skyscrapers," as Winter points out, air-conditioned internal spaces are often positioned as refuges from an external (ecological and social) environment increasingly ravaged by the impact of climate change. The "solutions" to these issues have tended to be sought in the domain of engineering or technological innovation rather than considering how air conditioning has become naturalized as part of the rise of globalized middle-class lifestyles. Building on alternative urban developmental models such as that of "tropical modernism" and on the insights of social practice theory, Winter discusses a range of sustainable cooling practices that have been prevalent historically across the region and many of which persist to this day, from the Planter's Chair of colonial times to the use of hand fans, slatted furniture, or the habit of sitting on the floor. Winter concludes that central to maintaining and/or reviving this low-carbon comfort heritage is an emphasis on historical accounts of socio-material arrangements and practices enabling the inhabitation of indoor spaces that are far less energy-intensive than the air conditioning paradigm prevalent today.

The next four chapters examine environmentalism in the context of consumption and market capitalism. In chapter 3, Devleena Ghosh and Amit Jain examine the rise of "consumer-citizens" driven by ethical and sustainable concerns. As they note, while research on green consumption and green marketing has tended to associate ethical consumption with the Global North with the South largely imagined as a site of production, the rise of the middle classes in South and East Asia complicates this picture. Focusing on the vast consumer market of India, the authors review consumer perceptions and preferences toward green marketing practices/products. Discussing the ubiquity of greenwashing, the chapter argues that the promotion of green marketing practices in a country such as India can only hope to bring corporate and philanthropic goals together if all actors make real and long-term commitments to social, ethical, and environmental objectives.

Scott Writer's chapter focuses on a very specific market aimed at high-end eco-consumers, naturally farmed tea in Taiwan. Based on ethnographic fieldwork with small-scale tea producers who draw on "natural farming" or the "ecological school" of tea cultivation, Writer's essay explains the way in which the farmers willingly submit to the vagaries of various "natural" forces and non-human agents, such as flavor-enhancing insects, a process poetically captured by the phrase "relying on heaven." As Writer points out, the taste, quality, and also brand status of the highly prized teas made through this process are intertwined not only with the particular environment in which they were grown but also with the specificity of the producer's own embodied taste and practices. For tea makers and consumers alike, then, the taste, experience, and value of different teas is linked to a complex and unpredictable ecosystem of tea production.

14   *Tania Lewis*

In chapter 5, Chris Hudson turns to the city-state of Singapore that, while once constructed as a Mecca for consumers, has been recently rebranded from a "Garden City" to a "City in a Garden." Central to this shift has been the reconstruction of Singapore as a kind of eco-theme park, a "dazzling green sensorium" heavily reliant on affect and the production of an eco-aesthetic, a process that has included developments such as the "naturalization" of spaces in the airport. While on the one hand this development can be seen purely as a value-adding exercise for global consumers and investors alike, Hudson argues that the long-term greening of Singapore has had real impact in terms of the conservation of bio-diversity and other environmental benefits, with the island's green cover growing from 36 per cent in 1987 to 47 per cent in 2007. The chapter thus illustrates the contradictory nature of attempts to tie green governance to the logics of consumption, with the Singaporean state's practices of conservation of rainforest cover and continued greening of urban areas tied to an ongoing investment in a carbon-intensive and globalized economy of consumption.

In chapter 6, Sarah Webb examines another type of ecotourism, based not in a city but on the island of Palawan in the Philippines. Drawing on a long-term multi-sited ethnography focused on an underground river on Palawan, she demonstrates the ways that ecotourism, while framed in part by globalized discourses and practices, is embedded within localized constructions of nature, nation, and economy. Examining a government campaign to have the site recognized as a "Wonder of Nature" through an international competition, she traces how the underground river became the focus of vast text and Internet voting endeavors, a process that saw not only Palawan transformed discursively into a site of national ecological significance but also saw significant material reshaping of place. As she notes, while ecotourism is framed as potentially contributing to the environmental and economic prosperity of the Philippines, such benefits are uneven, with indigenous Tagbanua and Batak families living in the region rarely benefitting from tourism revenue or related employment, pointing to the limits of narrowly economic and nationalist models of environmental place making.

Chapters 7 to 9 foreground the role of media in shaping, enabling and, in some cases, constraining environmental awareness, critique, and activism, from mainstream journalism to blogging and mobile games. Focusing on China and its media coverage of environmental issues, in chapter 7 Wanning Sun sets her discussion of Chinese media discourses and practices in the context of arguments concerning the country's emerging "green public sphere." Focusing on three key media and cultural contexts—the state news media, lifestyle television programs, and the realm of consumer behavior and the market—she suggests that while China's environmental journalism may have been more open to critical reflection in the past, this critical space has diminished rather than expanded in recent years as environmental problems caused by intensive industrialization and rising coal use have taken on a national and more politically sensitive dimension. Paradoxically, while the public has become more conscious than ever of the environmental risk they are living with (a recurrent theme in lifestyle media), Sun suggests that green activism and public debates on environmental issues may have much less space to maneuver than they did a decade ago, a concerning trajectory she terms "the greying of greenspeak."

Janice Hua Xu's chapter examines emerging forms of grassroots air quality–monitoring communities, largely enabled by digital media, in major cities in China, groups that have emerged in response to widespread public concerns regarding urban air pollution. In particular, she reports on NGO-organized monitoring activities related to airborne particulate matter, the results of which often challenge announced data from government environmental agencies. The chapter explores the way in which these fluid "green" communities, which are heavily reliant on digital and social media, have emerged through information sharing, consciousness raising, and various forms of mobilization. In doing so, she maps the complex relationship such grassroots organizations have with the state and with media. On the one hand, environmental activism has emerged as one of the earliest and most active areas of civil society in China, offering a significant critical voice in the context of state-dominated information flows and in some cases shaping policy making. On the other hand, Xu notes that NGOs necessarily have to engage with state environmental agencies and are potentially at risk of having their agendas reset by and through governmental pressures, reminding us of the distinct context in which forms of participatory civic politics are played out in China.

In their chapter on the Tokyo-based art project, *Shibuya: Underground Streams*, Hjorth and Kato discuss the role of mobile and personalized digital media in framing the way questions of environmentalism are being imagined and engaged with in contemporary post-3/11 Tokyo. Examining the key role played by mobile media and social media during the Fukushima disaster for both sharing disaster information and staying in touch with friends, relatives and the community at large, they note that after 3/11, many Japanese citizens created new accounts on social media in order to be prepared for future possible disaster situations. Through using a range of urban interventions including video projections and mobile games, *Underground Streams* sought to provide a space in which everyday commuters in the busy area of Shibuya could take time to reflect on the series of underground streams running under the city of Tokyo and to map a range of water-related native creatures. *Underground Streams* thus sought to consider the ways in which the environment is being imagined and practiced in contemporary post-3/11 Tokyo and the integral role of mobile media in the Japanese environmental imaginary.

The final three chapters in the collection examine various experiments in sustainable living and community in urban environments, all of which speak to the potential for alternative Asian urbanisms and future modernities. In chapter 10, Sun Jung maps the recent rise of cooperative living associations and associated green lifestyles in Korea. Modeled in part on Western co-ops, Jung links these contemporary developments to a nostalgia for rural Korean models of community based on cooperative labor (traditionally known as *dure*). Arguing that there has been growing public interest in Korea in new socio economic models that account for questions of social justice and environmentalism, she notes that numerous grassroots movements from alternative media to co-ops and social enterprises have emerged in the face of a perceived lack of political will and engagement in socioeconomic change. Discussing various examples of cooperative living associations, she argues that, while they draw on the philosophies of *dure*, in contrast to the hierarchical village-based arrangement of older-style community organizations, the new co-ops bring together participants from a range of class backgrounds in a largely horizontal structure that is in turn supported by the use of social media and grassroots-driven alternative media activities such as podcasts. The co-ops thus offer a complex and innovative hybrid model of adapting and blending old and new forms of community as a way of integrating environmental, social equity and participatory politics for urban living.

In chapter 11, Terada, Yokohari, and Amemiya offer another set of insights into emergent environmentally inflected practices and community, focusing on the rise of urban farming in Japan and especially Tokyo. While they observe that urban farming in Japan and globally can be understood in terms of an increasing engagement with everyday environmentalism, they argue that the growing interest in urban farming in Japan also needs to be understood in the context of a shift in work culture away from the "company man or woman" to a growing focus on individual lifestyles. In this context, they argue that a growing number of workers are choosing to be part-time farmers while maintaining their jobs, a lifestyle that dovetails well with the distinct mixed-use urban-agricultural landscape of Tokyo. They conclude by imagining how Tokyo as an urban-rural city might offer more socially and ecologically sustainable models for living in urban environments throughout Asia and beyond.

Finally Ka-ming Wu's chapter on the rise of organic farming in urban Hong Kong provides a fascinating comparison and contrast to emergent practices in Tokyo. Based on an in-depth case study of an organic farm set up in the New Territories, it analyses the rise, role, and impact of farming-based activism in Hong Kong. As Wu shows, these green activists' concerns are not only with supporting organic food and sustainable modes of living but also with contesting the hegemony of real estate developers in a city where there is very little local food production. Through extensive fieldwork, Wu shows how the activists have used a range of creative consumer and lifestyle-oriented activities and events from farm tours and farmer's markets to bread-baking classes in order to recruit members of the general public into a broader critical discussion and engagement with questions of local Hong Kong history, environmental activism, lifestyle consumption, and the "productive" use of space in Hong Kong. Like many of the contributions in this collection, Wu's chapter points to the complex imbrication of environmental issues and social practices in wider historical, socio-cultural and political contexts and the need for reflexive, flexible and localized "solutions" that engage with these contexts.

Notes

1 As *The Guardian* reported in 2015, China's continued coal dependence has seen growing problems with environmental deserts, noting that in one province, a quarter of a million "environmental refugees" have had to be relocated due to rising temperatures and drought (http://www.theguardian.com/environment/ng-interactive/2015/jun/05/carbon-bomb-the-coal-boom-choking-china?CMP=ema-60).

References

Abu-Lughod, Janet. 1989. *Before European Hegemony: The World System, A.D. 1250–1350*. Oxford: Oxford University Press.
Barry, John. 2012. *The Politics Of Actually Existing Unsustainability: Human Flourishing in a Climate-Changed, Carbon Constrained World*. Oxford: Oxford University Press.
Beck, Ulrich. 2006. *The Cosmopolitan Vision*. Cambridge: Polity Press.
Beck, Ulrich. 2015. "Emancipatory Catastrophism: What Does it Mean to Climate Change and Risk Society?" *Current Sociology* 63 (1): 75–88.
Bennett, W. Lance. 1998. "The Uncivic Culture: Communication, Identity, and the Rise of Lifestyle Politics." *PS: Political Science and Politics* 31 (4): 740–61.
Berkhout, Frans, Geert Verbong, Anna J. Wieczorek, Rob Raven, Louis Lebel, and Xuemei Bai. 2010. "Sustainability Experiments in Asia: Innovations Shaping Alternative Development Pathways?" *Environmental Science & Policy* 13 (4): 261–71.
Brand, Ulrich, and Markus Wissen. 2013. "Crisis and Continuity of Capitalist Society-Nature Relationships: The Imperial Mode of Living and The Limits to Environmental Governance." *Review of International Political Economy* 20 (4): 687–711.
Calhoun, Craig. 2010. "Beck, Asia and Second Modernity." *The British Journal of Sociology* 61 (3): 597–619.
Chakrabarty, Dipesh. 2007. *Provincializing Europe: Postcolonial Thought and Historical Difference*. Princeton, NJ: Princeton University Press.
China Daily. 2008. "Eco-Friendly China: *Economist Magazine*." *China Daily*, October 6. Accessed September 16, 2014. http://www.china.org.cn/environment/opinions/2008-10/06/content_16568827.htm
Choong, Mek Zhin. 2014. "Duo Turns Bungalow's Grounds into Permaculture 'Classroom.'" *The Star*, August 22. Accessed September 17, 2015. http://www.thestar.com.my/News/Community/2014/08/22/Their-educational-garden-Duo-turn-bungalows-grounds-into-permaculture-classroom/.
Chua, Beng Huat. 2016. "Foreword: Rethinking Consumption in Economic Recessionary East Asia." In *Lifestyle Media in Asia: Consumption, Aspiration and Identity*, edited by Fran Martin and Tania. Lewis. London: Routledge.
Dent, Christopher M. 2014. *Renewable Energy in East Asia : Towards a New Developmentalism*. New York: Routledge.
Dussel, Enrique D. 2002. "World-System and 'Trans'-Modernity." *Nepantla: Views from South* 3 (2): 221–44.
Eisenstadt, Shmuel Noah. 2000. "Multiple Modernities." *Daedalus* 129 (1): 1–29.
Geall, Sam, ed. 2013. *China and the Environment: The Green Revolution*. London: Zed Books.
Hoffman, Lisa. 2011. "Urban Modeling and Contemporary Technologies of City-Building in China: The Production of Regimes of Green Urbanisms." In *Worlding Cities: Asian Experiments and the Art of Being Global*, edited by Ananya Roy and Aihwa Ong, 55–76. West Sussex: Wiley-Blackwell.
Jungyun, Kwon. 2012. "Eco-friendly GreenCard Counts over 2 million Users." *Korea.net*, April 17. Accessed September 16, 2014. http://www.korea.net/NewsFocus/Policies/view?articleId=99987.
Ku, Dowan. 2011. "The Korean Environmental Movement: Green Politics Through Social Movement." In *East Asian Social Movements: Power, Protest, and Change in a Dynamic Region*, edited by Jeffrey Broadbent and Vicky Brockman, 205–29. New York: Springer.

Lewis, Tania. 2015. "'One City Block at a Time': Researching and Cultivating Green Transformations." *International Journal of Cultural Studies* 18 (3): 347–63.
Lewis, Tania, Fran Martin, and Wanning Sun. 2016. *Telemodernities: Television and Transforming Lives in Asia*. Durham, NC: Duke University Press.
Li, Vic, and Graeme Lang. 2010. "China's 'Green GDP' Experiment and the Struggle for Ecological Modernisation." *Journal of Contemporary Asia* 40 (1): 44–62.
Live Curiously Magazine. 2014. "Growing Towards a Sustainable Lifestyle." *Live Curiously Magazine*, September 26. Accessed September 16, 2015. http://livecuriouslymag.com/2014/09/grow-sustainable-lifestyle/#.VkJ1Fa4rJ7M.
May, Shannon. 2011. "Ecological Urbanization: Calculating Value in an Age of Global Climate Change." In *Worlding Cities: Asian Experiments and the Art of Being Global*, edited by Ananya Roy and Aihwa Ong, 98–126. West Sussex: Wiley-Blackwell.
Ong, Aihwa. 1999. *Flexible Citizenship: The Cultural Logics of Transnationality*. Durham, NC: Duke University Press.
Rofel, Lisa. 1999. *Other Modernities: Gendered Yearnings in China After Socialism*. Berkeley, CA: University of California Press.
Schatzki, Theodore R., Karin Knorr Cetina, and Eike Von Savigny, eds. 2001. *The Practice Turn in Contemporary Theory*. New York: Taylor & Francis Group.
Schlosberg, David, and Romand Coles. 2015. "The New Environmentalism of Everyday Life: Sustainability, Material Flows and Movements." *Contemporary Political Theory*, June 30. doi:10.1057/cpt.2015.34.
Shiva, Vandana. 2008. *Soil Not Oil: Environmental Justice in an Age of Climate Crisis*. Brooklyn, NY: South End Press.
Shiva, Vandana. 2013. *Making Peace with the Earth*. London: Pluto Press.
Shome, Raka. 2012. "Asian Modernities: Culture, Politics and Media." *Global Media and Communication* 8 (3): 199–214.
Shove, Elizabeth. 2004. *Comfort, Cleanliness and Convenience: The Cocial Organization of Normality*. Oxford: Berg.
Shove, Elizabeth, Frank Trentmann, and Richard Wilk, eds. 2009. *Time, Consumption and Everyday Life: Practice, Materiality and Culture*. Oxford: Berg.
Shove, Elizabeth, and Gordon Walker. 2010. "Governing Transitions in the Sustainability of Everyday Life." *Research Policy* 39 (4): 471–76.
Skillington, Tracey. 2015. "Theorizing the Anthropocene." *European Journal of Social Theory* 18 (3): 229–35.
Thompson, Leah. 2014. "A Map of China's Back-to-the-Land Efforts." *China File*, December 15. Accessed September 16, 2015. http://www.chinafile.com/reporting-opinion/earthbound-china/map-chinas-back-land-efforts.
Urry, John. 2011. *Climate Change and Society*. Malden, MA: Polity Press.
Vinken, Henk. 2010. "Fun with Consumers: Enjoying Anticonsumerism in Japan." In *Civic Engagement in Contemporary Japan: Established and Emerging Repertoires*, edited by Henk Vinken, Yuko Nishimura, Bruce L. J. White, and Masayuki Deguchi, 203–24. New York: Springer.
Weller, Robert Paul. 1999. *Alternate Civilities: Democracy and Culture in China and Taiwan*. Oxford: Westview Press.
Wittrock, Björn. 2000. "Modernity: One, None or Many? European Origins and Modernity as a Global Condition." *Daedalus* 129 (1): 31–60.
Yang, Guobin, and Craig Calhoun. 2007. "Media, Civil Society, and the Rise of a Green Public Sphere in China." *China Information* 21 (2): 211–36.

Zhang, Joy Yueyue. 2015. "Cosmopolitan Risk Community and China's Climate Governance." *European Journal of Social Theory* 18 (3): 327–42.
Zhang, Joy Yueyue, and Michael Barr. 2013. "Recasting Subjectivity through the Lenses: New Forms of Environmental Mobilisation in China." *Environmental Politics* 22 (5): 849–65.

2 From sustainable architecture to sustaining comfort practices

Air conditioning and its alternatives in Asia

Tim Winter

For many travellers to Asia, TripAdvisor has become a key resource for researching the quality and satisfaction levels of hotels and guesthouses. More recently, the website has begun identifying and tracking the environmental credentials of its hospitality register, encouraging users of the site to consider the issue of sustainability in their choice of accommodation; an initiative that forms part an industry-wide move toward the all-encompassing mantra of "sustainability". In recent years, the travel and tourism sector has developed a plethora of awards, guidelines, and policies directed at "greening" the industry in recognition of the need to curb energy and resource consumption. For many hotel owners, this has become a feature of market differentiation and helped encourage more people to partake in responsible tourism. Accordingly, as part of listings criteria and on the comments pages, TripAdvisor encourages readers to pay attention—through its GreenLeaders program—to issues such as water usage, laundry, landscaping, lighting, and the degree to which hotels and guesthouses consider the environment in managing their resources and energy consumption (TripAdvisor 2015). In the highly competitive and stratified world of hospitality, balances are constantly struck between luxury, cleanliness, and comfort on the one hand and saving costs and the environment on the other. While TripAdvisor's growing attention to the environmental implications of travel and tourism has helped encourage hotels and guesthouses shift this balance toward the latter, the question of how they manage their indoor climate has yet to be highlighted as an issue worthy of attention. In fact, the site considers indoor air, or more specifically its cooling and drying through electronic air conditioning, less as an issue of environments consequence and more a marker of quality and comfort. Many establishments highlight air conditioning (from now also AC and air-con) as a key feature of their product offering. As an indicator of reliable, optimum, all-year-round comfort, hotels in the four- and five-star sectors proudly proclaim their rooms as being not partially but "fully" air-conditioned. It is a situation that has led to the rise of tens of thousands of hotel rooms across Asia featuring inoperable windows, with guests having little control over their comfort levels beyond choosing between a narrow pre-set range of temperature settings on the thermostat.

I would suggest that such a situation represents a significant omission in the quest for more sustainable buildings and their usage. The absence of debate and critique on TripAdvisor, in contrast to concern given to the ways in which towels, showers, bedding, and plants are managed by service providers, begins to reveal the general lack of awareness of the issues surrounding indoor thermal comfort and the environmental consequences of creating and maintaining artificially chilled space. Indeed, while a number of incidents leading to a wider public debate concerning air-con usage in Asia in the last decade or so have occurred—most notably the "Cool biz" and "Super Cool biz" (post-2011 Tōhoku Earthquake and Tsunami) initiatives in Japan—the issue rarely receives attention within discussions about sustainability or climate change and development, particularly in Asia. As an increasingly invisible, normalized backdrop to urban life, the idea of air-con as a "necessity" invariably goes unchallenged with chilled, dried air seen as infinitely expendable resource, one that can be easily replenished with a flick of the switch. It is to such issues and challenges that this chapter turns its attention.

To put the question of indoor comfort in context, for the majority of countries, buildings account for around 50 per cent of their carbon footprint. Looking forward, the consequences for developing a more environmentally responsive and responsible built environment in Asia becomes apparent given the distinct shifts in global energy usage, as predicted by the International Energy Agency (IEA), with China, India, and the Middle East accounting for 60 per cent of an energy demand that is expected to grow from current levels by more than a third by 2035 (IEA 2012). For those countries lying in Asia's tropical and subtropical parts, it has been estimated that between 40 and 70 per cent of the energy used by buildings stems from cooling via electronic air conditioning (see Winter 2013). A host of factors are driving this increase in cooling-related energy consumption. Fast-paced high-rise urban development, rural-urban migration, population growth, together with a rapid ascendency of a middle class are among the trend determining factors shaping increased air-conditioning usage. The city-state of Singapore, popularly referred to as "the air-conditioned nation", is particularly revealing in this regard (Figure 2.1). Recent household surveys indicate that more than half of the energy costs (55 per cent) for Singaporean families is associated with keeping them and their food items cool, with 37 per cent and 18 per cent accounted for by air conditioning and refrigeration, respectively. As a consequence, for the average Singaporean household today, air conditioning and refrigerators consume more energy than all other electrical appliances and lighting combined (National Environment Agency 2012). Similarly, in neighboring Malaysia, a recent study by the Centre for Environment, Technology and Development (CETDEM) found that 66 per cent of average household electricity consumption is associated with cooling (CETDEM 2014). Given Singapore and Malaysia's principal cities are home to a high proportion of high-rise, middle-class urban residential accommodation, together they represent an important signpost for future usage in the wider region.

Figure 2.1 Thermal Modernity, Singapore
Photo by Tim Winter

In response to such trends, both countries have come to the fore as leaders in developing initiatives and forms of engineering and architecture designed to curb the reliance on energy-intensive methods of cooling. But while recent years have seen a number of "tropical skyscrapers" commissioned by high-profile architects and companies such as Ken Yeang and WOHA Architects, wider forces are at play in both countries serving to polarize how indoor and outdoor spaces are valued, discussed, perceived, and even marketed as spaces of comfort, risk, or security. The unwanted externalities of fast-paced urban growth and land clearance, and most notably airborne pollution, together with fears in the region concerning transmittable diseases, are among the vectors shaping how the indoors is framed as a safer, more sterile environment. As Figure 2.2 illustrates, it is an anxiety that is now both reflected and produced in the marketing campaigns of companies dealing with indoor air management products, in this case Samsung. It is in such devices that we begin to see some wider trends in how ideas, debates, and assumptions about indoor comfort and the governance of air have been framed in recent years in Asia. As we shall see, it is a space dominated by technology and engineering and, as such, hidden away from public view and scrutiny. And as the example of TripAdvisor indicates, the topic of air and air conditioning too often lies beyond debates about sustainable practice or the ethics of sustainable consumption. Accordingly, I would suggest that the lack of public awareness about air conditioning and its alternatives represents a significant obstacle in the development of a broad based critical debate about the future of architecture and urban development in the region.

Sustaining comfort practices 23

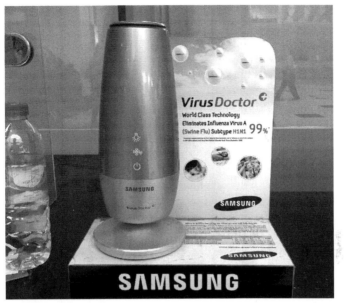

Figure 2.2 Airport advertisement for air sanitizer
Photo by Tim Winter

Engineering indoor comfort

As authors such as Cooper (1998), Arsenault (1984), and Cox (2010) have demonstrated, the rise of our modern air-conditioning regime starts in the hotels and cinemas of southern U.S. states and the creation of leisure spaces that offered respite from hot summer afternoons. Fascinatingly, such accounts trace how air conditioning was installed in the White House as part of the industry's lobbying as well as the economic and geographic directions it took in penetrating offices across the United States and its entry into the home in the post–World War II decades. In terms of understanding the internationalization of air-conditioned comfort, we can point to some key markers for a history that has yet to be adequately accounted for. Of particular importance here was the development of the first "Comfort Chart"—based on human subject responses to different combinations of temperature and humidity of human comfort—that proved critical in shaping a science of indoor comfort in the early 1920s (Cooper 1998, p. 71). But the geographical mobility of this knowledge regime was advanced most tangibly via the research of one man in particular, Ole Fanger. An engineer by training, Fanger undertook laboratory-based experimentation into thermal comfort and perceptions of indoor environments at the Technical University of Denmark from the 1960s onward, forming the highly influential International Centre for Indoor Environment and Energy in the late 1980s (Shove 2003). Fanger's thermal comfort equation centered around precise ideas about mean radiant temperature, relative velocity, and air humidity in order to create "an optimal thermal comfort for man". Crucially, and as authors such as Shove (2003) have shown, it was a methodology of physiological comfort measurement that would come to be adopted and embedded in codes and standards around the world from the 1970s onward. Perhaps most influentially, the idea of 22C as the most comfortable temperature for human productivity became critical to the standards adopted by the American Society of Heating, Refrigeration, and Air Cooling Engineers, which have been exported to numerous countries around the world including those in the Asia region (Shove, Chappells, and Lutzenhiser 2009).

The science of Ole Fanger had a particular approach to perspiration and the possibilities of banishing it and its associated smells through the conditioning of air. Accordingly, he identified two units of measurement: the first for measuring the scent emission of people and objects (the olf), the second for assessing the total sensory "load" produced by such scent emissions (the decipol). As Shove, Pantzar, and Watson explain,

> In technical terms, an olf is equivalent to the scent emitted by an average person at rest, i.e. someone who takes approximate 0.7 baths per day, has a surface area of 1.8 meters squared, wears clean underwear, works in an office environment, is healthy and is a non-smoker...Fanger's decipol represents the air pollution from 1 standard person (0.7 baths/day, 1.8m2, clean underwear daily, 80 per cent use deodorant) ventilated by 10l/s unpolluted air
>
> (2012, p. 65)

It was a laboratory-based methodology to thermal comfort that has come to define and prescribe international norms and ideas of normality; wherein culturally and historically blind definitions of normal bodies, normal activities, and normal conditions have been plotted and charted for the purposes of design and the efficient engineering of indoor space. And crucially here, it is the science by which many indoor spaces were designed and engineered in Asia from the mid-late twentieth century onward.

Indeed, as I have argued at length elsewhere, the issue of indoor thermal comfort in Asia has to date primarily been considered as a domain of engineering, technological innovation, or architectural design (Winter 2013). In both the building science and the architectural profession, there is a growing awareness of the need to counter the prevailing trend of energy intensive methods of cooling by promoting alternative modes of comfort for work, leisure, and domestic spaces. Southeast Asia has been at the forefront of the turn toward the "greening" of city planning and development via the introduction of legislation designed to encourage more sustainable commercial architecture, housing, and urban landscaping. In cities such as Singapore and Hong Kong, architects have been strongly encouraged to introduce more "green" elements into their design processes (Figure 2.3). Not surprisingly, this new wave of "green architecture" has introduced vegetation on, in, and around buildings in an attempt to reduce urban heat islands and humidity, remove airborne toxins, and create a sense of

Sustaining comfort practices 25

Figure 2.3 Urban Greening, Singapore
Photo by Tim Winter

more socially progressive architecture. Designers such as Jason Pomeroy are among those that have embraced vertical and rooftop gardens as an integral feature of high-rise construction (Pomeroy 2014). As a passive cooling method, the implementation of a green roof can absorb large quantities of solar energy, with the majority being soaked up by the plants and layers of substrate below (Kamarulzaman et al. 2014, p. 2). The aim is to lower the surface temperature of buildings and reduce the load on HVAC systems and thus the energy required to keep occupants cool and comfortable. Targeting both large-scale commercial architecture and domestic environments, heavy investments are also being made into the development of an infrastructure of indoor-comfort-smart technologies. As part of the emergent economy of the "internet of things" products such as "Nest", "Tado", and the "Ambiclimate" all promise to offer users a more fine-grained control of their thermal surroundings, and incorporate features that respond to the daily rhythms of occupants and the external weather (see Ambi Climate 2015). Interestingly, the home has become a key site of innovation for this bourgeoning sector. By tying into smartphones and "smart" control panels, these devices allow home owners to access usage information, change temperatures of different rooms, set location sensors to turn the device on or off, and create opportunities for energy savings (Nest 2015; Tado 2015).

Many further examples of innovative architectural design and air-conditioning technologies could be cited here, but in the limited space available, the themes of "green architecture" and smart technologies are noted to illustrate and acknowledge some key initiatives that will have a positive contribution in countering the energy consumed from electronic air conditioning in Asia in the coming years. In what is currently a highly inefficient and wasteful sector of building design, ongoing research and development in the engineering, design, and technical management of indoor comfort will deliver statistically significant efficiency gains and cost savings. However, in support of the critiques of Strengers (2013) and others regarding the overly deterministic optimism regarding the possibilities of smart technologies, I would suggest design and engineering approaches to indoor comfort will not in themselves be sufficient in curtailing the ongoing increase in air-con energy consumption in a region experiencing rapid and uneven development. While newly installed technologies might be heralded as offering a percentage saving of energy consumption over previous designs (Tado 2015), this does little to counter broader societal trends of rapidly increasing air-con usage and dependency. In fact, it is likely efficiency dividends may well serve to contribute to the further normalization of air-con usage in everyday life across many of Asia's cities. Interviews conducted with Malaysian householders in 2014, for example, suggested that where previously only the living space was cooled on a part-daily basis, additional units had been installed in bedrooms as well as cooking and dining spaces, with usage extending over much longer periods of the day.

To consider the future of indoor comfort in Southeast Asia and other parts of Asia then, we have to take a much broader perspective than that offered by design and engineering and consider air conditioning in relation to societal trends such as middle-class lifestyles, urban development, and how comfort relates to the more abstract concepts of modernity and nation building. In this respect, there is a need to excavate the broader socio-cultural and political associations of indoor thermal comfort in the region. From as early as the 1920s, air conditioning in Southeast Asia can be regarded as a transformative technology—with *The Straits Times* newspaper even predicting "that the introduction of air conditioning and its 'manufactured weather' would make the tropics more healthy and prosperous, transforming such regions from backwardness to civilisation" (*The Straits Times* 1929, p. 5). With air conditioning initially installed in the region's most prestigious office buildings, cinemas, and high-class hotels, it did not take long for the concept of luxury and comfort to be associated with the new technology. Over time, its adoption expanded substantially—workplaces, shopping centers, public transport, and private homes all embraced electronic cooling as a means to meet and alter thermal comfort expectations. In the case of Singapore, it was a technology that powerfully aligned with and advanced the discourse of productivity and efficiency that lay at the heart of the post-colonial nation-building project. Colonial ideas about climate, the tropics, and modernization had penetrated the thinking of key political figures, most notably Lee Kuan Yew. He instructed for electronic air conditioning to be installed in many of the offices of the newly formed Singapore civil service in the 1960s (Chang and Winter 2015). The high cost of installation and its operation at that time, however, meant it remained a privilege for a select few deemed critical to the proper functioning of the state. As planning regimes and architecture evolved over the coming decades, a clear inter-dependence emerged between building typology, architectural design, constructional systems, and air conditioning. Not only deemed pivotal to creating productive workplaces, air conditioning became integral to the creation of leisure-scapes and environments for all-year-round shopping and consumption. Air conditioning thus proved pivotal to both the development of the state, and an economic development strategy dependent upon ever-increasing levels of productivity and consumption. With Singapore far from unique in this regard, it can be argued that the idea of a particular thermal modernity—whereby indoor comfort has been the subject of strategic governance by the state and other actors—has been a defining characteristic of development for various countries in South, East, and Southeast Asia since the Second World War.

It is against this larger backdrop that I would argue the issue of thermal comfort and energy consumption needs to be viewed and debated. To more critically interrogate the present directions of our paradigm of air conditioning and its reliance upon energy-intensive cooling methods, there is a need to leverage the issue out of its current confines of engineering, architecture, or software design and provide platforms upon which its associations with urban development, consumption, identity, and so forth can be articulated more visibly. Complementing this, following Shove, Pantzar, and Watson (2012) and others, I would also suggest there are significant benefits of moving the focus away from the question of comfort provision to comfort practices. It is to such themes that I now turn.

Sustainability and tradition

One significant opportunity the emergent smart technology economy promises is its ability to offer building occupants a degree of control over their thermal envelopes. Giving a greater level of autonomy to the individual in this way may well open up an important space for incorporating a wider variety of comfort envelopes and a return to the idea that users negotiate and accomplish that comfort on an ongoing basis. In anticipating such directions, we can thus productively look more closely at comfort practices, an emphasis that raises the possibility of revisiting some of the ways in which people maintained thermal comfort in different parts of Asia prior to the widespread uptake of air conditioning.

To date, tradition based approaches to thermal comfort in Asia have overwhelmingly focused on the potential for conserving and adaptively reusing certain forms of architecture from a pre-air-con period. Indeed, in recent years, much has been written and discussed about the merits of the genres of "tropical modernism" and "tropical vernacular" as offering sustainable, low-energy alternatives to the modern regime of electronic air conditioning. Architects such as Geoffrey Bawa, Charles Correa, Stanley Jewkes, and Vann Molyvann have been celebrated for their approach to airflow and natural cooling features in response to their local climates. Spanning public, commercial, and domestic structures, these architects draw on an architectural vocabulary oriented around natural ventilation (large openings, stilts, heat escape devices); sun shading (overhanging rooflines, verandahs, solar orientation, greenery); and breathability (low-heat storage materials, latticed windows, slatted floors). In Cambodia, Vann Molyvann's buildings of the 1950s and 1960s were shielded from harsh climatic conditions through stilts and carefully positioned windows that avoided the path of the sun (Vann 2003). Like other architects of this period, he looked to those forms of cooling found in the country's vernacular architectural heritage. In Sri Lanka, Geoffrey Bawa's architecture became renowned for seamless flows between indoor and outdoor spaces and the incorporation of vegetation as an agent of cooling. From domestic homes with inner courtyards to hotels, schools, and churches, Bawa's designs were oriented by shade, water, air-flow, and the rhythms of the day and seasons. Such buildings represented the accumulation of a deep knowledge about building for the climatic conditions of the tropics that became popular across South and Southeast Asia in the decades leading up to widespread adoption of affordable air conditioning (Fry and Drew 1964; Fathy, Shearer, and Sultān 1986; Ford et al. 1998).

Of course, it was an approach that extended far beyond the practices of the region's iconic architects, with cities throughout tropical and subtropical Asia characterized by buildings oriented around their localized climatic conditions: a building stock that many contemporary architects and owners are now looking to for renovations and redevelopment through adaptive reuse. In cities such as Penang, Melaka, Phnom Penh, and Singapore, the shophouse typology of the late nineteenth, early twentieth centuries has proved popular for creating renovations that utilize airflow, internal courtyards, ponds, and overhanging rooflines (Yung 2014). In the tourism sector, the legacy of Geoffrey Bawa is still apparent in both the hotels and resorts he designed and those he inspired. Bawa designed resorts in Sri Lanka, Bali, and India, all of which featured long, open, naturally ventilated corridors, bungalows with courtyards and pools, as well as an abundance of vegetation and outdoor dining and seating spaces (Jazeel 2007). It is a design language that has been widely adopted across the region, with numerous high-end hotel and resort groups charging a premium for an accommodation and dining experience that features greenery and the fresh air that comes from an architecture that reduces the boundaries between indoor and outdoor space. Likewise in Malaysia, the architectural practice of Seksan Design has also designed smaller hotel properties using disused sheds, old buildings, and tiny houses. As part of the open-plan design narrative, Ng Seksan has sought to encapsulate a sense of local identity by promoting a Malaysian vernacular within a wider framework of environmental and social sustainability (Azizan 2012). It can be argued with some confidence that such initiatives—together with other forms of restoration, renovation, and conservation that allow the ongoing use of buildings of a pre-air-con era—hold real potential for countering the distinct trend toward rapidly increasing energy consumption associated with indoor comfort in countries such as Malaysia today. However, while fully acknowledging the benefit of these architectural based approaches, the critical point I wish to make here is that as the basis of a sustainability discourse, their potential as a large-scale alternative to the "hegemony" of AC is very limited. In order to activate a wider debate about indoor comfort, I would argue we need to see such architectural design as one part of a wider effort of sustaining tradition-based low-carbon comfort practices. One of the effects of electronic air conditioning is its transformative affect on everyday practices and routines. It is, therefore, helpful to consider how non-air-con comfort practices disappear, why habits and routines change, and why the material culture of everyday life alters as modes of comfort provision change. To approach such topics and questions, recent debates around social practice theory are instructive here.

Toward a framework of comfort practices

Citing Schatzki (2001), Yolanda Strengers (2012, p. 226) suggests that social practice theory aims to offer a distinct ontological account of the social, one that focuses not merely on norms and meanings or institutions and instead foregrounds relations between practices and material arrangements. In seeking to overcome the dualisms of production and consumption, and overly simplistic ideas of behavior and consumer choice, it is an approach that not only reads the material and social as interwoven and inherently entangled but sees that nexus as the starting point of investigation. As Schatzki points out, "practices are the source and carrier of meaning, language, and normativity", whereby everyday life is held together by and through particular material configurations (cited in Strengers 2012, p. 228). Clearly, here we see the intellectual traces of actor network theory and the emphasis it gives to human, non-human relations. The key realization here then is that—and as Shove, Pantzar, and Watson (2012, p, 10) put it—we need not only to have a "suitably materialized, theory of practice" but also understand that materiality as bundles or configurations of multiple elements. The authors give the examples of cooking, sports, and driving to argue that there is a need to critically focus attention on the links and breakages between materials—things, technologies, and material resources—competences, a term they use to fold in skills, techniques, and knowledge, and the meanings and values associated with particular practices. Accordingly, in proposing that "practices emerge, persist, shift and disappear when connections between elements of these three types are made" (Shove, Pantzar, and Watson 2012, p. 14), they offer private transport as an example to illustrate the analytical vantage point that needs to be adopted here:

> If we take the practice of driving rather than the car or the driver as the central unit of enquiry, it becomes clear that relations between the vehicle (along with the road and other traffic), the know-how required to keep it in motion and the meaning and significance of driving and passengering are intimately related, so much so that they constitute what Reckwitz refers to as a "block" of interconnected elements. Accordingly, novelty can come from any quarter and at any time
>
> (Shove, Pantzar, and Watson 2012, p. 31)

The key implication here is that we shift the point of focus away from air conditioning as technology or as an architectural design feature to the practices of comfort. Strengers has helpfully elaborated on this point in relation to thermal comfort in the home, arguing that a practice theory perspective might view the increase in residential air-conditioning as the changing practice of household cooling, involving the complex co-evolution of material infrastructures (changing housing formats, central heating and cooling, the affordability and availability of the air-conditioner); common understandings of air-conditioning as a normal and necessary service, and changing notions of "air" "health" and "wellbeing" [sic] associated with indoor climate and temperature; practical knowledge about how to cool the body and home; and rules about how to use and install the air-conditioner. This is distinct from accounts of the air-conditioner's rapid diffusion in western societies that privilege processes of market economics (affordability and availability), cultural symbolism (the air-conditioner's role as a "status" object), or changing individual choices and lifestyle needs

(2012, p. 228)

In considering such insights in relation to the rapid uptake of air conditioning in Asia, rather than focusing on the entanglements that lead to its adoption and incorporation into everyday life as Strengers, Schatzki, and Shove et al. have done, I want to focus on its alternatives, those low-carbon comfort practices that lie outside the comfort regime of electronic AC. To head in such directions and as noted earlier, we need to see comfort as something that is accomplished—as opposed to being delivered as a service—such that it is enacted by the occupants of building on an ongoing basis and reproduced over time. Prior to the widespread adoption of air-con, comfort practices relied upon an accumulated knowledge that was transmitted to others over time. In the hot and humid climate of Southeast Asia, maintaining comfort involved understanding the thermal properties of materials and the implications of habituated activities. In many cases, understanding the thermal properties of textiles formed part of clothing practices. Caution here should be made in not offering an overly climatic determinism, as the histories of clothing and dress by cultural group are layered with the traditions of religion, class, gender, different ethno-cultural heritages, and so forth. By recognizing such factors, it is possible to identify the practices of wearing certain textile fibers, styles of clothing, or seasonally based garments that all point toward an accumulated knowledge of maintaining bodily comfort in certain climatic conditions (Khoo 1993; Dhamija and Eicher 2010).

We can think of fans in a similar way. Some of the earliest examples of hand-held fanning originate from China, with woven bamboo ceremonial fans having been dated as far back as the second century BC. Accordingly, books by Irons (1982) and Hutt and Alexander (1992) document the extensive history of hand fanning in China and Japan, respectively, indicating how the practice of cooling also became deeply incorporated into the cultural fabric of their societies, allowing users to hide emotions, demonstrate etiquette and manners, and identify social hierarchies. Interestingly, across a number of Asian countries, together with the shade-providing decorative umbrella, fans became one of the accoutrements of royal and court culture, repeatedly featuring in ceremonies and processions. In India, the "punkah" began to appear from the seventeenth century onward.

Typically attached to the ceiling and composed of palm fronds or a cloth-covered wooden frame, the punkah fan would be operated by a human operator of "wallah" via pulleys and ropes. Now regarded as one of the iconic images of British colonialism, the punkah spread to other parts of Southeast Asia, and even as far as the houses and offices of nineteenth-century plantation owners in the southern states of America (Connors 2002; Gontar 2009). Electrification in Asia led to the installation of mechanical punkah and early versions of the electric fan familiar today. While the precise pathways taken by the different technologies of fanning across different societal contexts in Asia is difficult to track and scope for worthy further research, it has remained ever present in the practice of maintaining bodily comfort. Whether designed to provide comfort at the scale of the individual or the room, fans intended for the hand, desktop, floor-standing, or ceiling represent energy-efficient alternatives to electronic air conditioning (see, for example, Big Ass Fans 2015). But crucially, their effectiveness stems in part from the material combinations within which they are used. It has long been understood, for example, that the design of furniture has a notable impact on the degree to which comfort can be physiologically achieved and sensed.

To cite just one example, there is a long tradition across various parts of Asia of seating designed around slats and meshes, facilitating a through flow of air and the efficient dissipation of heat away from the body (Figure 2.4). One particularly noteworthy design was the "Planter's Chair", various versions of which became popular across the Caribbean, southern United States, as well as the European

Figure 2.4 Climate responsive furniture and fans, Melaka, Malaysia

Photo by Tim Winter

colonies of Asia. Designed as a recliner with mesh seating, its key innovation was the addition of elongated arms that would either swing out to the front or be fixed in position, allowing the user to benefit from the circulation of air around legs that were raised up and spread apart. Scanning archives for photographs of these in use tends to confirm it was a design that afforded comfort and relief for a select few. Primarily used by men, it would have no doubt caused an altogether different form of discomfort for the Victorian English lady, fearful of the risk of the embarrassing indiscretions the chair might pose. Equally, while photographic records of interior scenes from the nineteenth century confirm males from both Europe and the subcontinent adopted the convention of wearing the open lungi or sarong, the heavily reclined design of the chair spoke of relaxation, resting, and slumber, meaning it was appropriate only for those in charge of the household and their guests; a position of privilege that no doubt gave license to certain indiscretions. In both the punkah and the Planter's Chair, then, we gain some insight into the hierarchies and gendered practices of comfort of European colonialism. European practices and values would also intersect with more localized and existing practices, such as fanning noted above or the common custom of sitting on the floor, a practice that remains common today and speaks to a complex mix of social conventions and hierarchies and an accumulated knowledge of heat transfer and movement.

Of course, alongside these material worlds are various accompanying traditions of thermal comfort praxis. Indeed, numerous examples could be cited regarding habits and rhythms of bathing, working, resting, or shopping in accordance with the time of day and local climatic conditions. Much like elsewhere in the world, comfort practices in tropical and subtropical Asia have long involved quotidian rhythms of movement around the cooler spaces of home, utilizing the knowledge of shade, curtaining, and the cooling effects of vegetation to find comfortable spaces. Fergus, Humphreys, and Roaf elaborate on this point further, suggesting such daily practices include

> movement between buildings, between rooms, around rooms, out of the sun, into the breeze, closer to the fire, with the blinds shut, with the curtains open and so on…People who regularly occupy a particular space will have a customary temperature that they associate with that place for a particular time of date or year. It will be part of a thermal pathway they follow each day, a pathway that at times may be too hot or too cold, but on average constitutes a well-understood pattern for a generally comfortable life
>
> (2012, p. 69)

The examples of clothing and furniture are cited here as illustrative of a larger analytical path that can be adopted to consider those comfort practices that lie outside the current paradigm of electronic AC. Obviously, in highlighting examples from the contexts of nineteenth-century colonialism, any idea of reviving such cultural practices raises questions about nostalgia and the romanticization of the past—as it should with historic architecture. The point here then is not to valorize such nostalgia for a "golden era" of sustainable comfort but to identify the material and social entanglements by which comfort has been historically practiced in the region and to understand some of the key factors by which some practices remain stable and others disappear. Colonialism and empire gave particular socio-political and architectural contexts through which the Planter's Chair was popularized. Indeed, in looking at its usage today, one context where it remains particularly popular is in the lounges and verandas of the region's colonial era hotels that hark back to a "golden age" of European travel. Equally however, as a common feature of veranda houses of the elite and wealthier middle classes of India and elsewhere, they also speak to altogether different memories, as the following excerpt from the online blog of an Indian interior designer illustrates:

> This chair is exactly the kind of thing I picture when I hear my mom talk about the "good old days" growing up in Bangalore. The key feature of the planter's chair is its swing-out arm extension meant for putting your feet up on…My mom tells me we had two of these on the veranda of our family home on Museum Road. I imagine my grandfather sinking into it and his thoughts on a balmy afternoon, while his eleven kids tiptoed around him, planning the day's itinerary of scaling compound walls and climbing mango trees…The chair belonged to Amrit's grandfather. "I remember him sitting there, the man of the house, feet up and smoking his hookah," he says….As the Chennai sun streamed golden through the window, I closed my eyes to visions of hookahs and mango trees
> (Tiipoi Ltd 2014)

Such examples point toward questions about which material and social configurations enable such elements—in this case, a particular design of chair—to remain in use. Perhaps the Planter's Chair is an example of an element that has marginal use in today's high-density urban environments? In undertaking the task of understanding forms of longevity and persistence, we can, however, identify elements—such as hand fans, operable windows, slatted furniture, or the habit of sitting on the floor—that remain far more common and widespread. The key here, then, is understanding how particular material arrangements and social practices came to stabilize in ways that constituted a larger regime of thermal comfort, enabling the inhabitation of indoor spaces that are far less energy-intensive than the air-conditioning paradigm prevalent today. And critically, accounting for why certain practices fade or disappear while others remain popular allows us to begin to anticipate the degree to which they might be maintained or revived as part of a low-carbon comfort heritage, one that includes the forms of historic architecture highlighted above. As Shove, Pantzar, and Watson (2012) note, it is analytically productive to interrogate such questions through the lens of relations of bundles. Accordingly they ask, "How do bundles and complexes of practice form, persist and disappear? As elements link to form practices, so practices connect to form regular patterns, some only loosely associated, others more tightly bound" (2012, p. 17). One key question then in thinking about more sustainable forms of urban development in Asia pertains to the role of AC in breaking the links between existing bundled comfort practices and the degree to which old links might be restored or existing elements can be brought into new, more resilient associations.

Conclusion

To date, cultural geographers, planners, and sociologists working on Asia's cities have largely discussed sustainability in terms of exterior spaces. Considerable work needs to be done to integrate their analyses with the ideas and frameworks of architects and designers to construct a more critical analysis of "interior geographies". Along with escalators, elevators, and communications infrastructures, climate control systems have formed part of the matrix of technologies of construction across the region over the last half-century or so. In exploring one of these—air conditioning—this chapter has argued that the technology has proved pivotal in the expansion of high-rise architecture and rapid urban development across much of Asia and, as such, constituted a powerful element of urban modernity and economic development for many nation-states in the region. However, and as noted earlier, as a largely invisible backdrop to urban life, workplace, transport and leisure spaces, air conditioning very rarely receives the critical attention it warrants. I would suggest its rapid uptake in many of the region's cities and countries has significant implications for developing more sustainable, low-carbon futures. One key challenge here, then, is fostering a wider debate around such issues and a critical awareness as to the environmental implications of fast-changing comfort norms and expectations. A focus on comfort practices and the ways in which buildings are occupied and used is thus seen as an important step toward fostering wider awareness and debate.

To that end, this chapter has highlighted the need to develop a more critical reading of indoor comfort and suggested there is considerable merit in shifting attention toward the various ways comfort is achieved and practiced on a daily basis. The speed and scale of development and urbanization in many parts of Asia over recent decades has had a profound impact on everyday culture—both material and non-material, including those cultural practices associated with the habitation of indoor space. It has been suggested here that significant benefit arises from pursuing the maintenance of those comfort practices that lie outside today regime of electronic AC. Within this argument, the value of conserving and maintaining non-air-con architecture has been acknowledged, but by foregrounding comfort practices, it has been suggested that an architectural response is, in itself, not enough to destabilize current trends toward AC usage. Rather, by placing the built space within a wider analytical frame, it forms part of a more analytically expansive way of understanding how low-carbon alternatives can be more productively maintained and supported. As Tania Lewis in this volume argues have argued, there is a need to move beyond technological or science-based prescriptions of sustainability to more carefully consider how we might imagine and practice green modernities and forms of urban development. To that end, this chapter has highlighted the need to reframe indoor space as bundles and configurations of comfort practice as the means to revive and retain low-carbon alternatives to air conditioning.

Acknowledgments

This research was supported under the Australian Research Council's Discovery scheme (Cool Living Heritage in Southeast Asia: Sustainable Alternatives to Air-conditioned Cities, DP120102448). The author also thanks Toyah Horman for her assistance in preparing this chapter for publication.

References

Ambi Climate. 2015 *Ambi Climate: The smart add on for your air conditioner.* Accessed July 25, 2015. http://www.ambiclimate.com/.
Arsenault, Raymond. 1984. "The End of the Long Hot Summer: The Air Conditioner and Southern Culture." *The Journal of Southern History* 50 (4): 597–628.
Azizan, Farah. 2012. *Farah Azizan on Seksan for IFA Stuttgart-Berlin Exhibition Catalogue, 2012.* Accessed July 20, 2015. http://www.seksan.com/txt_stuttgart.html.
Big Ass Fans. 2015. *Summer Cooling.* Accessed July 20, 2015. http://www.bigassfans.com/au/summer-cooling/.
Center for Environment, Technology and Development, Malaysia. 2014. *Sustainable Energy Roadshow: 'Fit and Save' Exhibition & Workshop.* Accessed July 20, 2015. http://cetdem.org.my/wordpress/?page_id=1254.
Chang, Jiat-Hwee, and Tim Winter. 2015. "Thermal Modernity and Architecture." *The Journal of Architecture* 20 (1): 92–121.
Connors, Michael. 2002. *Carribean Elegance.* New York: Harry Abrams.
Cooper, Gail. 1998. *Air-Conditioning America: Engineers and the Controlled Environment—1900–1960.* Baltimore, MD: Johns Hopkins University Press.
Cox, Stan. 2010. *Losing Our Cool: Uncomfortable Truths about Our Air-Conditioned World (And Finding New Ways To Get Through Summer).* New York: The New Press.
Dhamija, Jasleen, and Joanne B. Eicher, eds. 2010. *Berg Encyclopaedia of World Dress and Fashion 4: South and Southeast Asia.* Oxford: Berg.
Fathy, Hassan, Walter Shearer, and Abd-el-rahman Ahmed Sulṭān. 1986. *Natural Energy and Vernacular Architecture: Principles and Examples with Reference to Hot Arid Climates.* Chicago, IL: University of Chicago Press.
Fergus, Nicol, Michael Humphreys, and Susan Roaf. 2012. *Adaptive Thermal Comfort: Principles and Practice.* Routledge: London.
Ford, Brian, Nimish Patel, Parul Zaveri, and Mark Hewitt. 1998. "Cooling Without Air Conditioning: The Torrent Research Centre, Ahmedabad, India." *Renewable Energy* 15 (1–4): 177–82.
Fry, Maxwell, and Jane Drew. 1964. *Tropical Architecture in the Dry and Humid Zones.* London: Batsford.
Gontar, Cybèle T. 2009. "The American Campeche Chair." *The Magazine Antiques.* Accessed July 20, 2015. http://www.themagazineantiques.com/articles/the-american-campeche-chair/.
Hutt, Julia, and Helene Alexander. 1992. *Ogi: History of the Japanese Fan.* San Diego, CA: Dauphin Publishing.
International Energy Agency. 2012. *World Energy Outlook 2012 Executive Summary.* Paris: International Energy Agency.
Irons, Neville John. 1982. *Fans of Imperial China, Hong Kong.* London: Kaiserreich Kunst in association with the House of Fans.

Jazeel, Tariq. 2007. "Bawa and Beyond: Reading Sri Lanka's Tropical Modern Architecture." *South Asia Journal for Culture* 1: 7–26.

Kamarulzaman, Noorazlina, Siti Zubaidah Hashim, Hasnan Hashim, and Alla Abdullah Saleh. 2014. "Green Roof Concepts as a Passive Cooling Approach in Tropical Climate—An Overview." *E3S Web of Conferences* 3 (01028): 1–7.

Khoo, Betty L. 1993. *Costumes through Time, Singapore*. Singapore: National Heritage Board and Fashion Designers Society.

The Straits Times. 1929. Regulating Tropical Weather. March 22.

National Environment Agency. 2012. *Household Consumption Survey 2012*. Singapore: National Environment Agency.

Nest. 2015. *Nest Thermostat*. Accessed July 25, 2015. https://nest.com/thermostat/meet-nest-thermostat/

Pomeroy, James. 2014. *The Skycourt and Skygarden: Greening the Urban Habitat*. Oxon: Routledge.

Schatzki, Theodore R. 2001. "Introduction: Practice Theory." In *The Practice Turn in Contemporary Theory*, edited by Theodore R. Schatzki, Karin Knorr Cetina, and Eike Von Savigny, 1–13. New York: Routledge.

Shove, Elizabeth. 2003. *Comfort, Cleanliness and Convenience: The Social Organisation of Normality*. Oxford: Berg.

Shove, Elizabeth. 2012. "Energy Transitions in Practice: The Case Of Global Indoor Climate Change." In *Governing the Energy Transition: Reality, Illusion or Necessity?* edited by Geert Verbong and Derk Loorbach, 51–74. New York: Routledge.

Shove, Elizabeth, Heather Chappells, and Loren Lutzenhiser, eds. 2009. *Comfort in a Lower Carbon Society*. London: Routledge.

Shove, Elizabeth, Mika Pantzar, and Matt Watson. 2012. *The Dynamics of Social Practice: Everyday Life and How It Changes*. London: SAGE.

Strengers, Yolande. 2012. "Peak Electricity Demand and Social Practice Theories: Reframing the Role of Change Agents in the Energy Sector." *Energy Policy* 44: 226–34.

Strengers, Yolande. 2013. *Smart Energy Technologies in Everyday Life: Smart Utopia?* Houndmills: Palgrave Macmillan.

Tado. 2015. *Tado-Smart AC Control*. Accessed July 25, 2015. https://www.tado.com/de-en/smart-air-conditioner.

The Straits Times. 1929. Regulating Tropical Weather. March 22, pg 5, accessed 22/3/2015: http://eresources.nlb.gov.sg/newspapers/Digitised/Article/straitstimes19290322-1.2.12.aspx

Tiipoi ltd. 2014. "Plantation Chair." Accessed July 20, 2015. http://tiipoi.com/blog/plantation-chair/.

TripAdvisor. 2015. *Greenleaders*. Accessed July 20, 2015. http://www.tripadvisor.com/GreenLeaders.

Vann, Molyvann. 2003. *Modern Khmer Cities*. Phnom Penh: Reyum Publishing.

Winter, Tim. 2013. "An Uncomfortable Truth: Air-Conditioning and Sustainability in Asia." *The Journal Environment and Planning A* 45 (3): 517–31.

Yung, Eesther H. K., Craig Langston, and Edwin H. W. Chan. 2014. "Adaptive Reuse of Traditional Chinese Shophouses in Government-led Urban Renewal Projects in Hong Kong." *Cities* 39: 87–98.

3 Green marketing and green consciousness in India

Devleena Ghosh and Amit Jain

In front of the Cornersmith Café in Marrickville, Sydney, there is a long queue of mostly black-clad young people waiting patiently for a table. Others have put their names down on a waiting list and promise to return later. The café is small, the food as good as many other inner-Sydney cafes, but its attraction lies mostly in its "green" credentials. Their website proudly announces, "We believe in sustainable and ethical food production and business practices. We have a seasonal menu and use locally-sourced produce from small-scale growers and makers, ethically produced meats, and a whole lot of our housemade pickles" (Cornersmith 2010). For between $140 and $150, you can learn to preserve, with or without sugar, make gluten-free products, or bake pastries.

Cornersmith is an apposite example of how successful green credentials can be. It has been able to deploy its focus on local produce and environmental concerns as responsible and ethical consumption, thereby attracting customers who pride themselves on their ecological priorities. The classes in pickling and baking add value to their enterprise and enhance their brand. A friend, on learning about the pickling classes, said in horror: "Our mothers fought patriarchy so we wouldn't have to do this any more!" She was only partially joking.

The Cornersmith patron is, on the other hand, an excellent example of the ecologically responsible consumer who is increasingly concerned about the protection of the environment. They are usually well-educated, middle-class citizens who are also aware that environmental problems are complex and persistent and willingly acknowledge that scattered individual efforts are not sufficient for significant change (Amine 2003). In this context, the consumer and the citizen are not discrete entities; the concerns of one inform the behavior of the latter.

These niche consumers value sustainably and ethically produced consumer goods. Since 1987, the Brundtland Report "Our Common Future" (World Commission on Environment and Development 1987) highlighted environmental issues, saying,

> We came to see that a new development path was required, one that sustained human progress not just in a few pieces for a few years, but for the entire planet into the distant future. Thus "sustainable development" becomes a goal not just for the 'developing' nations, but for industrial ones as well.

Since the 1992 Rio Earth Summit, governments, and major corporations have been conscious of sustainability as an important factor for their consumers and citizens. However, "powerful vested interests, a deeply entrenched and environmentally-hostile management paradigm, and a global economy on a trajectory to conventional economic growth" (Peattie and Charter 2003, p. 726) means that the greening of production is still a work in progress even though this rapidly growing section of consumers with high disposable incomes can no longer be ignored.

In the hyper-globalized and super-diverse twenty-first century, ethical consumption has both temporal and spatial ramifications. Commodity chains span transnational and virtual borders, material desires have far-reaching environmental consequences, and the relations of production also represent the complex positions of workers and consumers. Most studies dealing with these topics assume that consumers live in the Global North and producers in the Global South. This article argues, using an empirical survey, that such a framing is now outdated due to the growth of middle-class populations in emerging economies in the Global South and that the promotion of green marketing practices in a country such as India may align corporate and philanthropic goals only if all actors make long-term commitments to such objectives. Our survey consisted of a questionnaire to which we received 106 responses. The questionnaire covered topics such as awareness of environmental degradation, the gravity of such environmental problems, knowledge of government and corporate green initiatives, and skepticism toward such initiatives.

Background

In an illuminating article in the *Harvard Business Review*, Lubin and Esty claim that whereas "sustainability" is a business mega-trend, most business executives do not recognize it as a priority strategy (Lubin and Esty 2010) even though, over the past 10 years, environmental issues have had substantial impact on market value for customers, shareholders, and other stakeholders. Globalization of workforces and supply chains has added to environmental demands and business liabilities while the rise of new world powers, notably China and India, has intensified competition for natural resources (especially oil) and added a geopolitical dimension to sustainability (Lubin and Esty 2010). "'Externalities' such as carbon dioxide emissions and water use are fast becoming material— meaning that investors consider them central to a firm's performance and stakeholders expect companies to share information about them" (Lubin and Esty 2010). Green issues are now global phenomena and sustainable consumption a worldwide concern.

Green consumers and green consumerism began to enter mainstream research in the 1970s and 1980s. The upsurge of environmental concern in the 1970s regarding highly polluting industries produced the concepts of "ecological marketing" and environmentally conscious consumers (Henion and Kinnear 1976). Antil (1984) describes green consumerism as a specific type of socially conscious consumer behavior focused primarily on environmental protection, while Shah (2013) concludes that green consumers purchase only environmentally safe products because of their concern for the environment. Ottmann suggests that, to take advantage of this growing segment of the market, businesses should balance environmental issues with primary customer needs and that all aspects of marketing—including new product development and communications—should be integrated with environmental considerations (Ottman 1998).

Michael Polonsky (1994) defines green marketing as consisting of all activities designed to generate and facilitate the exchanges intended to satisfy human needs or wants with minimal detrimental impact on the natural environment.

> Green marketing is related not only with the marketing of the green products or environment friendly products, but it incorporates a broad range of activities ranging from product modification, changes in the production process, changes in packaging, as well as modifying advertising of the products or removing any activity that impacts the natural environment in negative way.

Peattie and Charter, on the other hand, define green marketing as the holistic management process responsible for identifying, anticipating, and satisfying the needs of customers and society in a profitable and sustainable way (2003, p. 727). There is an inherent paradox in both these definitions in that environmental concerns usually involve conservation, recycling, and re-use while marketing is focused at stimulating and facilitating consumption. Green marketing has to adopt an open-ended perspective, ascribing an intrinsic rather than instrumental value to the environment and focusing on global rather than local concerns. To market their products as truly "green", businesses must adopt ethical and green practices in production as well as with all stakeholders including employees, suppliers, dealers, customers, and so on. They must manufacture eco-friendly products that have minimal detrimental impact on the environment.

Lyn S. Amine quotes from Kermit the Frog's song in "The Muppet Show" in her article on green marketing: "It isn't easy being green", saying that business writers normally use this line "in an ironic sense to underline the challenges attendant upon supporting and implementing green business practices among individual consumers and corporations alike" (2003, p. 373). An example is the fact that, as stated above, green marketing is targeted at increasing consumption (even if such consumption is of sustainable products). On the other hand, rampant growth and consumerism are two of the main reasons for environmental crises. Paradoxically, consumers who change to green consumption habits are more influenced by the "green" quality of their purchases rather than the brand. Thus, green marketing practices, in theory, provide opportunities for corporations to meet consumer demands, concurrently address environmental issues, develop a competitive advantage, and create a loyal consumer base (Renfro 2010). Cause-related marketing, in particular, has evolved as one area wherein firms can link their corporate social responsibility activities with strategic marketing and charitable goals to gain competitive advantage and improve their long-term business prospects (Agarwal and Tyagi 2010).

Cause-related marketing

Many governments have now instituted environmental regulation mandating sustainable business practices. In India, the Environment Protection Act was implemented in 1986 (Government of India 1986), and the environmental auditing of industrial units was formally introduced in March 1992 with the overall objective of minimizing consumption of resources and generation of waste through the use of clean technologies in industrial production (Mahwar et al. 1997).

New Delhi, the Indian capital, was one of the most polluted cities until the Supreme Court of India intervened in favor of alternative fuels. A historic Supreme Court judgment in 1998 forced all public transport vehicles, an estimated 100,000, to switch to cleaner compressed natural gas (Ghosal and Chatterjee 2015). More recently, the Indian government passed the "The Companies Act 2013", a bill that (among other things) mandates corporate social responsibility (CSR) for companies over a certain size and registered in India. Beginning in the fiscal year 2014–2015, the Act requires corporate entities that meet the criteria to spend at least 2 per cent of their average net profit in the previous 3 years on CSR activities (Prasad 2014).

Such laws have helped to increase the popularity of cause-related marketing (CRM) as a model through which for-profit entities (for example, corporations), nonprofit entities (for example, non-governmental organizations [NGOs]), and consumers can intervene and ameliorate social issues. Under the CRM model, a corporation makes a donation to an NGO each time a consumer purchases their branded product. For example, each time a consumer in India buys a packet of Tide washing powder, Procter & Gamble donates to a group of education-focused NGOs, Project Shiksha. Since these donations are triggered by consumer purchases, cause-related marketing can be understood as a form of ethical consumption. It has become an important strategic tool for businesses wishing to build a positive corporate image among consumers and increase their sales and profits.

For consumers, alliances between for-profit firms and nonprofit organizations (with nonprofit causes) have become increasingly popular (Gourville and Kasturi Rangan 2004). Customers who were attracted to cause-related marketing were more likely to pay a premium price for the product promoted. These commercial and philanthropic sponsorships thus helped the corporations involved to achieve profits as well as improve their corporate image and brand recognition (Nicolau-Gonzalbez, Mas-Ruiz, and Calderon-Martinez 2005). Generally, commercial sponsorships generated positive returns for the organizations concerned and firms financing socially responsible activities as well as their core business improved their stock prices and were more competitive in the marketplace (Dennis et al. 2008). Increasing consumer concern about environmental issues (Juwaheer 2005) and with green values has translated their real-world changes in consumption patterns and a move to eco-friendly appearing products (Bhatia and Jain 2013).

The case of India

However, the choices offered to most consumers in wealthy countries such as Australia or the United States are very different from those available to buyers in low-income countries and emerging economies. World Bank figures for 2000 showed that nearly half the world's population lived on under $2 per day and, for them, notions of consumer choice or discretionary spending were risible (Peattie and Charter 2003, p. 726). Green marketing in India is, therefore, directed mainly at the middle classes, the fastest-growing segment of the population, estimates of which range from 30 million to approximately 300 million people. India's middle-class consumption is roughly equivalent to Ireland's total private consumption and is forecast to triple in its share of India's total consumption over the next 15 years (Saxena 2010). However, the definition of "middle-class" as a category is highly contested. It may be based on factors such as earning an annual income of more than 70,000 Rupees; speaking English and having private education; appetite for global culture and Western lifestyles; and/or being constituted in opposition to imagined categories of the slum-dwelling or rural poor (Hawkins 2015, p. 6).

Traditionally, in a largely agricultural, late-industrializing country, environmental concerns were the preserve of either the government or the philanthropic sector; in India the latter includes an increasingly diverse array of actors—corporations, NGOs, faith-based groups, entertainment celebrities, and so on. Indian traditions of philanthropy often incorporated a cause-related marketing model, such as local shops having a box available for customers to make charitable donations toward community cow sheds, orphanages, or other causes (Hawkins 2015, p. 2).

Green marketing in this context often involved celebrity endorsement. Leading Bombay film actor Shah Rukh Khan endorsed anti-poaching initiatives organized by the U.S.–based international wildlife conservation NGO WildAid, in cooperation with India's state authorities and broadcast media (WildAid 2007). Another Bombay cinema star, Aamir Khan, was involved in the campaign to save a wildlife corridor at Aarey Milk Colony (Jadhav 2015). Booker Prize–winning author Arundhati Roy lent her name and prestige to a number of environmental movements (Roy 1998). Along with her writings and lectures in support of these causes, Roy consistently donated money received as prizes, awards, or lecture fees to activist movements. For example, the Booker Prize money and the royalties from her novel, *The God of Small Things*, went to the Narmada Bachao Andolan, a protest movement against the Sardar Sarovar dam being constructed on the River Narmada (Frontline 1999).

An example of a government initiative on the environment is the "Mission Swachh Bharat" (Clean India) campaign that the Prime Minister of India, Narendra Modi, launched on October 2, 2014. He hoped that "the mission should become the agenda of the entire country in the form of a mass movement ... with the aim of creating a clean India by 2019". Besides promoting cleanliness of public areas and the collection and processing/disposal/reuse/recycling of municipal solid waste, this campaign tapped into one of the major concerns for both the urban and rural poor: the elimination of the open defecation that is endemic to India. One of the aims of the project is to build over 800 million toilets along with modern sewage treatment systems (Government of India 2014). Various celebrities including cricket icon Sachin Tendulkar, industrialist Anil Ambani, and several Bombay film actors such as Amitabh Bachchan, Aamir Khan, and Priyanka Chopra lent their support to this movement (*Times of India*

2014). Bachchan, whose endorsements are highly sought, publicly swept streets and picked up garbage in Mumbai as part of his contribution.

The Government of India also demonstrated excellent use of public communication and social media in promoting this campaign. The CEO of Facebook, Mark Zuckerberg, promised to help the government create a "Swachh Bharat" or "Clean India" app, but local entrepreneurs beat him to the game. The web is now flooded with a number of such free apps that are available in the Android Play Store. One of them promises to map the efficacy of local initiatives; another app marks out a city's debris hotspots. Another created by an engineering graduate who also holds an MBA in sustainable energy and product design management enables users to track and report unclean places in their locality (Inc42 2014). The Union Ministry of Drinking Water and Sanitation encouraged people to directly upload photos of unused or unclean toilets on their website and on social media through mobile phones or tablets (*The Hindu* 2015).

For businesses, making green marketing part of their core strategy poses several challenges (Welling and Chavan 2010). Green marketing implies that products and services are produced sustainably; this may, for example, involve appropriate technology, new or modified, and green power/energy as well as a change to branding (such as eco-labeling). These manufacturing transitions may initially be costly in contexts where many customers balk at paying premium prices for green products. Green marketing, to be effective, requires companies to undertake effective and innovative public relations to communicate the benefits of environmentally friendly products and persuade consumers to pay higher prices for obvious additional benefits (such as non-polluting, fuel-efficient vehicles and household products manufactured with non-hazardous materials). Most businesses, therefore, subsumed environmental concerns within community development and philanthropic activities, distinguishing them from core business objectives. It is only recently that sustainable development, production, and consumption have been linked to CSR, and there is widespread acknowledgment that business organizations have responsibilities not only to shareholders but also to the society within which they function (Agarwal and Tyagi 2010). As mentioned above, on April 1, 2014, India was the first country in the world to mandate CSR through new CSR guidelines requiring companies to spend 2 per cent of their net profit on social development (Prasad 2014).

In this context, most respondents to our survey rated the seriousness of environmental concerns highly but also concluded that environmental degradation had increased in the last decade (Tables 3.1 and 3.2). These responses show that consumers are concerned about environmental protection but think that not enough is being done by the appropriate and responsible actors to ameliorate such problems.

As far as Indian consumers are concerned, the 2012 Greendex survey found that 57 per cent of them were choosing to buy environmentally friendly products (National Geographic 2012), while Nielsen research puts India among the top three Asia Pacific countries, along with Vietnam and Indonesia, which showed a strong affinity for eco-friendly products (*The CSR Journal* 2014). Consumers showing the largest increase in environmentally sustainable behavior were in India, Russia, and the United States (Howe et al. 2010). In 2014, Fairtrade India, an organization that works to enable

Table 3.1 Consumer perception about environmental degradation and perceived state of environment in the next five years

Statements	Mean	Std. Deviation
Environmental Degradation has risen in last decade?	4.38	.980
In the next five years, state of the environment will be degraded more?	4.15	.814

Table 3.2 Consumer perception about seriousness related to various environmental concerns

Seriousness of environmental concern	Mean	Std. Deviation
Destruction of Ozone	4.33	.923
Industrial Air Pollution	4.32	.911
Industrial Water Pollution	4.28	.870
Warming up of Earth	4.26	.979
Drinking Water Contamination	4.25	.964
Destruction of Rain Forest	4.24	.972
Hazardous Waste	4.12	1.039
Auto Air Pollution	3.93	.959
Pesticides on Food	3.88	1.057
Oil Spills	3.81	.996
Ocean Contamination	3.77	1.026
Endangered Species	3.75	1.128
Solid Waste	3.74	.998
Destruction of Wet Lands	3.72	.974
Industrial Accidents	3.40	1.093
Genetically Modified Products	3.37	1.107
Indoor Air Pollution from Household Cleaners, Tobacco Smoke, Asbestos etc.	3.25	1.122

better terms of trade for small and marginalized farmers, conducted a survey about the sustainability issues that consumers felt were most important. Eighty-five per cent of respondents agreed that upholding the rights of workers and producers and protecting the environment was a joint responsibility of business and consumers. Young people in particular held businesses even more responsible than older consumers; of young respondents ages 18 to 24, none thought it was the law's responsibility to lead on ethical business practice. They were also willing to put their money where their mouths were: Ethical consumers were, on average, willing to spend 25 per cent more for a product they felt was ethical (Doane 2014). Our own survey found the levels of consumer awareness about green products/practices to be high (about 96 per cent of the sample; Table 3.3). The respondents rated the importance of green marketing practices of corporations highly (mean score 4.36 on a 5-point agreement scale) and were positive about the promotion of green products/practices.

Table 3.3 Awareness about green initiatives taken by various government and non-government entities

Entity	Percentage of people who know about the initiatives taken by various government and non-government entities
Ministry of Environment	38.7
State Government	35.8
NGOs	31.1
Large Business of India	23.8
Small Business of India	12.3
Others	3.8

Additionally, the *Re: Thinking Consumption* study by BBMG and others identified "aspirationals" as a category of "style and social status seeking" consumers in India who wanted to purchase brand-name products that "improve their own lives (through function and status) *and* improve society more broadly" (BBMG, GlobeScan, and SustainAbility 2012). These "aspirationals" account for 42 per cent of consumers in India and are more than twice as likely than consumers in developed countries to buy products because of social or environmental benefits (BBMG, GlobeScan, and SustainAbility 2012; Hawkins 2015, p. 6).

Indian businesses have responded to this growing niche market in many ways. Godrej Consumer Products gives incentives to buyers to exchange their old products for environmentally friendly ones. For example, the advertisement for the Godrej air conditioner emphasizes its energy efficiency—"India's most energy-efficient; less power than a hair dryer" (Godrej Appliances 2012). NDTV, a major media group, promotes green values through its campaign Greenathon, organizing various philanthropic and social activities to raise environmental awareness as well as contribute to developmental causes such as the electrification of rural areas (NDTV 2012). Many companies are now offering more eco-friendly alternatives for their customers; recycled products, paper, or cloth rather than plastic bags. Titan, Tanishq, and Fab India both have a corporate policy of using only carry bags made of recycled material. The NDTV Greenathon campaign mentioned above begins its television spot with the words "Today we declare a war on plastic" (NDTV 2012). Idea Cellular Limited, a mobile phone company, launched a campaign titled "Use Mobile Save Paper", urging their consumers to replace paper documents with mobile apps (Idea Cellular Limited 2013). Kansai Nerolac Paints emphasizes the fact that their paint is lead-free ("Do you know that paint with lead can damage your nervous system?") in their advertising in India (Nerolac Paints India 2012). Dell Computers in India now come in eco-friendly bamboo packaging bundled with a system-recycling kit. They offer special discounts toward the purchase of a new Dell system to consumers who send in their old systems for free recycling. Dell also initiated a 'Dell Go Green Challenge' to raise awareness and community involvement in green initiatives in India. This challenge invited users to share photographs, videos, and other innovative depictions of key issues, concerns, or thoughts on green technology at www.dellgogreen.com (*The Indian Express* 2010).

Cause-related marketing in India

In 2005, India's largest consumer goods company, Procter & Gamble (P&G), launched a cause marketing campaign called "Shiskha" ("education") in partnership with Child Relief and You (CRY) to bring education to underprivileged children across India. This issue was identified as a top concern through customer surveys, and the campaign was designed to trigger donations with each purchase of a Proctor & Gamble product. Funds collected through this campaign are directed to education NGOs such as Round Table India and Save the Children India. In the last 9 years of the Shiksha program, P&G made a cumulative donation of more than $4.5 million (Rs 270 million) to its NGO partners (CMF Global Voices 2013).

This campaign's success can be directly attributed to Proctor & Gamble India's commitment to a long-running and visible marketing campaign promoted by its media and public relations outfits. There are advertisements on different television channels and publicity at points of sale at large retail stores and local retail outlets to create customer awareness. The company has persuaded several eminent Indian celebrities to endorse Shiksha and encourages its employees to participate through hands-on volunteering. The campaign is active on social media; the P&G Shiksha Facebook page has more than 290,000 followers (CMF Global Voices 2013).

Another successful example of cause-related marketing is the Desh ko Arpan (DKAP) campaign that promotes a brand of salt marketed by the company Tata as the purest-tasting salt and at the same time "provid[es] consumers with an opportunity to contribute to a cause" (Shatrujeet 2002). Under this program, the company, in partnership with CRY, has promised to contribute 10 paise ($ 0.002) from every kilogram of Tata Salt sold toward the uplifting of underprivileged girl children. As a result of this CRM campaign, Tata salt sales rose by 16 per cent, and "consumers have begun to recognize the benefits of branded salt" (Hawkins 2015, p. 4). Like the Proctor & Gamble campaign, the DKAP campaign idea stemmed from a consumer insight linked to the idiomatic usage of the word *salt* across languages, from someone being "worth his salt" or "having eaten his/her salt" or "betraying salt". The DKAP campaign draws heavily on the values of patriotism and philanthropy in its advertising; the "purity" of its salt calls to mind Gandhi's defiance of British rule through his epic Salt March and becomes linked to a "purity of thought and action". The creative director of the campaign, Rajeev Raja (Shatrujeet 2002) commented that they wanted to draw a parallel between the way in which small amounts of salt could change the complexion of food to small acts of integrity and loyalty that could change a nation, thus "highlighting small deeds of selflessness that reflect a respect for the Greater Good. In the process, the campaign rises from being solely about Indianness to being about good citizens" (Hawkins 2015, p. 5).

Campaigns such as these successful and visible ones are the reasons why our respondents demonstrated a high level of trust (mean score of 3.57) in the environmental claims made by organizations. The implications of this finding are positive; corporations, government, and non-government entities have the social capital to undertake pro-environmental initiatives and may generally depend on consumer support for them (Table 3.4). In contrast, however, our survey

Table 3.4 Consumer skepticism about green practices of the organizations

Statement	Mean	Std. Deviation
Organizations manufacturing/promoting green products are really concerned about the environment?	3.57	1.024

found that the respondents were not familiar with many of the environmental initiatives undertaken by government bodies, NGOs, or corporations in India (see Table 3.3). Therefore, corporations, NGOs, and government bodies need to improve their public communication practices so as to better engage consumers in environmentally sustainable initiatives.

Conclusion

Both the empirical data and the secondary literature demonstrate that the level of awareness about and preference for green products is high among consumers in India and that they approve of green marketing practices; consumers generally feel that environmental degradation has escalated in the last decade and expect it to deteriorate further in the next 5 years and are of the opinion that governments and corporations are not doing enough to ameliorate environmental damage.

It is also evident that consumers approve of cause-related marketing and philanthropic activities undertaken by corporations. Such campaigns help to build trust and positive social capital for these organizations and enhance their profitability and competitive advantage. These findings demonstrate that corporations and governments should make the most of the opportunities to align their corporate and philanthropic goals with green marketing practices since this is likely to both enhance profit and fulfill their CSR objectives.

Dipesh Chakrabarty points out that in the age of the Anthropocene, humans have to be viewed simultaneously on contradictory registers: as a geophysical force and as a political agent, as bearers of rights and as an author of actions; subject to both the stochastic forces of nature (being itself one such force collectively) and open to the contingency of individual human experience; belonging at once to differently scaled histories of the planet, of life and species, and of human societies (Chakrabarty 2012, p. 15). In this context, green and/or cause-related marketing raises some interesting paradoxes about the moral economy of consumption in India. Is the Indian middle class in thrall to brand culture and conspicuous spending? Or are there significant sections of it that wish to differentiate themselves from the lower classes by purchasing goods that may have the desirable brand but also have the added value of contributing to a cause? In the latter case, such consumers are then in the win-win position of helping the underprivileged without compromising the safety of their middle-class status. Hawkins comments,

> Project Shiksha bridges this gap well by promoting itself as a "national consumer movement that empowers consumers across the country to participate and support education of marginalised children in India" (India

PR Wire, 2008), while at the same time increasing the sale of its branded household products (Agarwal, 2013). Similarly, the resolution of these contradictory notions (conspicuous versus moral consumption) is evident in the DKAP campaign where the double meaning of purity (as a brand qualifier and a description of philanthropic actions) attracts consumers from the "aspirational" category who wish to purchase brand-name products and simultaneously improve society. The ability of CRM to bridge this apparent divide in consumer culture is perhaps what makes it most appealing to for-profit, non-profit and consumer actors in the Indian context

(Hawkins 2015, p. 6)

At the entrance to one of the most contested coal mines in Central India stands a signboard: "We have only one earth; let us preserve it." This billboard, at a site producing the very fossil fuel that is a major contributor to global environmental damage, is also a double sign; it points both to the effectiveness of leveraging green credentials as part of a set of marketing strategies and to the ways in which such green tropes may be deployed as fig leaves to conceal unpleasant, sometimes catastrophic, environmental realities. Green or cause-related marketing can be a double-edged sword. It can attract media and consumer attention where otherwise the cause is absent in the public sphere. It may also enlist supporters who were previously ignorant or uninspired about that cause. However, unless there is ongoing and robust commitment from all actors involved, media focus is generally soon diverted elsewhere, and the cause becomes lost. Endorsement or support for green causes by corporations and governments make for limited politics if they are solely profit-driven. On the other hand, a well-thought-out realignment of corporate and social responsibility goals involving government, corporations, NGOs, and consumers may have truly transformative aspects—the ability for meaning making and an opportunity to reauthor the social and material world.

References

Agarwal P. K., and A. K. Tyagi. 2010. "Cause Related Marketing in India: A Conceptual Paradigm." *Advances in Management* 3 (12): 24–31.
Amine, Lyn S. 2003. "An Integrated Micro- and Macrolevel Discussion of Global Green Issues: 'It Isn't Easy Being Green'." *Journal of International Management* 9 (4): 373–93
Antil, John H. 1984. "Socially Responsible Consumers: Profile and Implications for Public Policy." *Journal of Macromarketing* 4 (2): 18–39.
BBMG, GlobeScan, and SustainAbility. 2012. *Re: Thinking Consumption: Consumers and the Future of Sustainability*. Accessed September 15, 2015. http://www.globescan.com/component/edocman/?task=document.viewdoc&id=51&Itemid=0.
Bhatia, Mayank, and Amit Jain. 2013. "Green Marketing: A Study of Consumer Perception and Preferences in India." *Electronic Green Journal* 1 (36). http://escholarship.org/uc/item/5mc39217.
Chakrabarty, Dipesh. 2012. "Postcolonial Studies and the Challenge of Climate Change." *New Literary History* 43 (1): 1–18.

CMF Global Voices. 2013. P&G India Addresses Education with Shiksha. Last Modified October 1. Accessed September 15, 2010. http://causeupdate.com/globalvoices/pg-india-addresses-education-with-shiksha.

Cornersmith. 2010. "Cafe." Accessed September 15, 2010. http://www.cornersmith.com.au/

Dennis, Bryan, Robert S. D'Intino, Jeffery D. Houghton, Christopher P. Neck, and Trish Boyles. 2008. "Corporate Social Performance: Creating Resources to Help Organizations Excel." *Global Business and Organizational Excellence* 27 (2): 26–41.

Doane, Deborah. 2014 "New Fairtrade India Survey Finds that Indian Consumers Care about Social Well-Being." Accessed September 15, 2015. http://www.thealternative.in/business/new-fairtrade-india-survey-finds-that-indian-consumers-care-about-social-well-being/

Frontline. 1999. "A novel gesture" *Frontline,* July 3–16. Accessed February 6, 2013. http://www.frontline.in/navigation/?type=static&page=flonnet&rdurl=fl1614/16140360.htm.

Ghosal, Aniruddha, and Pritha Chatterjee. 2015. "Seven Years Ago, Everyone Saw Delhi's Air Take a Deadly U-Turn but No One Did a Thing." *The Indian Express*, March 31. Accessed September 15, 2015. http://indianexpress.com/article/india/india-others/seven-years-ago-everyone-saw-delhis-air-take-a-deadly-u-turn-but-no-one-did-a-thing/

Godrej Appliances. 2012. "Godrej Eon Ac." YouTube video, 0:25, posted by Godrej Appliances, April 18. Accessed November 3, 2015. https://www.youtube.com/watch?v=PbcrDY0WuW8.

Gourville, John T., and V. Kasturi Rangan. 2004. "Valuing the Cause Marketing Relationship." *California Management Review* 47 (1): 38–57.

Government of India. 1986. *Environment Protection Act.* Accessed November 3, 2015. http://envfor.nic.in/legis/env/env1.html.

Government of India. 2014. "Swacch Bharat/My Clean India." Accessed October 30, 2014. https://swachhbharat.mygov.in/.

Hawkins, Roberta. 2015. "Shifting conceptualizations of ethical consumption: Cause-related marketing in India and the USA." *Geoforum.* doi:10.1016/j.geoforum.2015.05.007.

Henion, Karl E., and Thomas C. Kinnear. 1976. "Measuring the Effect of Ecological Information and Social Class on Selected Product Choice Criteria Importance Ratings." In *Ecological Marketing*, edited by the American Marketing Association, 145–56. Chicago, IL: American Marketing Association.

Howe, Jeff, Steve Bratkovich, Jim Bowyer, Kathryn Fernholz, and Sarah Stai. 2010. *Green Marketing-Growing Sales in Growing Markets.* Minneapolis, MN: Dovetail Partners Inc.

Idea Cellular Limited. 2013. "Use mobile save paper." YouTube video, 1:26, posted by Nilesh Gohil, August 28. Accessed November 3, 2015. https://www.youtube.com/watch?v=jEvZ-UBUf50.

Inc42. 2014. "The App that is Trying to Keep Indian Streets Clean." *Inc42 Magazine*, November 11. Accessed December 3, 2014. http://inc42.com/startups/swachh-bharat-app/

Jadhav, Ranjeet. 2015. "Now, Bollywood Star Aamir Khan Pledges Support to Aarey." *Mid-Day*, March 29. Accessed September 15, 2015. http://www.mid-day.com/articles/now-bollywood-star-aamir-khan-pledges-support-to-aarey/16099180.

Juwaheer, Thanika Devi. 2005. "Emerging Shades of Green Marketing Conscience Among the Population of a Small Island Economy-A Case Study on Mauritius." Accessed September 15, 2015. http://irfd.org/events/wfsids/virtual/papers/sids_tdjuwaheer.pdf.

Lubin, David A., and Daniel C. Esty. 2010. "The Sustainability Imperative." *Harvard Business Review*, May. Accessed September 15, 2015. https://hbr.org/2010/05/the-sustainability-imperative#.

Mahwar, Ranveer Singh, N. K. Verma, S. P. Chakrabarti, and D. K. Biswas. 1997. "Environmental Auditing Programme in India." *Science of the Total Environment* 204 (1): 11–26. doi:10.1016/S0048-9697(97)00161-7.

National Geographic. 2012. "Greendex Indians." Accessed September 15, 2015. http://images.nationalgeographic.com/wpf/media-live/file/Greendex-Indians_FINAL-cb1409255777.pdf

NDTV. 2012. "The best of Greenathon 4." YouTube video, 17:45, posted by NDTV, May 21. Accessed November 3, 2015. https://www.youtube.com/watch?v=PbcrDY0WuW8.

Nerolac Paints India. 2012. "Nerolac TVC-Lead free paints." YouTube video, 0:20, posted by Nerolac Paints India. Accessed November 3, 2015. https://www.youtube.com/watch?v=_lUzjt5Qq-w

Nicolau-Gonzalbez, Juan L, Francisco J. Mas-Ruiz, and Aurora Calderon-Martinez. 2005. "Commercial and Philanthropic Sponsorship: Direct and Interaction Effects on Company Performance." *International Journal of Market Research* 47 (1): 75–99.

Ottman, Jacquelyn. 1998. *Green Marketing: Opportunity for Innovation*. Chicago, IL: NTC Business Books.

Peattie, Ken, and Martin Charter. 2003. "Green Marketing." In *The Marketing Book*, edited by Michael J. Baker, 726–56. Oxford and Burlington: Butterworth-Heinemann.

Polonsky, Michael Jay. 1994. "An Introduction to Green Marketing." *Electronic Green Journal* 1 (2). http://escholarship.org/uc/item/49n325b7.

Prasad, Ashok. 2014. "India's New CSR Law Sparks Debate among NGOs and Businesses." *The Guardian*, August 12. Accessed September 4, 2015. http://www.theguardian.com/sustainable-business/india-csr-law-debate-business-ngo.

Renfro, Leigh Ann. 2010. "Green Business Operations and Green Marketing." *Gatton Student Research Publication* 2 (2), Gatton College of Business & Economics, University of Kentucky.

Roy, Arundhati. 1998. "The End of Imagination." *Outlook India*, August 3. Accessed September 11, 2013. http://www.outlookindia.com/article.aspx?205932.

Saxena, Rachna. 2010. "The Middle Class in India." *Deutsch Bank Research*, February 15. Accessed September 10, 2015. http://www.dbresearch.de/PROD/DBR_INTERNET_DE-PROD/PROD0000000000253735.pdf.

Shah, Priya. 2013. "Green Consumerism." *Asia Pacific Journal of Management and Entrepreneurship Research* 2 (1): 51–5.

Shatrujeet, N. 2002. "Tata Salt Expands 'Purity' Proposition with Desh Ka Namak Campaign." *Afaqs!*, August 19. Accessed 11 September 2013. http://www.afaqs.com/news/story/4771_Tata-Salt-expands-purity-proposition-with-Desh-Ka-Namak-campaign

The CSR Journal. 2014. "Ethical Consumerism: Look Before You Buy." *The CSR Journal*, August 1. Accessed September 15, 2015. http://thecsrjournal.in/ethical-consumerism-look-before-you-buy/.

The Hindu. 2015. "Unused Rural Toilets to Face Public Scrutiny." *The Hindu*, January 1. Accessed January 5, 2015. http://www.thehindu.com/news/national/swachh-bharat-goes-hitech-govt-to-track-toilet-use-in-realtime/article6742186.ece?utm_source=RSS_Feed&utm_medium=RSS&utm_campaign=RSS_Syndication.

The Indian Express. 2010. "Dell India's Green Steps!" *The Indian Express*, June 4. Accessed September 15, 2015. http://archive.indianexpress.com/news/dell-indias-green-steps-/629530.

Times of India. 2014 "PM Modi Ropes in Celebrities for his 'Swachh Bharat' Challenge." *The Times of India*, October 2. Accessed October 5, 2014. http://timesofindia.

indiatimes.com/india/PM-Modi-ropes-in-celebrities-for-his-Swachh-Bharat-challenge/articleshow/44121679.cms.

Welling M. N., and S. Chavan Anupamaa. 2010. "Analyzing the Feasibility of Green Marketing in Small and Medium Scale Manufacturers." *Asia Pacific Journal of Research in Business Management* 1 (2): 119–33.

WildAid. 2007. "Shah Rukh champions the cause of India's unsung heroes," July 13. Accessed November 3, 2015. http://www.wildaid.org/news/shah-rukh-champions-cause-india%E2%80%99s-unsung-heroes-forest-guards.

World Commission on Environment and Development. 1987. "Report of the World Commission on Environment and Development: Our Common Future." Accessed September 15, 2015. http://www.un-documents.net/our-common-future.pdf.

4 "Relying on Heaven"
Natural farming and "Eco-tea" in Taiwan

Scott Writer

Just to look at Mr. Zhang's tea fields is to see that they are different. Arriving at his small farm after a bumpy half-hour ride in a flat-bed truck through the hills above the town of Beipu, you notice first the long grass growing between the rows of tea plants; if left unchecked, it seems the grass will soon cover them entirely. Looking closer, you see that a host of animal species has taken up residence among the tea. Zhang points them out as he walks among the bushes: a spider's web traced across the face of one plant, a dense cluster of caterpillars hidden beneath the foliage of another. It is a far cry from the neatly manicured rows of tea bushes commonly seen in Taiwanese tourism campaigns. Yet what at first appear to be signs of neglect—tea plants converged upon by weeds, a crop riddled with pests—are in fact manifestations of a particular approach to agriculture that in Taiwan is known as "natural farming" (自然農法 *ziran nongfa*), or what Zhang calls the "ecological school" (生態派 *shengtai pai*) of tea cultivation.[1] For farmers of this stripe, the plant and animal life that surround their tea plants are not pests to be eradicated but constituents in a complicated and contingent play of agencies, a tea-field "ecosystem", whose dynamism is thought to determine the quality of each tea crop.

This chapter focuses on practices of "natural" tea farming and tea manufacturing in and around Beipu, a small town in the southeast of Hsinchu County in Taiwan. My argument is based primarily on ethnographic fieldwork and interviews carried out there in 2011 and 2012. During this time, I was granted access to the fields and factories of several small-scale tea producers, who instructed me in tea-making procedures and shared with me their thoughts about growing, manufacturing, and selling tea.[2] My primary tutors in the art of tea making were the farmers whom I refer to here as Mr. Zhang and Mr. Lin.[3] Their centrality to my fieldwork experience is reflected by the prominence I grant them in this chapter, albeit deploying their views in counterpoint with those of other tea producers whom I visited for interviews or participant observation during my research. All of these farmers are engaged in growing, manufacturing, and selling tea directly to customers under the "produce your own, sell your own" (自產自銷 *zichan zixiao*) model of small- to medium-sized home-factories that has been prevalent since the liberalization of Taiwan's tea manufacturing industry several decades ago (some operate larger-scale businesses that also process raw leaves purchased from other farmers in Beipu and adjacent tea-growing areas).

The tea that these farmers produce is commonly and widely known as "Oriental Beauty" (東方美人茶 *dongfang meiren cha*). However, it is also known locally as "Peng Feng Tea" (膨風茶 *pengfeng cha*) and as "White Down Oolong" tea (白毫烏龍 *baihao oolong*), the latter a reference to the distinctive silver-white down that coats the leaf-buds of the tea after it is processed. In keeping with this volume's interest in ways of imagining ecologically attuned "green" living in Asia, my immediate concern in this chapter is to think through how "ecological" practices of growing and manufacturing Oriental Beauty are also ways of understanding and rendering sensible qualities of local tea-growing and tea-manufacturing environments. To produce high-quality tea requires tea producers apprehend the relationships that hold between particular tea-growing environments, received styles of tea manufacturing, and the optimal taste and fragrance of each tea. And it is only by successfully coordinating these different contingencies that the tea maker can be confident that his or her tea will command a viable price when it enters into systems of market exchange. This conjunction of ontological and economic contingency is neatly summarized by a vernacular expression commonly used by tea producers, 靠天吃飯 *kao tian chi fan*: "to rely on heaven for sustenance." In what follows, I take up the notion of "relying on heaven" (*kao tian*) as a way of conceptualizing how tea production practices are tangled up within relations that hold between the qualities of tea and the environmental qualities particular to its space of cultivation and manufacture. The first part of this chapter situates these concepts in the context of the "ecological" methods of tea cultivation as carried out in and around Beipu, paying special attention to the way in which relying on heaven in practice requires tea producers to admit into the tea-growing process a raft of non-human actors whose interventions can play a decisive part in determining the quality of the raw tea leaves. In the second part, I change tack to consider how practices of tea manufacturing transpose this engagement with the tea field ecosystem into a concern with the materiality of each batch of tea leaves and the sensory effects that skilled tea manufacturers are able to elicit from such material.

Framing my inquiry into tea production in this fashion puts me in debt to several currents in recent scholarship. On the one hand, in conceptualizing the tea field as a site for contingent articulations of human and non-human agency and granting that the latter is often decisive to the outcomes of cultivation and manufacturing practices, I am echoing not just the views of my tea farmer informants but also a concern with the agency of non-humans that animates a wide range of recent social theory. The import of this work is captured to some extent by Bruno Latour's remark that a full rendering of social life must also account for "the capacity of artefacts to construct, literally and not metaphorically, social order" (2000, p. 113). Accordingly, I have endeavored to give sufficient weight to the various agential capacities of the plants, animals, and natural forces: the "things" that constitute the tea-field "ecosystem." In the field of cultural geography, an allied concern with the cross-hatching of the human and non-human worlds has animated the work of scholars such as Sarah Whatmore, whose concern for how plants and animals are "routinely caught up within multiple networks of social life," (2002, p. 9) is reflected by my account of tea production and especially my interest in how the products of "natural farming" are transformed by the tea-manufacturing process.

On the other hand, my interest in how ecological specificities influence the afterlife of tea in its guise as a material and commodity links this chapter to debates in cultural studies, sociology, and anthropology that have been gathered under the banner of "new materialism" (Braun and Whatmore 2010; Coole and Frost 2010; Bolt and Barrett 2012) or united by a concern with "materiality" as a field of inquiry (for example, Miller 2005; Ingold 2007; Holbraad 2011). From this work, as well as that of Deleuze and Guattari (1987), I derive an analytical orientation towards the way that the *expressivity* of particular materials influences social practices, aesthetic strategies, and political subjectivities. Crucial here are the ways in which tea production depends on the tea maker's enmeshment within the scales and temporalities immanent to each tea as a material, such that an account of the production process is necessarily also an account of a corporeal and affective encounter between humans and materials. Finally, I share with Jensen and Blok (2013) the view that the theoretical issues animating these fields of inquiry can be placed in a fruitful dialogue with ontological and epistemological orders different from those of the Euro-American societies from whence these debates issue. In this light, let us return to the tea fields to see in more detail how the tea farmers of Beipu take up questions of non-human agency and materiality in practice.

The tea field as "ecosystem"

As the seasons turn over into summer, Mr. Zhang visits his fields with increasing frequency. Walking up and down each row, he checks not only the health of his plants but also looks to confirm the arrival of an important, if not entirely reliable, visitor to his fields: the "small green leaf hopper" (小綠葉蟬 *xiao lü ye chan*; *Jacobiasca Formosana Paoli,* sometimes rendered in English as the "tea jassid"). These cicadas, measuring just a few millimeters long, thrive in Taiwan's tea fields, their populations peaking in the early summer and again to a lesser extent in late autumn (Tan 2009, pp. 149–50). Tea farmers often refer to them as 浮塵子 *fuchenzi*—"floating dust"—a name indicative of both their size and also their pervasiveness when their population is at its peak. Small green leaf hoppers feed on tea plants, which is why in many parts of Taiwan they are treated as a pest best eradicated (Lai 2005, p. 159). Producers of Oriental Beauty tea in Beipu and neighboring tea-growing regions across Hsinchu, Miaoli, and Taoyuan counties, however, count these insects as a crucial ally. The reason for this is that the damage done to leaves that have suffered *fuchenzi* infestation results in their producing tea with a radically different taste and fragrance than would otherwise be obtained. Although research continues into the exact mechanism by which this occurs, recent biochemical studies indicate that the damage induced by the cicada's feeding results in a defensive stress response on the part of the tea plant that spurs the production of certain aromatic compounds (Cho et al. 2007; Yazaki 2008). To tea farmers, these changes are easily recognized by the yellow, stunted leaf-buds that develop after the cicadas have fed, a transformation that they describe using the term 著蜒 *zhuoyan*.[4]

Tea leaves with a sufficiently high degree of *zhuoyan* produce a finished tea that is qualitatively different from that made using undamaged leaves. The first, and most crucial, consequence of *zhuoyan* is the production of Oriental Beauty's distinctive "honey fragrance" (蜜香 *mixiang*). As Beipu tea producer Mr. Tan told me, "Only with that really insect-damaged tea leaves can you produce honey notes, only if they have *zhuoyan*. If you don't have any *zhuoyan*, then you simply don't get that floral, honey fragrance." Also, when these tea leaves are processed in the traditional fashion, the surface of the tea buds develop a fine layer of silvery "white down" (白毫 *baihao*). The tea farmers I visited during my fieldwork routinely pointed to the presence of such "white down" as an indicator of the degree of *zhuoyan* (and thus the quality) of their tea. Finally, the presence of tea jassids in early summer stunts the growth of the tea leaves, producing small, supple leaf-buds with a greater intensity of flavor. These tea plants do not experience the rapid growth otherwise typical of summer tea crops, and so their leaves do not display the thin and astringent taste that is consequently a hallmark of many summer teas. Taken together, we can see how the *zhuoyan* transformation brought about as a result of the small green leaf hoppers' activity makes them crucial to the elicitation of Oriental Beauty's defining material and sensory characteristics.

The imperative to allow for *zhuoyan* necessitates that producers of Oriental Beauty practice certain modes of tea cultivation that in Taiwan have come to be known as "natural farming." In contemporary Taiwan, "natural farming" refers in essence to approaches to agricultural production that eschew the use of pesticides or fertilizers, even organic varieties.[5] In the case of tea production, these methods are of a piece with traditional cultivation practices historically pioneered by tea producers in Beipu and surrounding areas (Fan n.d).[6] Accompanying a "natural farmer" such as Mr. Zhang on a walk through his fields, one realizes the constraints that this mode of cultivation places on its practitioners. Where a conventional tea farmer can call upon an arsenal of techno-scientific weapons to encourage plant growth or eliminate invasive insect species, the adherent of natural farming cannot. When the grass and weeds between the tea plants grows too high, it is cut with a hoe and spread between each row to serve as mulch to hold moisture in the soil and provide nutrients to the plants. To combat particularly ravenous insect species, Mr. Zhang has few weapons but the heel of his boot: Harmless spiders live to see another day; potentially devastating caterpillars are not extended such courtesy. Beyond these minor interventions, his fields are left to develop of their own course.

Growing Oriental Beauty, and "natural farming" more widely construed, involve a reworking of the relationship between the tea producer and the non-human world in which their cultivation practices are embedded. Whether conceived of as a return to traditional methods of cultivation or a deepening of a more contemporary vogue for organic agriculture, "natural farming" is routinely conceptualized as an alternative technological lineage to intensive, mechanized, fertilizer- and pesticide-heavy styles of tea production that might otherwise prevail (Chen and Lin 2001, pp. 64–5). "Natural" approaches to tea growing pare human intrusion back to a bare minimum, allowing the tea field "ecosystem" ever-greater influence over the eventual quality and yield of each season's crop. It is for this reason that teas produced in this fashion are commonly marketed as "eco-tea" (生態茶 *shengtai cha*), an appellation that has come to define a kind of *uber*-organic niche within Taiwan's domestic tea market (Lin n.d.).

By attenuating their power over the tea's development, tea farmers submit more directly to the contingency and caprice of the natural world. Keeping a space open in their fields for the play of non-human agencies admits not only the small green leaf hoppers but an entire "ecosystem" of potential allies and adversaries, some of which can critically impact the quality and yield of their harvests. Mr. Lin summarizes succinctly the dilemma that tea farmers like him face, saying that,

> If you want honey aroma, you must have insect damage. And if you want insect damage you need to [follow] the old methods of cultivation; you can't use pesticides or fertilizers. [But] then you are going to have a lower yield.

Having relinquished more powerful means of control in the pursuit of *zhuoyan*, tea farmers thus learn to live with the risk of their tea being wiped out. Zhang emphasizes that

> There's nothing you can do to stop insect-damage, it's up to them (隨便它 *suibian ta*) . . . In terms of the ecosystem, there are a lot of things happening that I am not able to control. For example, there's a bug called the "tea mosquito bug" (盲椿蟓 *mang chun xiang*) [Helopeltis fasciaticollis Poppius], they go through your fields like cars up a highway; within two or three days they've eaten everything. And then there's no tea left to pick.

To farm tea "naturally" is to do without the safety net of modern agro-science. Instead, one must adopt a stance of relying on heaven. Zhang sketches what this means to him:

> [W]hen you are "relying on heaven", heaven is going to give you what it does and you have to accept that. You take it year by year . . . So I am a person without goals . . . When you are "relying on heaven," what's the point of having a goal? I don't know what the "goal" could be. You can only dream: if each year my tea fields could produce thirty or fifty *jin* of that really top grade tea with a good degree of *zhuoyan*, wow, that would be really amazing!

To "rely on heaven" is, in this sense, to open tea production to the chance interactions of the tea-field ecosystem, signaled by the distinction between the goal-directed behavior of the mainstream tea farmer and the open-ended "dreaming" of the natural farming practitioner.

To some, to jump so suddenly from the practicalities of tea field management to invocations of "heaven" might seem overly abrupt. However, it is important to recognize that the Chinese concept of 天 *tian* or "heaven," as invoked here, refers to naturally occurring forces. More specifically, *tian* traces a field of forces that is immanent to and constitutive of the life-worlds of humans, plants, and animals (the reason why *tian* and its derivative words can also be translated into English as "nature"). This term's appearance in Zhang's comment above itself reflects a longstanding interest among tea makers and drinkers alike in how unique relations of "heaven, earth and human" (天 *tian*, 地 *di*, 人 *ren*) produce teas with individual tastes. For example, an instructional manual for tea producers issued by Taiwan's government informs us that, in the tea industry, "we often say that to produce a fine tea of outstanding colour, fragrance and flavour, the triad of 'heaven, earth and human' must be in coordination" (Lai et al. 2002, p. 3). This statement takes for granted that tea processing requires humans to be attuned with "heaven" and "earth." What further distinguishes natural farming and "eco-tea," however, is that the tea farmers allow their crop's development to be determined primarily via the agencies of "heaven" and "earth." It is this deliberate opening of a space for the agency of the non-human world to register its effects that allows Zhang to tell me that his method of tea farming is also a way of "venerating nature" (*chongshang ziran* 崇尚自然).

To rely on heaven is not, then, simply a rhetorical maneuver on the part of tea farmers but a way of fashioning their relationship with their tea and the wider tea-field ecosystem. And inasmuch as the tea producer's capacity to align with the productive dynamic of nature is indexed by the taste of their finished tea, this relationality must manifest not only as concepts but also in tea-making practices (Ingold 2000, p. 45). For tea farmers, notions such as "heaven," "earth," and "human" pose "problems of value that signify not only rhetorically and semiotically, but above all pragmatically" (Farquhar and Zhang 2012, p.243). To grapple with the contingency of these relationships—by worrying whether the crop will be wiped out by insects; by gauging the degree of *zhuoyan* in each field; by identifying the most timely moment to harvest the tea; by training the eye and hand to pick only those leaves that display the traces of *zhuoyan*; and via the manufacturing processes that translate *zhuoyan* into "honey fragrance" and "white down"—requires that tea producers synchronize the rhythms of human labor and its attendant social formations with those of the non-human world. Chen and Lin (2001, p. 49) call this, "following heaven's timing" (順天時 *shun tianshi*).[7] "Relying on heaven" refers to the farmer's exposure to the contingencies of the natural world and points to how the intensive relations between "heaven" and "earth" govern a constantly changing *situation* in which the tea and the tea farmer are embedded. The qualities of fine tea, in this sense, attest to the quality of the relationship humans have established with heaven and earth.

Making Oriental Beauty

If the material changes wrought by the *zhuoyan* process stand as indices of each tea field's "ecological" dynamic, they also transform the expressive trajectories available to these leaves when they are taken up in the factory and subjected to the processes of withering, tossing, heating, and pressing by which Oriental Beauty's finished state is achieved. Tea producers refer to this expressive aspect of each tea's materiality as its "quality" (質 *zhi*). As is the case in Euro-American discourses of *terroir* (Trubek 2008), farmers concerned with issues of "quality" take for granted that local environmental specificities modulate the materiality, and thus potential taste, of each tea. An example of this is the contrast Mr. Tan drew for me between Beipu-grown tea leaves and those produced across the county line in the town of Longtan. He told me that

> being used to local leaves, you get the feeling that the quality [of Longtan leaves] is not so good… because of the different soil and climate, the red clay soil there, we would think that kind of quality doesn't really match what is needed to make Oriental Beauty.

In addition, some farmers believe that using "ecological" modes of cultivation amplifies the place-bound distinctiveness of raw tea leaves. Mr. Zhang makes the distinction between the "quality" of naturally grown tea and that of conventionally grown leaves thus:

> I don't really go in for the kind of tea that uses pesticides and fertilizers. The thing is that with a tea, you can usually assume that fermentation will naturally produce a reddish color [around the leaf's edge], but I feel that with those teas the transformation of its color is not so nice. What I mean by "transformation" is that as we go through each step in the tea-making process—sun withering, indoor withering, all the way to tossing—if you use too much fertilizer, you'll get a dark, blackish tinge instead of the bright red color that is produced in organically grown leaves.

Here, the signature effects of each tea-field ecosystem are imbued in each batch of leaves as a differential potential for transformation.

Although tea producers rely on a particular configuration of non-human agencies to produce *zhuoyan*, the transformation of these raw leaves into a finished tea that possesses "honey aroma" and "white down" depends, in turn, on the efficacy of particular tea-making conventions. As a "partially fermented" (部分發酵 *bufen faxiao*) oolong tea, it is only by subjecting the leaves to sustained heat, motion, and moisture that the farmer can achieve a desired taste, fragrance, and appearance that are significantly different from that of the raw leaves.[8] It is *zhuoyan*, as a material signature, that serves as a link between these ecological and technological systems. Mr. Zhang touches upon this interplay between when he states that

> what we produce here [in Beipu] is mostly heavily fermented tea . . . to about fifty to sixty per cent. If you don't have a good degree of *zhuoyan*, tea produced like that—its honey fragrance note, or its ripe or fresh fruit notes—they won't be so apparent, and the tea won't be considered very good.

It is particular methods of manufacture, then, that actualize the expressive potentiality encoded by "ecological" modes of cultivation. Until the tea-making process has been completed, the tea's taste exists primarily as a theoretical object. But what is often called a tea's "original taste" (原味 *yuanwei*) is not an abstract ideal held in the mind of the tea maker but a pattern of responsive transformation the material displays under the perturbing interventions of the human and non-human agents it encounters.[9] As Mr. Lin explains,

> Understanding fermentation really means looking into the tea making process. Taiwanese teas, oolong style teas like Oriental Beauty, High-Mountain Oolong or Baozhong, are all "semi-fermented." So when you are making tea, the tossing, that's done in order to incite fermentation [i.e., oxidation]. But what I often say is that the real significance of "fermentation" is "decomposition" (分解 *fenjie*), that is, to break down the material constituents in the tea, so that when we brew the tea its taste can be more fully apparent.

Here tea making is not just an elaboration of a preexisting, essential flavor but the unraveling of a trajectory of becoming that proceeds by engaging with what might be called the *invariances* immanent to each tea's materiality: an "original" taste that is "more fully apparent" only in and through its patterns of transformation (DeLanda 2002, pp. 75–6). The technical manual issued by Taiwan's public-sector tea research agency supports this framing of the slippery ontology of tea's taste when it states that

> Each tea leaf has its own inherent (本身 *ben shen*) fragrance and taste. In tea manufacturing the leaf goes through the complex series of chemical reactions that allows the leaf to express its elegant fragrance and produce its sweet and mellow taste. These aspects of a tea's quality—its fragrance and its taste—can only be attained through the interplay between factors including a suitable cultivar; favourable soil and climate; proper cultivation techniques and appropriate tea manufacturing procedures and equipment
> (Lai et al. 2002, pp. 34–5)

From the point of view of the tea producer, then, the "inherent" flavor and taste attributed to a finished tea is not *just* an essence but also the expression of a network of ecological and technical agencies—including the tea producer's own labor—whose interplay allows the tea to express "itself."[10]

Guiding each batch of tea toward a desired conjunction of taste, scent, and color requires the tea maker to continually "attend to the situation" (看情況 *kan qingkuang*). Successfully managing the passage between different stages of tea processing—from laying the leaves out to wither in the sunlight, to tossing them by hand and machine, to firing, rolling, and drying them—requires by the tea producer registering the various "decisive points" (判斷點 *panduandian*) that the tea reaches along its trajectory of oxidation. These points manifest as material changes in the tea but also implicate shifting properties of the tea-making environment. For example, if a dry northerly wind is blowing at the time the tea enters the factory, then the tea makers must increase the speed of activity to avoid the tea's drying out. Conversely, an increase in humidity will slow and prolong each aspect of manufacturing as the speed of evaporation from the leaf decreases. Another example is how, when the tea is left out for withering, the tea maker traces the speed of evaporation by attending to material changes in the leaf: a decrease in the leaves' weight and increasing dryness to the touch, the wrinkles that emerge on each stem, and a darkening of each leaf around its edge. This same logic entails also that tea farmers attend to the impact of *zhuoyan* on the leaves. As another Beipu tea producer, Mr. Du, told me, the reduced water content of heavily insect-damaged leaves makes them softer and more prone to bruising or drying out, necessitating an extra care and finesse when they are tossed by hand. If, on the other hand, a tea producer detects a low degree of *zhuoyan* than that required to successfully elicit a "honey fragrance," they might instead settle for a more easily achieved "ripe fruit" fragrance (熟果香 *shuguoxiang*). These are some of the many ways that tea producers register and respond to the material transformation of each batch's "quality" via the sensations (scents, textures, and so on) that this material produces as it undergoes oxidation. As one farmer regularly stressed to me, "there is no timetable" to be followed in the tea factory: The tea itself determines the speed and duration of processing. In place of a timetable, tea producers thus substitute a pragmatics of attention.

Making tea requires that the tea producer learn how to sense both the ecologically freighted qualities of the tea "itself" (as a material) and the features of each batch's processing environment that will impinge upon the speed and intensity of its physical transformation. For the tea maker, these are registered as experience (經驗 *jingyan*) rather than disembodied knowledge (知識 *zhishi*). A degree of affective sensitivity thus distinguishes the bodies of the novice and master tea maker

> If the humidity today is a bit high, then it will slow down the evaporation process. If the temperature today is relatively cool, then it will be slower to dry. How do you grasp all of these together? Is there an answer? There isn't. Lot's of stuff has no answer. Even when you produce the finished product, you still don't know the answer . . . It depends on your degree of sensitivity and harmonization (協調性 *xietiaoxing*)
>
> (Mr. Zhang, interview)

To make tea successfully, one must acquire the ability to identify the traits of expression that emerge through the tea-making process and project from these to the taste of the finished tea. Likewise, the tea maker must adjust (or "harmonize") his or her own behavior or elements of the factory set-up (for example, altering the speed or intensity of tossing the tea; adjusting the temperature at which the tea is fired) to hold each batch of tea on the desired trajectory (Yu 2013). On this point, Mr. Peng confessed to me that early in his tea-making career, although he had been able to understand the concepts behind each stage of processing, he was still not able to "link up" each stage to elicit the desired taste. It was through trial and error that he acquired in practice a sense of how the steps related to one another and to the materiality of the tea. Only with experience was he able to learn how to guide each batch of tea toward its optimal taste. Tea making thus hinges on the cultivation of forms of "bodily resonance" that bind the tea maker and each tea. These resonances are both thoroughly corporeal and yet defiantly abstract, or perhaps abstract precisely because of their stubborn corporeality (Hsu 2008; Yu 2008).[11]

In conversation, producers of Oriental Beauty acknowledged the complexity of tea production most typically by gesturing toward the ineffability of experience. Their attempts to explain to me the corporeal, sensory, and affective encounters by which the taste of their tea came about marked precisely the point at which technical explanations foundered and gave way instead to appeals to tacit, embodied ways of knowing that they had built up through years of experience at the tea farm and factory. For example, Mr. Zhang cautioned me that

> really to make tea encompasses temperature, humidity, and includes your own state of mind, your degree of sensitivity, so it is really abstract. If you ask me for a set answer, I'll tell you there isn't one . . . How would you explain the moment when you've eradicated the grassy taste [of the raw tea leaves]? . . . I can describe it, but how would you write it, how could you do it? . . . I think you're better off just describing the process, because to grasp the internals (裡面的掌控 *limian de zhangkong*), that's just too abstract.

Zhang's emphasis here on the abstraction he sees as inherent to tea making highlights how each tea's materiality is distinguished by the producer's direct experience of the unique sensations and affects produced by the tea as it transforms from raw leaves to a finished tea. Here my informant echoes Hsueh's (2003, pp. 156–7) suggestion that for tea farmers, once one has grasped the rudiments of *zhuoyan* and basic tea-processing procedures, making tea became instead about "observing the tea as you make it" (看茶製茶 *kan cha zhi cha*) while at the same time "observing heaven as you make tea" (看天製茶 *kan tian zhi cha*). That is, the "abstract" (抽象 *chouxiang*) element in tea production is the tea maker's attunement to the tea's materiality, an attachment that allows them to follow and respond to the material and environmental contingencies that impinge upon each tea's taste-trajectory. These responses draw upon acquired dispositions and endowed sensitivities as much as conscious deliberation (Ingold 2000, p. 197; Hinchcliffe 2010). In this sense, the labor of tea making is a way of actualizing a particular relation between the human and non-human (or "heaven," "earth," and "human"), the affective affinity between the tea maker and his or her tea represented or indexed by the tea's taste, fragrance, and other material signatures. To "follow the material" (Deleuze and Guattari 1987, p. 409) in this fashion is to eschew the recipe in favor of open-ended practice: a way of thinking and working within the envelope of contingencies inherent to each material. To figure tea making in this way both opens this account of tea production to the agential capacities of things and materials and equally allows us to appreciate the way in which tea makers are caught up in the "situationality" of life experienced as "an ongoing process that includes agency within it" (Ames 1998, p. 227).[12]

Heaven and the market

Having a sense now of how each tea maker's affective and practical acumen is crucial to eliciting the optimal taste from each batch of tea, we can appreciate why questions of personal style and its theorized relation to taste are central to the understanding of each tea in its guise as a product. The taste of a finished tea is understood as the result not only of the environmental qualities specific to its space of cultivation but of each tea producer's sensitivity to such specificities as embodied in their tea-making practice. Each tea maker invests his or her tea with qualities that are expressions of their personal style of tea making. As Mr. Zhang put it to me,

> All we can say is that for tea, left on its own, dried naturally, it will have a very bland (淡 *dan*) taste and color. It's because after being subjected to human labor that it can be bitter or astringent . . . Producing tea, I actually think that the main technical challenge is to get rid of the bitter or astringent flavors [that are produced] and preserve the sweetness and freshness. This is what we who are serious about tea are after. But the changes [in the tea] that this involves, how to control the timing and distribution (調配 *diaopei*), that will differ from person to person.

In keeping with this conception of artisanal "style," Beipu tea producers were typically keen to link the taste—and by extension the value—of their tea with their personal approach to tea making: the care and attention that they lavished on their own teas, the extended time spent tossing the leaves by hand, the higher degree of oxidation that is achieved, and the richer, deeper "honey aroma" that eventuated. This conception of the tea maker's labor dovetails with the Deleuze and Guattari definition of "style" and its relationship to materiality as being "no longer a question of imposing a form upon a matter but of elaborating an increasingly rich and consistent material, the better to tap increasingly intense forces" (1987, p. 329). Tea made with this requisite level of attention, Beipu farmers claimed, produced a singular taste that surpassed that of the lightly-fermented teas currently most popular among Taiwanese tea drinkers.

Often my informants contrasted their own painstaking pursuit of "honey aroma" with what they alleged were faster, lightly oxidized, and less carefully manufactured teas produced by farmers in the neighboring town of Emei or in the high mountain areas of central Taiwan, techniques that they felt were ill-suited for producing Oriental Beauty. These differences were understood as more than just differing taste preferences or manufacturing conventions. Instead, the alleged embrace of more economically expedient manufacturing techniques was taken to indicate a deficit of personal attainment that rendered these farmers oblivious to the "heavenly" environmental contingencies that condition the singular materiality of each tea. Making tea without adequate care was a sign of an insufficiently resonant connection between the producer and his or her tea. And in the views of many Beipu tea farmers, this deficiency was in turn manifest in what they claimed is an insufficiently robust "honey fragrance" in their competitors' teas, which more often possess the "fresh and delicate fragrance" (清香 *qingxiang*) typical of the lightly oxidized oolong teas that dominate Taiwan's domestic tea market. Thus, the way of ecologically engaged tea making that I have characterized as relying on heaven traces a field of practice and disputation that chimes in both ontological and economic keys.

For my informants, as producers and sellers of Oriental Beauty, the trajectory of each tea is one that draws together not just the ecological and technological agencies mobilized in the tea field and factory but also those operations that invest each tea with economic value. The products of "heaven" accrue economic value only if their naturally endowed qualities are elicited and transformed by the hands of the tea producer, who makes a corresponding claim for his or her technical mastery. In turn, if each tea maker's distinctive way of recognizing and configuring tastes, smells, and textures accrues some sense of personalization to each tea, it also constitutes a way of positioning tea as a product in the market. A final example from Mr. Lin helps to clarify these relations. Speaking of autumn tea, usually considered an inferior crop due to that season's lower rainfall, he suggests that

> If you adopt as your model lightly-fermented "competition" tea,[13] then autumn tea will definitely be very bitter and astringent, and you won't be able to sell it for much, and with Taiwan's labor costs being what they are, you simply won't make a profit. But if you process this tea with [a higher degree of] fermentation, you can still produce some pretty nice tea. And if the tea is good, then you can definitely make a profit.

Here, the "ecological" contingencies of the tea's making are transformed using the technical procedures of the tea factory in order to address contingencies of market relations. The production of desired qualities or traits of expression freights the material from a purely "ontological" frame into a frame that is at least partly "economic." In this sense, the dynamic of materiality specific to oxidation serves as a way to translate material qualities of raw tea such that the tea farmer can enact a new relation between taste and value, all the while retaining, in the sense that tea's taste remains immanent to its ecologically conditioned materiality, each tea's relationship with an abstract "nature."

The presence of particular tastes signifies to tea makers and drinkers alike both the "ecological" singularities of particular places and the quality of the relationships that hold between that place, the tea it produces, and the tea maker who has produced it. In this sense, Oriental Beauty (and eco-teas more generally) serve as indices of a productive but highly contingent affiliation between "heaven," "earth," and "human" through which each achieves its form of actualization. Things are not rendered mute (nor infinitely mutable) in the face of masterful human agency, just as human agency is not rendered passive and inconsequential by the vitality of the non-human world. Rather, careful processes of accommodation entangle the life of Oriental Beauty within "ecological," technical, and practical forms of agency, in the process elaborating the immanent qualities of each tea and equipping it to travel in ever-wider circulations of affective and economic exchange. When "heaven" and

Notes

1. For a description and analysis of representations of "natural farming" and "eco-tea" in Taiwanese lifestyle media, see Writer (2013).
2. This fieldwork was supported by a Taiwan Fellowship granted by Taiwan's Ministry of Foreign Affairs.
3. All of the names used for my informants are pseudonyms. For names of informants and in citations I have used the pinyin system of Romanization, except where authors have an existing usage. Place names are rendered following the most commonly used convention (for example, Hsinchu rather than Xinzhu).
4. This is a transliteration into Chinese characters of a Hakka word, pronounced *chogrhan* in the Hailu-dialect spoken in Beipu. Hoklo speakers in Taiwan use the term 「蜓仔」 *iân-á*.
5. Unsurprisingly, opinions varied among tea farmers as to how zealously such prohibitions needed to be observed. For example, some farmers I spoke with would admit to the use of organic fertilizers at certain points in the tea plant life-cycle and certain times of the year (typically those most distant from tea-picking seasons).
6. Thus it is not unusual to see more recently developed lines of "eco-tea" packaged for sale using descriptors such as "honey-fragrance oolong" or "honey-fragrance black tea" in order to link their tea with the "honey fragrance" most commonly identified with Oriental Beauty.
7. The word *tianshi* 天時 can simply mean "the seasons," but I am here following the translation of Farquhar and Zhang (2012, p. 164) to emphasize the intensive and affective aspect immanent to the concept of seasonality itself.
8. More precisely, oolong teas such as Oriental Beauty can be defined as a style of partially-*oxidised* tea, in contrast to, among others, non-oxidized "green" tea (綠茶 *lü cha*) and fully-oxidized "red" tea (紅茶 *hong cha*, which is known in English as "black tea"). However, for historical reasons, in Taiwan it is most common to refer to the oxidation reaction as "fermentation."
9. My analysis here is aligned with Farquhar and Zhang's analysis of "originary *qi*" 元氣 in traditional Chinese medicine: "Originary *qi* is a kind of theoretical object, but it expresses only as particular forms, and these forms are always undergoing transformation" (Farquhar and Zhang 2010, p. 276).
10. This conception of a tea's "essence" dovetails neatly with the classical Chinese concept of 性 *xing*, or an entity's "nature" or defining character. Angus Graham notes of this concept that "*xing* will be spontaneous process with a direction continually modified by the effects on it of deliberate action" (Quoted in Hall and Ames 2001, p. 28).
11. To think of tea making this way thus dovetails with the sense with which "feeling" (感 *gan*) has been employed recently by Sinophone scholars investigating the historically and culturally situated relationships between the senses, the body, and culture, or what they call 身體感 *shentigan* (Yu 2008). I follow Elisabeth Hsu's elegant translation of this term as "bodily resonances" (Hsu 2008).
12. This quote is drawn from Roger Ames's definition of the Chinese word 勢 *shi*, a term that captures some of the complexity of the tea-making experience. He translates it as "situationality": "at once 'situation,' 'momentum,' and 'manipulation.' *Shi* includes all of the conditions that collaborate to produce a particular situation, including place, agencies, and actions" (Ames 1998, p. 227).
13. Lin is here referring to the biannual "Fine tea competitions" held across Taiwan, which he—and several other Beipu farmers—identifies as the major factor encouraging

producers to shift from making orthodox, heavily oxidized "honey aroma" Oriental Beauty to a lighter, fresher style of tea.

References

Ames, Roger T. 1998. "Knowing in the *Zhuangzi*: 'From Here, on the Bridge, over the River Hao.'" In *Wandering at Ease in the Zhuangzi*, edited by Roger T. Ames, 219–30. Albany, NY: SUNY Press.
Bolt, Barbara, and Estelle Barrett, eds. 2012. *Carnal Knowledge: Towards a New Materialism of the Arts*. London: I. B. Tauris.
Braun, Bruce, and Sarah Whatmore, eds. 2010. *Political Matter: Technoscience, Democracy and Public Life*. Minneapolis, MN, and London: University of Minnesota Press.
Chen, Huantang, and Lin Shih-Yu. 2001. *Taiwan cha (Formosa Oolong Tea)*. Taipei: Maotouying.
Cho, Jeong-Yong, Masaharu Mizutani, Bun-ichi Shimizu, Tomoni Kinoshita, et al. 2007. "Chemical Profiling and Gene Expression Profiling during the Manufacturing Process of Taiwan Oolong Tea 'Oriental Beauty'." *Bioscience, Biotechnology and Biochemistry* 71 (6): 1476–1486.
Coole, Diana, and Samantha Frost, eds. 2010. *New Materialisms: Ontology, Agency, and Politics*. Durham, NC, and London: Duke University Press.
DeLanda, Manuel. 2002. *Intensive Science and Virtual Philosophy*. London and New York: Continuum.
Deleuze, Gilles, and Felix Guattari. 1987. *A Thousand Plateaus: Capitalism and Schizophrenia*. Translated by Brian Massumi. Minneapolis, MN, and London: University of Minnesota Press.
Fan, Hongjie 范宏杰. n.d. "Mixiang cha (Honey-fragrance Tea)." Taiwan Tea Research and Extension Station. http://teais.coa.gov.tw/view.php?catid=1558.
Farquhar, Judith, and Qicheng Zhang. 2012. *Ten Thousand Things: Nurturing Life in Contemporary Beijing*. New York: Zone Books.
Hall, David, and Roger T. Ames. 2001. *Focusing the Familiar: A Translation and Philosophical Interpretation of the Zhongyong*. Honolulu, HI: University of Hawai'i Press.
Hinchcliffe, David. 2010. "Working with Multiples: A Non-Representational Approach to Environmental Issues." In *Taking-Place: Non-Representational Theories and Geography*, edited by Ben Anderson and Paul Harrison, 303–20. Farnham: Ashgate.
Holbraad, Martin. 2011. "Can the Thing Speak?" *Working Paper Series #7*. Open Anthropology Cooperative Press. http://openanthcoop.net/press/http://openanthcoop.net/press/wp-content/uploads/2011/01/Holbraad-Can-the-Thing-Speak2.pdf
Hsu, Elisabeth. 2008. "The Senses and the Social: An Introduction." *Ethnos* 73 (4): 433–43.
Hsueh, Yun-Feng 薛雲峰. 2003. *Pengfeng cha—dongfang meiren, baihao wulong (Pengfeng Tea—Oriental Beauty, White Down Oolong)*. Taipei: Zihe Wenhua.
Ingold, Tim. 2000. *The Perception of the Environment: Essays on Livelihood, Dwelling and Skill*. London and New York: Routledge.
Ingold, Tim. 2007. "Materials Against Materiality." *Archaeological Dialogues* 14 (1): 1–16.
Jensen, Casper B., and Anders Blok. 2013. "Techno-Animism in Japan: Shinto Cosmograms, Actor-Network Theory, and the Enabling Power of Non-Human Agencies." *Theory, Culture & Society* 20 (2): 84–115.
Lai, Zhengnan 賴正南, ed. 2002. *Chaye jishu tuiguang shouce–zhicha jishu (Tea Industry Technical Handbook: Tea Manufacturing)*. Taoyuan: Taiwan Tea Research and Extension Station.

Lai, Zhengnan, ed. 2005. *Chaye jishu tuiguang shouce–cha zuo zaipei jishu xiudingban (Tea Industry Technical Handbook: Tea Making and Tea Growing Techniques (Revised Edition))*. Taoyuan: Taiwan Tea Research and Extension Station.

Latour, Bruno. 2000. "When Things Strike Back: A Possible Contribution of 'Science Studies' to the Social Sciences." *British Journal of Sociology* 51 (1): 107–23.

Lin, Ru-Hong 林儒宏. n.d. "Shengtai chayuan dongzhiwu xiang diaocha yu fenxi" (Surveying and analyzing the relations of animals and plants in eco-tea plantations). Taiwan Tea Research and Extension Station. http://teais.coa.gov.tw/view.php?catid=1508

Miller, Daniel, ed. 2005. *Materiality*. Durham, NC, and London: Duke University Press.

Tan, Hung-jen 譚鴻仁. 2009. *Pengfeng cha de dilixue (Geography of Pong-Fong Tea)*. National Taiwan Normal University Department of Geography Research Monographs no. 37. Taipei.

Trubek, Amy. 2008. *The Taste of Place: A Cultural Journey into Terroir*. Berkeley and Los Angeles, CA: University of California Press.

Whatmore, Sarah. 2002. *Hybrid Geographies: Natures, Cultures, Spaces*. London: Sage Books.

Yazaki, Kazufumi. 2008. "Molecular mechanism of plant-insect interaction via plant volatile compounds and its application." Institute of Sustainability Science, Kyoto University. http://iss.iae.kyoto-u.ac.jp/iss/eng/researcher_k.yazaki.html.

Yu, Shuenn-Der 余舜德. 2008. "Cong tianye jingyan dao shentigan de yanjiu" ("From Field Experience to Researching Bodily Resonances"). In *Tiwu ruwei: wu yu shentigan de yanjiu (Embodying Things: Objects and Bodily Resonances)*, edited by Yu Shuenn-Der, 1–43. Hsinchu: NTHU Press.

Yu, Shuenn-Der. 2013. "Taiwan dongding wulong cha zhi gongjiang yishu, keji yu xiandaixing" ("Craftsmanship, Technology and Modernity of Taiwan Dongding Oolong Tea Production"). *Taiwan Journal of Anthropology* 11 (1): 123–53.

5 The Urban Wilds
Ecoculture, consumption, and affect in Singapore

Chris Hudson

Shop eat chill

Of all the marketing strategies deployed by the Singapore Tourism Board in recent years, the slogan "Shop Eat Chill" perhaps best encapsulates the marshaling of affect for an economy of consumption. Singapore has long had a well-deserved reputation as a Mecca for shopping and eating, but in a world where the global proliferation of clothing chains such as Topshop, Zara, and Uniqlo can offer relatively cheap consumer goods at any number of locations around the world, the nation can no longer style itself as an Asian bazaar and a haven for tax-free electronic goods. If some visitors still see Singapore as the "only shopping mall with a seat on the UN council", as writer William Gibson allegedly said, they have missed the point. Since the 1990s, Singapore has rebranded itself as a "Renaissance City" (Singapore Government 2002) and a "Global City for the Arts". The reality has not failed to live up to the promise of a city of culture. For the annual Singapore Arts Festival, it seems that no expense is spared to attract an impressive array of international theatre and dance companies, philharmonic orchestras, and other smaller-scale local and imported performances. The plethora of arts and cultural events appears with such frequency and on such an extravagant scale that public life in Singapore imparts a sense of continuing carnival and a dramatization of urban life (see Hudson 2012). The collective affect generated by such an array of spectacles that appear not only in theatres but also in parks, shopping malls, and other public spaces is one of the keys to the government's economic agenda in the post-industrial era. Culture is now a strategy for capitalist accumulation and instrumental for private interests (see Kearns and Philo 1990; Zukin 1995), or as Lash and Urry express it, the economy is increasingly culturally inflected while culture is more and more economically inflected (Lash and Urry 1994, p. 64).

A symbolic regime that relies on eco-culture and the commodification of the natural environment has also become a salient feature of Singapore's marketing strategy and an important component of the affective register of Singapore. It has facilitated a mode of place making that allows Singapore to rebrand itself as an urban wilderness. Its success is contingent upon a vibrant eco-aesthetic that has made the intensification of the senses part of the quintessential Singapore experience and an important aspect of its affective allure.

This chapter considers the creation of an eco-culture in Singapore, one of the key characteristics of which is the deployment of the natural environment for the exploitation and manipulation of the senses in the promotion of a pervasive culture of consumption. To begin with, I examine some of the discursive and material strategies deployed in the branding and construction of Singapore as an eco-landscape with buzz; the subsequent section investigates the role of the senses in the naturalization of certain spaces and the production of eco-aesthetics. Following that is a consideration of the ensemble of affects on offer in Singapore where taste sensations combine with other sensations to create a culinary eco-adventure as part of the expansion of the consumer experience. Finally, this chapter concludes that the production of Singapore's eco-culture and the lucrative commercial prospects that accompany it rely on a complex regime of the senses, a synaesthetic extravaganza where consumers can immerse themselves in the urban wilds while eating, shopping, and chilling.

Eco-landscape with buzz

Singapore's renaissance in the global era has produced new symbolic goods and new ways of defining the national character. An important aspect of this is the generation of excitement and the production of "cool" spaces where people can not only shop and eat but also "chill". Bungee jumping, hip-hop competitions, and the hundreds of cultural events and festivals and other excitement-generating activities provided by the government and the private sector are vital elements of the consumer economy in Singapore. Excitement itself is a commodity, and is now part of the national narrative. When former prime minister and then senior minister Goh Chok Tong addressed students at the Nanyang Technological University in 2010, he inscribed Singapore as a "Global City of Buzz" and identified affect as a component of economic success: "We [are] talking about the positive vibes of a place, where the environment is vibrant and exciting, and where people feel energized, engaged and happy. Some call such a place 'happening', 'funky', or simply 'lively'" (Goh 2010). Positive vibes and funkiness precipitate emotional responses aligned with certain embodied reactions such as feeling energized, but a competitive market demands ever more novelty and ever more sophisticated aggregations of affective prompts to produce such responses. Commodities, as Nigel Thrift puts it, "are increasingly carefully designed to produce strong affective cues that will amplify their effectivity by lodging them firmly in the phenomenal register" (Thrift 2005, p. 7).

Despite the functional housing tower blocks that are typical of the city state, the ubiquitous shopping malls, and the seemingly ceaseless construction of the built environment, Singapore—unlike many other Asian cities and mega-conurbations—has not suffered so much a destruction of the "natural" environment during economic development as a relocation of it (see Yuen, Kong, and Briffet 1999, p. 323). The planting of millions of trees, plants, and shrubs in an island-wide planting program begun by founding Prime Minister Lee Kuan Yew in 1963 has been accompanied by the development of an extensive network of national parks and gardens. Far from being transformed into a Bangkok- or Jakarta-style concrete jungle, much of Singapore is a real jungle, with green cover of the island growing from 36 per cent in 1987 to 47 per cent in 2007 (Lee Siew Hua 2011). The reputation of Singapore as a clean environment where fines are imposed for littering is apparently as enduring as its reputation as a paradise of shopping and eating. Now renowned for being not just clean but also "clean and green", the long-term greening process has had important consequences for the conservation of bio-diversity and the amelioration of a tropical climate, among other environmental benefits.

The rise of the Global City for the Arts and the Global City of Buzz has been paralleled by the transformation of Singapore from "Garden City" to "City in a Garden" (as the National Parks Board has it), a strategy designed not only to keep the city clean and green but also to instill a sense of environmental order that would appeal to global elites, tourists, and investors. The president of the Republic of Singapore, Tony Tan Keng Yam, is quoted as saying that "Our reputation as a City in a Garden enhances Singapore's attractiveness as a destination for tourists, foreign businesses and global talents [sic]" (National Parks Board 2013, n.p.). Lee Kuan Yew said of the project that "greening was positive competition" (Lee Kuan Yew 2000, p. 177). "Nature", like excitement, is now highly marketable and has been mobilized in the interests of continuing economic development. Macnaghten and Urry suggest that in the context of global capitalism nature has become a mere artefact of consumer choice (1999, p. 25). In Singapore, the cultural capital generated by the Global City for the Arts collaborates with environmental capital to produce a powerful sensory mode for the creation of the affective spaces so crucial for an economy of consumption. The potent combination of culture, nature, and affect is exemplified in Orchard Road. As one of the premier shopping precincts in Singapore and, in Ritzer's terms, a landscape of consumption (2010), Orchard Road is also a horticultural landscape featuring an abundance of tropical trees and shrubs, a constant reminder that Singapore now styles itself not only as a Global City for the Arts but also as an eco-culture. This has been facilitated by the actions of the National Parks Board, under the Ministry of National Development. The Ministry's stated aim was "to bring parks and green spaces right to the doorsteps of people's homes and workplaces" as a way of "enhancing lifestyle experiences" (Ministry of National Development n.d., pp. 30–2).

The intrusion of greenery into city spaces as paradoxical "urban wilds" blurs the distinction between what is conventionally understood as rural and what is normally seen as urban and serves to reinforce the pervasive sense of eco-culture. The official Singapore Tourism website, YourSingapore.com, promotes this dissolving of the boundaries. Under the headings "Nature Lover, Step into the Wilderness" and "Be One with Nature," it exclaims

> Don't let the gleaming skyscrapers fool you; bursts of lush green lie interspersed within Singapore's cityscape. Hear the hustle and bustle of the city fade away as you step into ancient rainforests and nature reserves situated a short hop away from the central business district. Explore the myriad nature trails, wildlife parks and landscaped gardens that Singapore has to offer, or venture out to the neighbouring islands for a spot of snorkelling or

diving. For a more rustic getaway, head out towards Pulau Ubin or the Kranji Countryside—fondly dubbed "the last remaining slice of rural life"
(YourSingapore.com 2013b)

Ash Amin and Nigel Thrift point out that the concept of shopping malls as the battleships of capitalism that can bludgeon consumers into unconsciousness fails to acknowledge that consumers may be not so much be bludgeoned as "enchanted" (Amin and Thrift 2002, p. 40) into a heightened awareness or affective response. It is not only the battleships of capitalism and the "happening", "lively", and "funky" events that enchant but, in Singapore, an environment of lush tropical vegetation, even in the commercial and shopping districts, helps to provide this enchantment. This dazzling green sensorium has generated what Thrift terms "affective senses of space, literally, territories of feeling" (Thrift 2010, p. 292), produced through various uses of eco-aesthetics designed to engage and captivate for the purposes of stimulating consumption. While tourists and locals can "chill out" along nature trails, in botanical gardens and rainforests, and on beaches and jungle canopy walks, they are rarely far from a food or shopping outlet.

A spectacular and ambitious project to reinforce the image of Singapore as an eco-culture and create enhanced territories of feeling is the Gardens by the Bay project. The three gardens at Marina South, Marina East, and Marina Central—located on 101 hectares of reclaimed land at the mouth of the Singapore River—form a linked series of magnificent parks complete with two lakes that provide homes for waterbirds and aquatic and wetland plant species, several climate-controlled conservatories housing thousands of exotic and regional plant species, and themed gardens. In addition to a number of event venues, at least 11 food outlets and various gift shops on the site, there is an ongoing program of eco-culture related buzz-generating events, including sound-and-light spectaculars, photography exhibitions, eco-explorer adventures for primary school children, and high school programs. All "eco-experiences", or, as the Ministry for National Development calls it, "plant-based edutainment" (Ministry of National Development n.d., p. 35). The YourSingapore website acknowledges the importance of affect when the gardens are promoted as "an awe-inspiring green space for Singapore" (YourSingapore.com 2013a). The Gardens by the Bay are adjacent to the Marina Bay Sands Hotel and a few minutes' walk from a shopping mall incorporating both high-end restaurants and shops and the more affordable global and local chains, known as The Shoppes at Marina Bay Sands. New territories of feeling in Singapore have been created by the "renaturalization" of urban space that has the capacity to create an affective eco-culture that can help form an alliance between nature and consumption.

Sensational nation

Singapore has constructed itself as a space of nature, of consumption, of leisure, culture, the arts, and business, with a pervasive sense of buzz in the air. This has been facilitated by the promotion of sensory delight as a one of the predominant modes of representation and place-making. Affects, defined as those forces that are visceral rather than conscious or knowing (Seigworth and Gregg 2010, p. 1), are well suited for deployment as part of the symbiotic relationship that capitalism has developed with nature—notable in the growth of eco-tourism—since they do not have clear boundaries, are not easily controlled, and do not have easily identifiable origins. Affect is contingent upon aesthetics, because, as Virginia Postrel defines it, "Aesthetics is the way we communicate through the senses. It is the art of creating reactions without words, through the look and feel of people, places and things. . . . The effects are immediate, perceptual and emotional" (Postrel 2003, p. 6). An eco-aesthetic, now a significant feature of life in Singapore, is a form of affect that simultaneously exploits a range of senses through the production of an urban sensorium in combination with the relentless promotion of the consumption of food and consumer goods.

It has been noted that the power of vision and the "dictatorship of the eye" (Macnaghten and Urry 1999, p. 111) once dominated tourist interactions with nature to such an extent that "the tourist gaze" (Urry 1990) came to be understood as the primary mode of engagement. Places were generally consumed visually (Urry 1990, p. 1). Martin Jay has argued that modernity has been characterized by "scopic regimes" and vision should be understood as the master sense of the modern era (Jay 1992, p. 179). In the postmodern era, however, the perceptual field has widened, and other senses have increased in importance. This change can be related to new forms of political economy, particularly in Singapore where the early post-independence modernizing and industrializing strategies of the People's Action Party government were replaced by forms of post-Fordist flexible production and a symbolic economy characterized by the promotion of the arts and other intangibles such as "buzz".

The work of David Howes and others (2004) has challenged the previous hegemony, of the visual in favor of an approach that privileges the sensual. The "sensory turn" has precipitated a greater emphasis on understanding the sensational and embodied elements of social phenomena such as place making, the multi-sensory nature of cities (Adams and Guy 2007) and culture in general (Pink 2009). The exploitation of the senses is crucial for the production of an eco-culture because senses can be discursively organized for the purpose of constructing diverse natures that can then be exploited in various ways and deployed for different purposes (Macnaghten and Urry 1999, pp. 107–8). The greening project can simultaneously help temper the effects of the urban heat island, for example, and also provide the natural beauty designed to generate affects.

Singapore's greening project has aestheticized the urban environment and transformed extensive tracts of urban space into enchanted environments where the generation of an eco-culture can also mean the almost unremitting excitement of the senses (Hudson 2014). The marketing of "buzz" and "funky" and the generation of affects such as "happiness" have tapped into a now-global marketing strategy known as "the experience economy" (see Pine and Gilmore 2011). The staging of experiences can transform space into "experiencescapes", that is, sites of market production, stylized landscapes that are strategically planned, laid out, and designed to produce experiences of pleasure, enjoyment, and entertainment (O'Dell 2005, p.

16). Experiencescapes are organized spatially to accommodate senses and embodied manifestations; they are landscapes saturated with powerful affective markers.

The commodification and exploitation of Singapore's natural beauty is partly achieved through the provision of an affective map that can alert tourists—and remind citizens—of the eco-experiencescapes they can expect to encounter. The organization of space in Singapore and the emotional and embodied responses that one should anticipate are foreshadowed on arrival at Changi Airport. Singapore as a space of eco-culture is prefigured in a series of engagements with a re-naturalized world at the very boundary of the nation. At Terminal 3, Changi Airport, in the public spaces that locals can visit and where travellers pass through customs and passport control, there is a "jungle campsite" where children can enjoy a staged "Rainforest Adventure" (Figure 5.1). A sign at the site announces an experiential encounter with nature:

> Welcome to the Changi Airport Campsite! We have created the experience of camping in a rainforest without the need for you to sweat or get muddy! Have fun exploring and learning about plants in our tropical rainforest. Do look out for unique plants like the Staghorn Ferns, carnivorous Pitcher Plants and the Tiger/Pigeon Orchids. We hope you would enjoy your holidays with Changi Airport's Rainforest Adventure!

Once travellers have gone through customs and security and are actually waiting to travel, the "naturalization" of an otherwise industrial space continues, in the form of a Butterfly House. Passengers can commune with nature in a strange heterotopic world in which they are surrounded by hundreds of colorful butterflies in a

Figure 5.1 Terminal 3, Changi Airport Campsite

controlled-climate mini-rainforest and from which they can watch flights come and go in one of the busiest airports in the world. Indeed, Terminal 3—and Terminals 1 and 2 to a lesser extent—is an immense green space that belies its industrial purpose. The most obvious signs of this are the "vertical gardens", extensive walls covered in creeping vines and flowers (Figure 5.2), that impart the sense that Terminal 3 is a microcosm of Singapore itself in the way it combines a tropical rainforest safe from mosquitoes and snakes with shopping and eating (see Figure 5.3).

Terminal 3 is promoted locally as a mall and a weekend destination for family fun and for the purposes of eating and shopping in the Asian bazaar–like public spaces outside the immigration hall. Shopping and eating are the standard practices of those waiting for flights and for those locals who make the weekend expedition. The sweat-free rainforest experience is perhaps the first indication for the visitor that in Singapore nature will be packaged along with other consumer goods to provide a controlled experience of the environment in which the boundaries between nature and culture are blurred. For the citizen on a weekend quest for the excitement of shopping and eating, it is a reminder that the city state is also a "comfort zone", an "air-conditioned nation" where habitats are centrally controlled (George 2000) and where one need never get sweaty. Part of Terminal 2's multi-sensory experience is an extensive indoor garden where flowers bloom and birds chirp. Known as The Enchanted Garden, it is complete with sensors that activate the sounds of the rainforests of Borneo as passengers walk through it. One traveller commented that it was "great to see nature where you least expect it" (Cheong 2013, p. B5) even though some of the flowers that spring into bloom, such as the anthuriums, are mechanical, and driven by sensors.

Figure 5.2 Passport Control, Terminal 3

Figure 5.3 Terminal 3, Changi Airport

The experience of Singapore is preceded by a script that preempts and prescribes forms of knowledge and emotional response. The Changi Airport campsite and staged Rainforest Adventure, the vertical gardens, and Butterfly House all help to prefigure the affective spaces that visitors will encounter. The simulated campsite provides the means for the production of Singapore as a green space, through the narrative address provided by the signage but also through the anticipation of the embodied experience and the senses associated with it. Tourists can be assured that while they will be entering a green space of a City in a Garden, it will be sanitized, tamed, and contained in a micro-environment that has been transformed into a comfort zone. The eco-cultural spaces of Terminal 3 and other terminals provide excitement for those locals on a family outing or shopping trip; a prefiguring of Singapore as a green space for those entering the country; and nostalgia for Singapore as a sensuous tropical paradise of eating and shopping for those leaving.

Alan Bryman argues that more and more aspects of society are exhibiting the characteristics of Disney theme parks (2004). "Theming" of specific environments and spaces imparts an overarching narrative unity, creates distinctive features to distinguish it from other products and services, and helps create affect for the experience economy. Themed environments are entertaining environments; theming also provides meaning and symbolism that transcends the original purpose (Bryman 2004, pp. 16–18). The vertical green walls, the gorgeous orchids, the Butterfly House, and the Changi Airport Campsite are all designed to incite the imagination and stimulate the senses to establish a narrative unity that constructs "green" as the "theme" of Singapore.

A culinary eco-adventure

The excellence and multi-cultural variety of food in Singapore are a national fetish and one of the key ways the nation represents itself (see Tarulevicz 2012). Eating intersects with other forms of sensory excitement to help produce the combined power of eco-culture, consumption, and affect. The convergence of sensory regimes is part of what has been identified as "the eatertainment experience" (Pine and Gilmore 2011; Ritzer 2010, p. 19). The term captures the notion of the aestheticisation of eating as a new commodity form that arises out of embodied experience and the merging of sensations, with taste making up only part of the sensory response. Eating occupies a significant place in the program of buzz-generating attractions that crowd the Singapore calendar of events. Along with the Singapore Arts Festival, the Singapore Garden Festival, the National Day Rally Parade, and many other major events, the Singapore Food Festival not only engages consumers through the generation of culinary excitement, it also intensifies and magnifies it in the way that Thrift suggested (2005, p. 7). The integration of eating into the "City in a Garden" environment makes possible a seemingly infinite array of eatertainment experiences in eco-enhanced territories of feeling. There is a considerable number of food-focused annual events in Singapore, including the World Gourmet Summit (established in 1997 and encompassing culinary masterclasses, gourmet safaris, vintner and celebrity dinners); Ganbarou Nippon (Taste of Japan); Food Fiesta@Expo; Halal 2012 ("food, lifestyle, wedding, Indo Xtravaganza"); and Crave! Singapore. "Crave! Singapore" was a program of culinary adventures associated with the 2012 Singapore Food Festival. Its website addressed the individual consumer directly and promised not only food but also adventure, satisfaction, and delight in a "natural" experiencescape:

> We are offering a culinary adventure of major proportions ... Embark on an exotic, epicurean journey ... take a trip down to an authentic fishing *kelong* [in the Malay language, a wooden platform built over water] where the best catch of the day will be transformed into a sumptuous seafood dish, just for you!
> (Crave Singapore! 2012)

"Crave! Singapore" promises no less than an odyssey of major proportions that requires consumers to embrace the adventure and allow their senses to be assailed by the environment as well as the taste and smell of food.

Popular travel website Travel Wire Asia lists food as one of the "top ten reasons why we adore Singapore" and claims that "Singapore is a food paradise" (Travel Wire Asia 2012). Eating, it seems, is still one of the prime reasons for visiting Singapore. Jonathan Kandell, writing in the *Los Angeles Times*, calls Singapore a "city for the senses" while subscribing to the widely held myth that Singaporeans hardly ever have sex; he asserts that food has replaced sex as the major passion. Food, he proposes, has become the ultimate object of desire (Kandell 2002). As a visitor to Singapore, he elevates food to the level of fetish and depicts his own relationship to food that is not just sensual but ecstatic:

> I wandered the stalls, leering at the fried oyster omelets, the black pepper crab meat . . . the Penang laksa noodles . . . In the end, I chose . . . Singapore's national dish, Hokkien mee . . . Draped limply over a chair in a postprandial daze, I briefly considered a small portion of kaya [an egg-and-custard jam dessert]
> (Kandell 2002)

Those promoting culinary tourism in Singapore would no doubt be delighted by this appeal to the senses. It might also be the sort of inscription of place that John Frow had in mind when he argued that, due to certain entrenched modes of narrativizing, what the traveller sees is already given, the responses to place and experience already authorized. Preconceptions sometimes have greater force than the appearances of the world (Frow 1997, p. 66) and this and other similar descriptions of ecstasy and excess promote Singapore as a prime site for the stimulation of the senses through a culinary adventure of exorbitant delight.

Zoos and bird sanctuaries offer perhaps more than any other spaces the tamed and sanitized experience of nature that a lucrative, urban eco-culture demands. As territories of feeling and themed spaces for both adults and children, they are prime locations for eatertainment experiences and a wide range of modes of embodiment, generated by the combination of the tropical urban sensorium with the consumption of food. The Singapore Night Safari, a specialized themed space open only between 7 p.m. and midnight to showcase nocturnal animals, offers the Gourmet Safari Express:

> This Night Safari dining adventure is the first of its kind in the world where you can experience fine dining amongst the creatures of the night, all on board a moving tram. Your experience kicks off with a mocktail and a little mingling with our animal stars before the captivating tram ride begins. Then, get ready for a scrumptious 5-course meal served in a candlelit setting that complements your wildlife encounters across 7 animal kingdoms of the world. With choices from international to Indian and even vegetarian fare, the menu caters for diners of every taste and preference . . . Then, get ready to cap off your night at our popular Creatures of the Night Show. It's a moveable safari adventure feast not to be missed
> (Wildlife Reserves Singapore 2014c)

The Jurong Bird Park currently offers what are now standard food and wildlife encounters, combined. Lunch with Parrots is a "Beak Performance at Lunchtime" promising

> When you lunch with parrots, you can expect to be out-talked. You can also have a great spread of food and a buffet of hearty laughs while our colourful personalities (and their trainers) demonstrate to you that birds are beauties with brains. Feast on a sumptuous spread of Asian cuisine or have an a la carte meal as you marvel at the natural talents of our feathered performers in a highly interactive 30-minute show
> (Wildlife Reserves Singapore 2014a)

Like the Night Safari with its candlelit setting, the bird park uses metaphors of food (a buffet of hearty laughs) to exaggerate the appeal to the senses (sumptuous) to help the food and nature combination create an affective space of eco-culture and consumption. If that wasn't enough, you could enter another themed experiencescape and have a sense-stimulating Dinner with Penguins in the urban wilds of Jurong:

> As the sun goes down, soak in the amazing views with a pre-dinner cocktail in the African Wetlands. You and your guests will then be whisked away on an exciting Penguin Expedition where dinner will be served. Against the 30-metre panoramic backdrop of rocks, cliffs and nestling alcoves, enjoy a delectable feasts [sic] in the company of our adorable penguin . . . meet Pinky the Humbolt Penguin . . . and "experience" the four seasons cleverly simulated by our special lighting system
>
> (Wildlife Reserves Singapore 2014b)

Charlene Ng, writing for the travel section of AsiaOne online, notes the possibilities for consuming taste sensations and the aesthetics of nature at the Breakfast with the Birds event at Jurong Bird Park:

> Singapore's Jurong Bird Park recently revamped its Early Bird Breakfast show, which now comes with a new line-up of dining options and acts . . . Lighter foods such as croissants and Danish pastries, and a diverse array of main courses, including Western dishes like Songbird's Egg Benedict and "Owl"melette, and local ones such as Nasi Lemak, will be available . . . In addition, guests will get to enjoy an interactive show at 9.15 a.m., which highlights the important role forests play in maintaining a healthy ecosystem. To kick-start the performance a scarlet, hyacinth, and blue-and-gold macaw will swoop past the audience. Guests can also expect to see Butter, a sulphur crested cockatoo, which will suggest ways to save the earth . . . and Stanley, a green-winged macaw that can crack nuts with its beak . . .
>
> (Ng 2011)

With the addition of kitsch nomenclature for the dishes, designed to amuse, the promotional rhetoric, the spatial arrangements and the fetishizing of eating combine to produce an experiencescape conceptualized through the narrative unity referred to by Bryman. Perhaps to prepare them for the anticipated affective responses, AsiaOne's website also asks its readers, "How does this story make you feel?" Readers can then choose from a range of emotions expressed as emoticons: enlightened, shocked, saddened, amused, indifferent, angry, and disgusted.

All these eatertainment experiences, and many more like them, help to construct re-naturalized spaces in an otherwise urban landscape. They are versions of the diverse natures alluded to by Macnaghten and Urry that have been discursively organized by websites, tourist brochures, advertising, and other media that prefigure and circumscribe affective responses. These natures are consumer spaces; they offer the spectacle of staged nature and an experience involving a reorganization and reconfiguration of the senses. While eating outdoors is a traditional feature of life in Southeast Asia and hawker-style street food has never lost its popularity, eatertainment experiences of the sort found in zoos and other wildlife locations help to create new spaces of nature for the promotion of an eco-culture in its association with consumerism. Frow's "entrenched modes of narrativizing" are reinforced by travellers' tales such as Kandell's as well as official discourse and the Singaporeans' own food obsession.

Conclusion: A synaesthetic extravaganza

All cities offer multi-sensory experiences; all are the "roiling maelstroms of affect" that Thrift describes (2004, p. 57), but Singapore seems able to offer more methodically manufactured memorable moments than most, for tourists and visitors alike. Sensory experiences are prefigured at the very entryway to the nation, and the island is a riot of tropical color provided by birds, trees, butterflies, and flowers. In an ongoing extravaganza of affect, carefully curated rainforest paradises are combined with the promotion of food—a national fetish—to produce eatertainment experiences that help to reconfigure and reinscribe spaces of nature. These elements, allied with the omnipresent lure of shopping, create an elaborate form of synaesthesia: that is, a confusion of the senses where the stimulation of one sense triggers a response in a different sensory modality (see Harrison 2001).

In addition to the activities of theming that help impart an overall narrative unity to the marketing campaigns as described above, Bryman also lists hybrid consumption and merchandising as key features of the overall package of experiences. He defines hybrid consumption as a marketing strategy in which forms of consumption typical in one sphere interlock or overlap with forms of consumption normally found in another sphere. Hybrid consumption brings together different domains of consumption in unusual ways and is typical of hotels, museums, theme parks, shopping outlets and zoos (Bryman 2004, pp. 57–77). This chapter illustrates the importance of the strategy for Singapore, revealing the centrality of the green aesthetic and its close alignment with the government's environmental practices of conservation of rainforest cover and continued greening of urban areas.

If the merging of shopping, eating, and chilling in various forms of synaesthesia is an important marketing strategy and a key feature of Singapore's affective allure, it is because food is one of the most effective modalities for the creation of positive memories—one that will, moreover, generate nostalgia and encourage return visits. The tourism board of Singapore, the managers of zoos and wildlife parks, and others involved in the tourism industry are clearly well aware of the importance of food for memory. In studies of ritual in daily life, David Sutton (2001) has outlined the importance of food for cultural memory and for the recalling of rituals and other significant community and family events. The links he identifies are culture-specific and vary across cultures, but the memories that may be triggered by the "Breakfast with the Orangutans" or "Dinner with the Penguins" are less culturally specific and more globally oriented, particularly when the food on offer includes "international and local favourites". One does not have to be familiar with the story of Proust and the madeleine to understand the power of the taste, smell, and look of food to stir the memory and to raise vivid recollections of significant or pleasurable life events such as holidays, leisure, and family outings. The conflation of food, fun, and other forms of pleasures such as chilling and shopping in a model of hybrid consumption that memorializes holidays is evidenced by the seemingly endless images of meals posted by individuals on Facebook in the vein of "this is the lobster I had on my holidays in Bali" or "this is the croissant I ate in Paris". Food memorializes experience.

In Singapore, as elsewhere, these memories may be retrievable because the experience of stimulation of the senses is intensified by ensembles of affective activities and sites. The zoo, for example, offers not only constellations of sensations with its eating-with-wildlife possibilities but also makes available a range of spectacles to intensify the experience, and create lasting memories. The Splash Safari Show, for example, promises "a high-energy splash parade filled with many special moments that will tickle your funny bone and tug at your heartstrings at the same time" (Wildlife Reserves Singapore 2014d). The many wildlife experiences offered by the zoo create memorable moments characterized by hybrid consumption practices that produce hybrid affects. Participants are exhorted to anticipate various forms of affective response, embodied experiences, and sensory excitement. The zoo, the Jurong Bird Park, and other sites of urban wilds also offer a chance to contribute to maintaining bio-diversity and saving the earth. These are all themed experiencescapes that rely on a combination of culinary stimulation and context-specific affective responses for their power to encourage consumption.

The fusing of the everyday, visceral, pre-articulate action of eating with aesthetics and the generation of hybrid consumption is, of course, hardly an innovation. Nevertheless, the place of food in Singapore's national culture, its enduring reputation amongst tourists, and the state's commitment to an economy of consumption combined with a natural environment that no visitor or citizen could fail to admire, however much it is exploited for profit, have generated the means to elicit emotional responses. The eating-with-wildlife model—which is, given the Breakfast with the Orangutan tours in Borneo and elsewhere, not unique to Singapore—demonstrates the ease with which eco-experiences seem to be available for varieties of hybrid consumption. These elements of global consumer society come together as part of a strategy to remake the nation as a cohesive, integrated eco-landscape—a move in the development of the paradigm of the Disney theme park—in which various forms of consumption combine in an ensemble of sensations to delight and excite. All the events, affective spaces, emotional and physical gratification, and embodied experiences described above point to a complex and pervasive sensory regime, a synaesthetic extravaganza in which people can satisfy their desires to shop, eat, and chill.

References

Adams, Mags, and Simon Guy. 2007. "Editorial: Senses and the City." *The Senses and Society*, 2 (2): 133–36.
Amin, Ash, and Nigel Thrift. 2002. *Cities: Reimagining the Urban*. Cambridge: Polity.
Bryman, Alan. 2004. *The Disneyization of Society*. London: SAGE.
Cheong, Kash. 2013. "Senses Come Alive at Airport Enchanted Garden." *The Straits Times*, "Home," July 16. B5.
Crave Singapore! 2012. "About Crave Singapore!" Accessed March 3, 2012. http://www.cravesingapore.com.
Frow, John. 1997. *Time and Commodity Culture: Essays in Cultural Theory and Postmodernity*. Oxford: Clarendon Press.
George, Cherian. 2000. *Singapore: The Air-Conditioned Nation*. Singapore: Landmark Books.
Goh Chok Tong. 2010. "Global City of Buzz, Home for Us." Speech given at the Nanyang Technological University Students' Union, October 29. Accessed November 3, 2011. http:www.news.gov.sg/public/sgpc/en/media_releases/agencies/micacsd/speech/S-20101029-1.html.
Harrison, John E. 2001. *Synaesthesia: The Strangest Thing*. New York: Oxford University Press.
Howes, David, ed. 2004. *Empire of the Senses: The Sensual Cultures Reader*. Oxford and New York: Berg.
Hudson, Chris. 2012. "Life as Theatre in Singapore." *Access: Critical Perspectives on Communication, Cultural & Policy Studies* 31 (2): 53–64.
Hudson, Chris. 2014. "Green is the New Green: Eco-Aesthetics in Singapore." In *Green Consumption: The Global Rise of Eco-Chic,* edited by Bart Barendregt and Rivke Jaffe, 86–99. London: Bloomsbury.
Jay, Martin. 1992. "Scopic Regimes of Modernity." In *Modernity and Identity*, edited by Scott Lash and Jonathan Friedman, 178–95. Oxford: Blackwell.
Kandell, Jonathan. 2002. "Singapore: A City for the Senses." *Los Angeles Times*, March 17. Accessed March 3, 2013. http://articles.latimes.com/2002/mar/17/magazine/tm-33262.
Kearns, Gerard, and Chris Philo, eds. 1995. *Selling Places: The City as Cultural Capital, Past and Present*. Oxford: Pergamon Press.
Lash, Scott, and John Urry. 1994. *Economies of Signs and Space*. London: SAGE.
Lee Kuan Yew. 2000. *From Third World to First: The Singapore Story: 1965–2000*. New York: HarperCollins.
Lee Siew Hua. 2011. "High 5 for LKY: Singapore's Chief Gardener." *The Straits Times*, May 28. Accessed January 12, 2013. http://global.factiva.com/ha/default.aspx.
Macnaghten, Phil, and John Urry. 1999. *Contested Natures*. London: SAGE.
Ministry of National Development. n.d. "From Garden City to City in a Garden." Accessed February 27, 2012. http://www.mnd.gov.sg/MNDAPPImages/About%20Us/From%20Garden%20City%20to%20City%20in%20a%20Garden.pdf.
National Parks Board. 2013. "Foreword." In *Living in a Garden: The Greening of Singapore*. Singapore: Editions Didier Millet.
Ng, Charlene. 2011. "Breakfast with the Birds at Jurong Bird Park." *Asia One*, June 19. Accessed January 17, 2014. http://www.relax.com.sg/article/news/breakfast-with-the-birds-at-jurong-bird-park#sthash.1yZ04eOd.dpuf.
O'Dell, Tom. 2005. "Experiencescapes: Blurring Borders and Testing Connections." In *Experiencescapes: Tourism, Culture and Economy*, edited by Tom O'Dell and Peter Billing, 11–33 Copenhagen: Copenhagen Business School Press.

Pine, Joseph, and James H. Gilmore. 2011. *The Experience Economy*. Boston, MA: Harvard Business School Press.

Pink, Sarah. 2009. *Doing Sensory Ethnography*. London: Routledge.

Postrel, Virginia. 2003. *The Substance of Style: How the Rise of Aesthetic Value is Remaking Commerce, Culture and Consciousness*. New York: HarperCollins.

Ritzer, George. 2010. *Enchanting a Disenchanted World: Continuity and Change in the Cathedrals of Consumption*. London: SAGE.

Seigworth, Gregory J., and Melissa Gregg. 2010. "An Inventory of Shimmers." In *The Affect Theory Reader*, edited by Melissa Gregg and Gregory J. Seigworth, 1–25. Durham, NC: Duke University Press.

Singapore Government. 2002. *Renaissance City Report: Culture and the Arts in Renaissance Singapore*. Accessed January 15, 2014. http: www.nac.gov.sg/resources/policy.

Sutton, David. 2001. *Remembrance of Repasts: An Anthropology of Food and Memory*. New York: Berg.

Tarulevicz, Nicole. 2012. "'Let Lifeguard Milk Raise Your Child': Gender, Food and Nation in Singapore's Past." *International Journal of Asia Pacific Studies* 8 (2): 55–71.

Thrift, Nigel. 2004. "Intensities of Feeling: Towards a Spatial Politics of Affect." *Geografiska Annaler Series B* 86 (1): 57–78.

Thrift, Nigel. 2005. *Knowing Capitalism*. London: SAGE.

Thrift, Nigel. 2010. "Understanding the Material Practices of Glamour." In *The Affect Theory Reader*, edited by Melissa Gregg and Gregory J. Seigworth, 289–308. Durham, NC: Duke University Press.

Travel Wire Asia. 2012. "Top 10 Reasons We Adore Singapore." February 22. Accessed March 7, 2014. http://www.travelwireasia.com/2012/02/top-10-reasons-we-adore-singapore.

Urry, John. 1990. *The Tourist Gaze*. London: SAGE.

Wildlife Reserves Singapore. 2014a. "Lunch with Parrots". Accessed January 15, 2014. http://www.birdpark.com.sg/special-experiences/lunch-parrots.html.

Wildlife Reserves Singapore. 2014b. "Dinner with Penguins". Accessed January 15, 2014. http://www.birdpark.com.sg/special-experiences/dinner-penguins.html.

Wildlife Reserves Singapore. 2014c. "Gourmet Safari Express". Accessed January 15, 2014. http://www.nightsafari.com.sg/special-experiences/gourmet-safari-express.html.

Wildlife Reserves Singapore. 2014d. "Safari Splash Show". Accessed January 23, 2014. http://www.zoo.com.sg/shows-feedings/splash-safari-show.html.

YourSingapore.com. 2013a. "Gardens by the Bay". Accessed January 15, 2014. http//www.yoursingapore.com/content/traveller/en/browse/see-and-do/nature-and-wildlife/stroll-among-trees/gardens-by-the-bay.html.

YourSingapore.com. 2013b. "Nature Lover". Accessed January 10, 2014. http://www.yoursingapore.com/content/traveller/en/browse/see-and-do/nature-and-wildlife/wall-nature-lover.html.

Yuen, Belinda, Lily Kong, and Clive Briffett. 1999. "Nature and the Singapore Resident." *GeoJournal* 49 (3): 323–31.

Zukin, Sharon. 1995. *The Cultures of Cities*. Oxford: Blackwell.

6 Domestic "Eco" tourism and the production of a wondrous nature in the Philippines

Sarah Webb

Introduction

Important attention has been given to the ways eco-branded tourism has been shaped by flows of neoliberal capitalism and Western consumption, but fewer studies have acknowledged how domestic consumers in countries such as the Philippines have powerfully produced certain places as "wonders" of nature. In the Philippines, "eco"-branded tourism is an emerging market that is certainly oriented toward attracting international tourists. However, Philippine ecotourism remains a market that is actually supported predominantly by *domestic* consumers. What this means is that ecotourism ventures in the Philippines mediate consumers' experiences of nature through significant national influences and markets and are by no means shaped exclusively or most importantly by Western tastes (see Winter, Teo, and Chang 2009). Here, I examine a case study of a campaign that successfully resulted in the Puerto Princesa Underground River (PPUR) becoming inaugurated as one of the "New 7 Wonders of Nature" (N7WN). I argue that the practices that made the PPUR into a "wonder of nature" might be situated globally but were always grounded in the cultural production of daily life in the Philippines.

So, why is it important to consider how efforts to promote such places as globally significant are realized through the labor of nationals, as they engage in everyday activities such as text voting in international competitions or circulating photographic images via social media? I suggest that it is precisely through such practices that some Filipinos reproduce the social meanings that tangibly and intangibly transform spaces as they become more broadly valued as places of exceptional nature. In doing so, I draw on key studies that have examined how places become materially remade to better conform to the images and ideals that have been created and circulated elsewhere (Carrier and Miller 1998; Carrier and West 2009). I join scholars who have suggested that ecotourism is an important entry point for understanding the relationships between these practices and their resulting transformations (West and Carrier 2004, p. 485). Key here is the critical notion that researchers cannot understand ecotourism via an "ecotourism bubble" that extracts ecotourism from the broader contexts in which it exists (West and Carrier 2004, p. 484; Carrier and Macleod 2005, pp, 316–18). As Fletcher suggests, "ecotourism is about much more than just ecotourism . . . the phenomenon can be understood as a manifestation of dynamics central to contemporary social life in general" (2014, p. 14). However, many of these critical works are based on case studies that largely concern the experiences of Western tourists in international tropical destinations, particularly a demographic of "white, upper-middle-class, politically liberal/leftist members of postindustrial Western societies" (Fletcher 2014, p. 2; see also Mowforth and Munt 2009). When scholars instead concentrate on how certain nationals promote places of nature through everyday practices, what stories emerge about the contexts in which ecotourism in Southeast Asia is situated?

By examining certain Filipino engagements with a site located on Palawan Island—declared the "ecotourism capital of the Philippines"—I suggest that practices associated with the promotion of this place provide important insights into how ecotourism is embedded within nature, nation, and economy within the Philippines. In order to explore these dynamics, I position the everyday consumption and media practices of Filipinos as vital to understanding how such places are made within national imaginaries. Specifically, I examine two interrelated sets of practices: first, the importance of Filipinos participating in and encouraging the text voting that made the Puerto Princesa Underground River (the "lone Philippine entry") a winner in an international voter-determined competition (the N7WN), and second, the huge increases in domestic tourism to the PPUR that occurred as part of promotion efforts during and after the PPUR-N7WN campaign. My purpose in doing so is to provide an empirical account of the ways in which certain Philippine nationals shape understandings of nature within global flows of people, places, revenue, and images. I offer a case study that demonstrates how, even when the promotion of natural sites is oriented toward transnational markets, these connections are made and situated within the everyday practices through which some Filipinos imagine and realize the economic and environmental futures of the nation.

These aspirations, their related practices, and the resulting transformations of space provide the context within which associated ecotourism is situated in the Philippines. The phenomenon of ecotourism is, then, a means of using sites of natural heritage (apparently belonging to the nation) in order to produce economic benefits, which it has been suggested will be shared not only by local residents of Puerto Princesa City but also by the Philippine nation and Filipino citizens more broadly.[1] These dynamics contribute toward understanding how the social and spatial production of the Underground River became a concern owned by two important groups of Filipinos: first, those who could not afford to travel to the Underground River but who promoted its entry in an international competition (through text voting, sharing images via social media, and discussing the campaign in everyday conversations), and second, the many middle-class Filipino tourists who considered travelling to the Underground River both as an act of support and as an opportunity to visit a site of their own Filipino natural heritage.

But what does it mean for these Filipino citizens and consumers to adopt such concerns within the context of Philippine ecotourism? In considering the powerful ways in which nationals shape the production of a "wondrous nature," I suggest that significant forms of disjuncture have emerged as the spaces associated with the Underground River have been materially remade to better resemble broader, national understandings of what places of nature should look like and how they should be accessed and experienced. In particular, the "Philippine nature" produced through ecotourism consumption and media practices often differs significantly from the lived experiences of local indigenous residents, who are often simultaneously presented as a tribal fantasy for Filipino tourists, while being actually excluded from the spaces of increasingly valuable "natures" and their associated economic benefits.

Methodology

This case study is drawn from more than 20 months of anthropological fieldwork focusing on the commodity flows of forest resources (primarily between 2010 and 2012, with scoping and follow-up trips during late 2008 and late 2013, respectively). The bulk of this fieldwork was based in Puerto Princesa City, on Palawan Island, particularly the Puerto Princesa Subterranean River National Park (PPSRNP). However, more than a month of research was undertaken in Metro Manila and Los Baños, principally during October-November 2011 and February 2012. The research is based on a multi-sited ethnographic methodology, with main research methods including participant observation, qualitative interviews, and business and livelihood surveys. Interviews and participant observation with domestic tourists were conducted predominantly on Palawan Island during their visit. The ethnographic research that this case study is drawn from was undertaken during the voting, promotion, and aftermath of the PPUR-N7WN campaign (largely between 2011 and 2012). During the campaign, additional research activities included the compilation and analysis of media reports of the campaign and Internet promotional content (including travel blogs, social media, and advertisements).

Situating the case study: Domestic ecotourism on Central Palawan Island

Attracting revenue from international tourists remains a key objective for the Philippine Department of Tourism and is often articulated as an aspiration of Philippine local governments and those who work in tourism-related businesses. However, it is domestic tourism that "serves to realise the potentials" of tourism within the Philippines—particularly in buffering vulnerabilities to waning international tourist arrivals after events such as natural disasters, kidnappings, and disease outbreaks (Rodolfo 2009, p. 235). This was certainly the case when tourism on Boracay (often considered the national cautionary tale for ecotourism) suffered a serious decrease in international visitors after a 1997 coliform outbreak in the waters along the region's iconic beachfront (Ong, Storey, and Minnery 2011, pp. 551–52). On central Palawan, similar concerns were felt after the May 2001 kidnapping of tourists and employees from the luxury Dos Palmas Resort (in Honda Bay, Puerto Princesa City) by members of the Abu Sayaff Group (Alampay and Libosada 2005, p. 146; Austin 2003, p. 98). Tourism markets on

84 Sarah Webb

Palawan[2] have subsequently recovered, and the region has been reaffirmed as the "Ecotourism capital of the Philippines" through government promotion and business branding (see Rasch 2014). However, the targeted levels of international tourist arrivals have yet to be achieved; since the 1990s visitors to key locales on central Palawan Island (such as the Puerto Princesa Subterranean River National Park) have been predominantly domestic tourists (Table 6.1).

The PPUR is located in the PPSRNP on central Palawan Island. The Park (as it is referred to locally) is within the jurisdiction of Puerto Princesa City but is a 2-hour drive from the "downtown" of the capital city (where the airport, government offices, and much of the City's infrastructure are located; Figure 6.1). Downtown "Puerto" and the Park's ecotourism hub of Sabang are now connected by a concrete road, but certain tourists nostalgically recall a time when an unpaved road from Puerto reached only partway across central Palawan Island, and the remainder of the journey to Sabang was undertaken by hiking or boat (see Broad and Cavanagh 2001, pp. 40–3). On Palawan Island, the relatively high level of forest cover has made the island's tropical rainforests iconic throughout the Philippines. However, the idea that traversing Palawan's forested landscape might constitute a pleasurable leisure activity is a relatively recent one. Palawan was once considered a remote and undesirable destination within the Philippines (a reputation due in part to the region's endemic malaria, hosting of a leper colony, and history of piracy). The region became dramatically reimagined and transformed before becoming a popular tourism site: first, as a land and resource frontier; then, as the site of significant logging concessions; and, finally, as a hub for civil society and environmental movements (Eder and Fernandez 1996; Broad and Cavanagh 2001, pp. 39–55). During the 1990s, key events resulting from these movements (the UNESCO designation of Palawan as

Table 6.1 Registered domestic and foreign visitors to the PPSRNP, compiled and substantiated from PAMB 1999; PPSRNP Registered Park Visitors (published at local office, 2008); Goodwin 2002; Dressler 2011; Seiler 2014.

Year	Domestic visitors		Foreign visitors	
Historical overview				
1985	392	40.2%	583	59.8%
1995	12809	73.9%	4518	26.1%
2005	26920	78.8%	7222	21.2%
From the commencement of the N7WN competition				
2007	49185	77.74%	14086	22.26%
2008	76065	81.42%	17363	18.58%
2009	122501	84.94%	21718	15.06%
2010	148760	86.1%	24067	13.9%
2011	197773	83.8%	38097	16.2%
2012	248468	84.3%	46112	15.7%

Domestic "Eco" 85

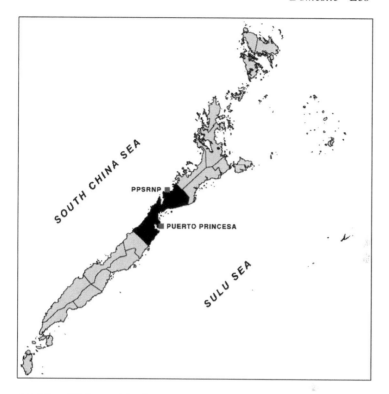

Figure 6.1 Map of Palawan Island

a Man & Biosphere Reserve during the early 1990s, and the establishment of a moratorium on logging in 1992) provided a foundation for eco-branded tourism to become heralded as an alternative to resource extraction. The flagship site for ecotourism on central Palawan Island has been the PPSRNP; previously called St. Paul's, the PPSRNP was established as a national park in 1971. In 1999, the Park was expanded from 3901 ha to 22202 ha in order to be inscribed as a UNESCO World Heritage site (see Dressler 2009, pp. 156–59 and 243). As the potential for the Park to attract tourism and revenue became apparent, entrance fees were introduced in 1994; however, indigenous Tagbanua and Batak families living in the region were rarely the beneficiaries of tourism revenue or jobs as Park employees (Dressler 2009, p, 159).[3] It has subsequently been argued that eco-branded tourism has exacerbated the historical and ongoing socioeconomic marginalization of indigenous residents, who have been dislocated and persecuted for practicing livelihood activities that are not seen to align with market-based conservation (Dressler 2011). During a household livelihood survey conducted as part of my research in late 2011, none of the indigenous families surveyed in the three *barangays* (municipalities) surrounding the PPSRNP were found to have livelihoods primarily oriented around tourism.[4] The marginalization of many local indigenous families from the benefits of eco-branded tourism in the

PPSRNP is certainly not unique within Palawan province. The exclusion of local residents from many of the benefits of ecotourism has raised the question of whether what is labeled "eco" tourism on Palawan is better understood as tourism *of* the environment rather than tourism that is "environmental" (Alampay and Libosada 2005, pp. 127–31; Eder 2008, p. 151; Fabinyi 2010, p. 422). What these politics of ecotourism suggest is that the ways places such as the Underground River are imagined by some to potentially contribute to the environmental and economic prosperity of the Philippines is often very different to the experiences of many who do live (or *have* lived) adjacent to these sites.

Voting for a wondrous nature

The PPUR has long been described as a "Cave of Wonders" within national discourses (Sablan 2003). However, more recently the Underground River has became branded as a Philippine "Wonder of Nature" through inauguration of the site within a Swiss-based international competition. During 2011, local government and business efforts to promote the site as one of the N7WN gained the support of the Philippine president (Figure 6.2). Through the resulting campaign to secure a Philippine title in the voter-determined competition, the Underground River became the focus of vast text and Internet voting endeavors—and a subject of not only Palawan but also *Filipino* pride. Many of the promotional activities surrounding the campaign targeted support in urban centers, often outside of Palawan and even the Philippines—especially through the encouragement of Overseas Foreign Workers to vote. President Benigno S. Aquino requested all government employees to support the campaign and appointed a national task force to support the endeavor (Proclamation no. 182). The dominant branding of the billboards and banners (coming from both official promotions, and adopted by supporting businesses) centered on the Underground River eventually becoming the "lone Philippine entry" in the competition, and as such, a source of "national pride".

The campaign was incredibly productive—not only in terms of generating votes for the PPUR as an entry within the N7WN competition, but also in promoting the Underground River more broadly. Filipinos who had spent small amounts of time in very specific parts of Palawan—and those who had never visited Palawan at all— were curating images and meanings of Palawan nature via text, blogs, social media, and everyday conversations. While some companies and agencies produced printed or digital banners to demonstrate their support of the campaign and prompt voting, others began to promote their own business by using images of the entrance to the PPUR as the backdrop to websites and signage. The Underground River's virtual and visual presence within Metro Manila increased through a plethora of images displayed in offices, malls, and airports and circulated through computers, tablets, and mobile phones (see also Dressler 2011). Support of voting for the Underground River in the N7WN campaign was further encouraged by phone carrier "promos", particularly a lottery called *Pera sa Kweba!* (money in the cave). This lottery was referenced in billboards (such as the one depicted in Figure 6.3) that suggested that when Filipinos stand together and vote, everyone can win.

Figure 6.2 A sign encouraging visitors to vote in the N7WN at the entrance to the PPUR portrays an image of the cave entrance behind it, January 2011

Photo by Sarah Webb

Figure 6.3 A billboard on the road between downtown Puerto and Sabang. The sign features then Puerto Princesa City Mayor Edward Hagedorn urging Filipinos to vote, declaring, "Let us carry the banner of our National PRIDE!" March 2011

Photo by Sarah Webb

In both appreciative acknowledgments of citizens' support for the campaign and more cynical commentaries, the success of the PPUR-N7WN campaign was largely attributed to the text-voting capacity and willingness of mobile-savvy Filipinos. In a speech given during his own text vote-casting, President Aquino III declared, "In the Philippines, we have no less than 80 million cellphone users, sending nearly two billion text messages every day. All we need is one billion votes—so that is half a day" (Aquino 2011).

The President's confidence referred to the pivotal role of text messaging in mediating everyday life across the Philippines (see Pertierra 2002). The potential to "mobilize" this expertise and familiarity with texting on such a national scale was enhanced by the high value placed by many Filipinos upon "standing together" and the importance accorded to the prestige of awards and competitions. For many, practices of supporting the campaign through voting or promotion embodied the pride associated with a *bayanihan*-spirited communal pursuit of a nationally desirable and beneficial goal.[5] As such, it was not only the integrity of the Underground River as a Wonder of Nature that was a source of pride but also the collective ability of Filipino people to make a Philippine nature globally recognized and appreciated. Additionally inspirational was the notion that this recognition offered potential productive opportunities for the nation's environmental and economic future, particularly through ecotourism revenue. A key aspiration of the promotion was the attraction of the spending by more foreign tourists. During the aforementioned speech, President Aquino suggested that voting enabled Filipinos to "take part in this democracy-in-action on behalf of our own environment" and "help the Puerto Princesa Underground River, as well as the Philippines, garner a distinct spot on the international tourist map" (Aquino 2011). Similar ambitions were publicized by the chairman of the PPUR Task Force, Department of the Interior and Local Government Secretary Jesse M. Robredo and then Puerto Princesa City Mayor Edward Hagedorn (Santos 2011; Philippine Information Agency 2012).

While the voting and promotion of the Underground River was largely located beyond central Palawan, these practices spurred two important flows to and from the region: first, the traffic in images and meanings of the Underground River throughout the Philippines and beyond; and, second, a dramatic increase in tourists visiting the Underground River. Yet, despite the emphasis on attracting foreign tourists, it was the mobilization of enormous numbers of (largely middle-class) Filipino tourists who not only supported tourist markets but transformed what it meant to visit this particular site of national, natural heritage.

Visiting a wondrous nature

The PPUR-N7WN campaign significantly impacted on tourist flows to central Palawan (particularly between downtown Puerto Princesa City and the Underground River via Sabang) and furthered the reputation of Palawan as the "ecotourism capital of the Philippines" (Rasch 2014, p. 242). In the lead-up to the November 2011 announcement of the N7WN winners, Filipino tourists from throughout the country and overseas travelled to visit a place of nature they considered part of their own Filipino heritage. A Puerto Princesa government official who worked extensively in the National Park describes how visitor numbers increased dramatically, "especially during the times when the Park was inscribed as a UNESCO World Heritage site and as finalist to the New 7 Wonders of Nature" (see also Table 6.1). He explains how the subsequent changes to visitor dynamics resulted in extensive transformations of visitor experiences of the National Park:

> During the start of the management of the Park when it was still with the DENR[6] more tourists are foreign tourists—before. But now more tourists are Filipinos. Of course the number before is very, very minimal but now the numbers of tourists are high. And the time they spend in the Park—before, they spend long times. One foreign tourist before will spend about three to four days in the Park, just reading books, watching birds, writing. But now most of the tourists, the visitors going in, just want to see the Underground River. Before they want to see the whole Park area. So of course we have to shorten the time of travel inside the Park because of the many tourists
> (Puerto Princesa City, August 2011)

As this account indicates, the surge in visitors associated with the N7WN campaign has dramatically transformed what it means to visit the Underground River. While in the 1980s more registered visitors to the Park were foreigners, by the early 1990s domestic tourists were the majority of visitors. This majority has increased as total visitor numbers have dramatically risen, first as a result of the 1999 inscription of the Park as a UNESCO World Heritage site but especially during the recent PPUR-N7WN campaign.

Ways of traversing space that were once key to the experience of "seeing" the Underground River, like hiking to the entrance, have been largely eliminated from most tourists' experiences of visiting the Park (see, for example, Sablan 2003)[7]. While there are other niche activities on the local tourism circuit (a mangrove paddleboat tour, spelunking, trekking, and bird watching), the majority of tourists spend a very minimal part of their "day" trip to the Park actually inside it. A recent zipline attraction makes a particular perspective of Palawan's iconic forest visible to visitors who need not spend extensive time walking around inside the forested Park to "see" it. While more tourists once stopped at local institutions like the Ethnographic Museum adjacent to the central *barangay* park office while they collected their park permits locally, now vans pass directly by (having already secured park permits in downtown Puerto Princesa). These permits are increasingly in demand as the surge in visitor numbers has resulted in new limitations on accessing the Underground River. By March 2012, the Park management board issued a travel advisory to notify potential visitors that the carrying capacity of the Park (900 visitors per day) was to be strictly enforced through a "No Permit, No Entry" policy (PAMB Resolution No. 06–2012). To accommodate this number of visitors, tourists were allocated specifically timed trips to visit the Underground River. As a result, it has become difficult for visitors to visit the Underground River without prior planning and booking or travelling via a private tour company. These private day tours have recently emerged as the dominant mode for tourists to visit the Park.[8] In order to consider how practices of visiting and making nature have become influenced by these trends, I give the following ethnographic account of such private day tours to the PPUR during 2010.

Day-tripping to the Underground River

The journey begins early in the morning. An air-conditioned mini-van collects visitors from their accommodations in pension houses surrounding Puerto Princesa City. Guests are told where to sit as they enter the van by our tour guide—an important consideration, as all the seats in the van have been allocated via the booking agency. Once the driver has collected all the passengers, the tour guide introduces herself (Teri) and the driver (Jose).[9] She jokes that all the guests will need to remember her, because once we reach Sabang, all of the vans look the same. She tells the guests if they cannot remember her name, not to worry, just to call her "Beautiful" and her colleague "Handsome". Her jokes, spoken in a mixture of English and Tagalog, initiate the comfortable congeniality essential to the enjoyment of such a trip for many of her guests. Although many middle-class Filipinos visiting Palawan travel in multi-generational family groups large enough to book their own transport or tour, the style of today's tour allows those travelling in smaller groups to join together with unknown travelers to share the expense of transport, guides, and food. As such, tourists pay an inclusive, per-person rate that includes these costs as well as their Park permit. Aside from myself, today's tour is composed of Filipino tourists: three single female friends in their early twenties, a woman in her sixties accompanied by her daughter, and two professional husband-wife couples in their late twenties.[10] Teri hands around a snack to each passenger—a sandwich of Lady's Choice (a nationally iconic sandwich spread of sweet mayonnaise and small pieces of meat) and two keychains (a wooden mask with "Palawan" carved into the forehead and a dream-catcher). She tells all the guests that now they have their souvenir, they need not spend their money buying souvenirs in Sabang—and besides, if anyone would like to purchase *pasalubong* (a gift for family, friends, or colleagues) we will be stopping at a specific *tiangge* (grouping of covered stalls) on the return journey.

The three friends travelling together and I discuss their trip to Palawan so far, particularly their island-hopping tour of the previous day. We look through the photographs from the excursion on one of the women's small digital camera. Few of the photographs show landscape shots; the majority of images are of the women posing in their beachwear holding starfish (transported to the shallows on islands for precisely such photographs). Many of the photos foreground staged iconic beach holiday items: an empty San Miguel beer bottle or a white conch shell. Such objects are often carried on tours by staff who include them as props when they take similarly composed photographs for their guests. The direct drive to Sabang takes less than 2 hours, but today our journey is lengthened by making short stops along the way. These include visiting one of the "view-decks" that has recently been sponsored by the City government as a livelihood venture. Teri warns us to take our change for the CR (*comfort room*, toilet) which has been built as part of tourism projects, so that community groups can collect revenue from users. As we exit the van, one of the young women I have been chatting with suggests we climb the stairs to the viewing platform to have our photograph taken together on her digital camera—"for Facebook"—against the backdrop of the mountain range and bay. One of the couples examines the beachwear for sale in front of the view deck café. A monkey walks along the balcony of the restaurant, its movements partially restricted by a long chain.

Upon first setting off, Teri warned against a possible inclination to sleep during the ride, as there would be plenty of scenery to observe and information to hear. Now that we are back in the van continuing the trip, she narrates the journey through a series of anecdotes. As the limestone karst range of the Park begins to dominate the landscape Teri tells us about the "native" Batak who, she explains, inhabit the upland, interior of the forest beyond the road. She describes Batak peoples through points of supposedly exoticized difference: their "Negrito" origins, "dark skin", "curly hair", and "short stature" (for a similar account during such van trips, see Dressler 2011). Her descriptions rely on a Batak absence to inscribe their imagined presence upon the passing landscape in a way that is uncomfortably similar to the spectacle evoked in her previous story (pointing out to us a river where supposedly a local child was eaten by a crocodile). When we approach the small section of the road before Sabang that remains unpaved, Teri warns passengers of the upcoming discomfort by drily telling them that if they had instead availed of the multi-cab journey (a small jeepney-style vehicle with open windows and doors) to Sabang, they could have received a "free massage" (a reference to the rough road) and "free powder" (dust). Her visitors shriek with loud laughter at what is a common genre of self-deprecating jokes told across the Philippines, humorous comments that Fenella Cannell suggests, "play on the gap between aspiration and reality" (1999, p. 21). As we cross over a stream where women are washing clothes via a small wooden bridge of rickety appearance, Teri announces to us that it is called the Miracle Bridge. "Do you know why it is called Miracle Bridge?" she asks smiling, "that is because it is a miracle that the government built it!" This joke is met with further laughter, and upon passing back the same way later in the day, several passengers call out "Miracle Bridge" as we cross it.

Taking the same trip the next week with another guide, Ramon, his own anecdotes reference not the state in a general sense but a specific politician—Puerto Princesa City Mayor Edward Hagedorn, who is famously portrayed as an illegal logger turned environmentalist. Ramon explains Hagedorn's commitment to a "clean and green" Puerto Princesa City by recounting a popular story about the Mayor's *oplan linis* (anti-littering) program: After the Mayor was allegedly caught by a janitor throwing away a cigarette butt, he paid the PHP 200 fine as evidence that "even those who make the laws must follow them". Ramon dramatically describes to guests how he believes Mayor Hagedorn has defended the Park against mineral extraction by promoting ecotourism as an alternative mode of generating revenue. However, Ramon suggests, such a venture relies upon promoting the Park to foreign tourists, as "only 25 per cent of tourists are locals [nationals]". Ramon stresses that the need for this promotion cannot be underestimated because, "the River is our future".

Once Ramon's tour arrives at Sabang, we exit the van, and he takes our group photograph on a guest's digital camera as a remembrance of the trip, at her request. The van has dropped us at the recently reconstructed concrete pier, and from here we are to take a short motorized *bangka* (boat) ride to the mouth of the Underground River. An alternative access to the mouth of the Underground River is via a four-kilometer hike. While this trail was once a popular alternative to travelling via *bangka*, it is not included as an option on the organized tours that include the cost of *bangka* transport and do not allocate time for walking to the River. Upon arriving at the beach near the mouth of the River and walking to the entrance, visitors are organized by tour guides, boat operators, and Park staff into smaller paddleboats and given life vests and hardhats. As we enter the cave, the guide's joke that bumps against the boat are "only crocodiles" is met by screams. He continues joking with his knowing guests by telling them not to look up if they feel water dripping on them, in case it is urine from the bats or birds that inhabit the cave. Inside the darkness of the cave, staff operate a powerful light to make certain features visible to guests. These formations are always identified by guides as familiar objects or famous figures—various fruits, Sharon Stone ("that sexy lady"), Jurassic Park (a dinosaur), and many images of the Virgin Mary and Jesus. Upon returning to Sabang beach from the Underground River, tour guests take a buffet lunch of Filipino foods at one of the outdoor beachfront restaurants. An older woman on the tour encourages Ramon to eat with the group. Ramon politely explains he will be taking his own lunch with the other tour guides and reminds the guests that buffet means not "all you can eat", but rather "eat all you can". The final activity at Sabang beach before returning to the van is to consider a vendor's offer of a renowned local delicacy—*tamilok* (a mangrove woodworm reputed to enhance fertility). Those who are "brave" enough to do so pose for photographs in the act of eating the mollusks.

This day-tripping account provides insight into how flows of revenue, national projects, and the tastes and aspirations of some Filipinos converge to shape the practices and meanings of commodifying nature. Central to understanding this nexus is considering how a "wondrous" nature is packaged as accessible, recognizable, and pleasurable for certain Filipino consumers—who themselves labor to produce the Underground River as an essentialized nature in accordance with their own aspirations of national benefits. Central to shaping this process has been the increasing privatization of visiting nature on central Palawan Island. As the above account suggests, it is private tour guides who provide the major facilitation of tourist experiences of the Park and the Underground River. These tour guides, on behalf of their absent employers, make a certain nature identifiable and pleasurable for new masses of visitors (for example, by facilitating encounters with invisible crocodiles, convenient starfish, urinating bats, captive monkeys, and exotic mollusks). Indeed, the ways this nature is made visible or consumable might better be characterized as spectacle rather than environmental education, given that guides' focus is on making their guests comfortable and entertained. Private tours are highly structured navigations through time and space that capture or direct much of tourist revenue as well as attention (through transport to specific sites, arrangement of meals, suggestions of where and when to purchase souvenirs, and even showing visitors how to capture themselves with certain backdrops or animals to reproduce commonly composed photographic images). So, while extensive economic activities center around Sabang, the "local" experience of travelling to the Underground River is largely facilitated for domestic tourists by external enterprises and their agents, few of whom are residents.

Guides also position the acts of ecotourism in which they and visitors are participating within everyday political discourses about central Palawan environments and economy. Ramon, for example, suggests in his speech about the need of international tourists to support ecotourism as an alternative to resource extraction that only 25 per cent of tourists to the Underground River were domestic tourists, when actually in recent years domestic tourists have comprised approximately 85 per cent of the total visitor numbers (see Table 6.1). Of course, Filipino tourists are in no way passive recipients of these meanings. Domestic tourists actively shape encounters of tourism and are co-participants in the related social reproductions of valuing nature and nation. In my interviews and conversations with domestic tourists on Palawan during the N7WN campaign, well-versed and knowledgeable citizens thoughtfully articulated the national significance and exceptional "nature" of the Underground River and made these meaningful to their own lives and experiences. The ambiance and activities described in the "day-tripping" account speak to the way these productions are embedded within important Filipino socialities—and how aspirations for the future are often discussed through shared, critical and, at times, self-deprecating humours about the nation's present and past.

Essentially, it is these important Filipino socialities and values that shape day-trips to a wondrous nature. My day-tripping account is filled with the small, everyday extensions of hospitality through which Filipino guides and guests work to produce such social interactions (telling jokes, eating together, engaging a lone traveller in conversation). Guides must be apt at monitoring and caring for their guests, and many of the more recent ways of traversing space relate to notions of comfort, which include avoiding the need for guests to walk extensive distances, providing snacks and meals, and directing the activities of guests. Despite articulated aspirations for international tourists, these features of tours largely cater to certain Filipino (often middle-class) tastes. The emerging experience of day-tripping to the Underground River is increasingly less appealing to many of the foreign "eco"-tourists identified elsewhere in this chapter (see descriptions by Fletcher and the government official).

Transforming a wondrous nature

The revenue flows, aspirations, and consumption practices I have outlined have not only shaped how domestic tourists visit the Underground River, the Park and Sabang—They have also resulted in transformations of these spaces. As the Underground River itself has travelled through images and more visitors than ever before have travelled to see a certain Underground River, the surrounding region has come to more closely resemble domestic tourists' expectations of what a gateway to a natural, national heritage should look like (with a concrete pier, a beach that is swept daily before tourists arrive, the planting of coconut trees, and the emergence of businesses such as souvenir stands and massage huts; Carrier and Miller 1998; West and Carrier 2004; Dressler 2011). With the increasing privatization of space and access, public places on Sabang pier and beachfront have been claimed for the use of "guests" of specific establishments, and signs discourage occupation of these areas by others. Transformations of the Sabang beachfront landscape have made certain "natures" more recognizable, accessible, and enjoyable for middle-class Filipino tourists but often in ways foreign to socioeconomically marginalized local peoples, such as indigenous Tagbanua and Batak residents of Sabang and surrounds (Dressler 2011). Many of the forms of pleasurably experiencing nature I describe as a feature of day-trip tours are significantly disconnected from the lives of indigenous farmers (for whom an encounter with a monkey is more likely to mean protecting fields from a pest rather than interacting with nature). One of the Tagbanua families I worked closely with often discussed the clothing and habits of tourists, particularly because they considered the bikini swimwear of some tourists to be quite immodest, and commented that those travelling for leisure were visiting the region without purpose, having "nothing to do".

In many ways, the lives of indigenous peoples are also foreign to domestic tourists within ecotourism encounters. The presence of indigenous peoples in Sabang as they travel across the Park, purchase groceries, or sell the products of their livelihoods is largely unrecognizable to any tourists who rely on the descriptions of Batak portrayed as a Palawan attraction by tour guides. The images of indigenous peoples compiled for these descriptions reflect less the reality of everyday or ceremonial life for indigenous peoples on Palawan and more the way markers of ethnicity and indigeneity are assembled for broader Filipino public consumption (see Alcedo 2014). As tour guides narrate the journey from downtown Puerto to Sabang, their descriptions project upon central Palawan landscapes an imagined indigenous presence that relies on the actual absence of Tagbanua and Batak residents who could challenge essentialized representations of contemporary indigenous upland lifeways[11] (Brosius 1999; Tsing 1999; Li 2002; Dove 2006).

Conclusion

The remaking of the Underground River as a site of national, natural heritage has occurred across not only spatial distances but also significant social divisions. The internationally recognized status of the site has relied upon the labor and cultural production of many Philippine citizens who cannot afford to visit the place themselves but who texted votes or circulated promotional images. Further national activations of the site through a massive increase in largely middle-class, domestic "eco"-branded tourism have fundamentally transformed what it means to visit this place. Although political agendas and increasing privatization shape how Filipino citizens and consumers can see the Park, neither voters nor visitors of "wondrous nature" are passive recipients of meanings. Rather, their practices of consumption are integral to the broader cultural productions of nationally significant meanings. These consumers are active in placing themselves within nature in ways that are desirable and reproducing places of nature in ways that they understand as beneficial for certain national environmental and economic futures—even if these aspirations do not necessarily incorporate the everyday economic and environmental experiences of many local residents.

Much of the extant work on ecotourism examines how Western-oriented expectations of culture and environment transform local people and places. By contrast, this case study speaks to the powerful transformations that occur within tropical Asian countries through emerging domestic "eco"-branded tourism. As more Filipinos than ever before visit the Underground River, this place has become further established in national images as a site of Philippine natural heritage. In creating, circulating, and consuming Palawan environments, socially differentiated and spatially distanced Filipinos produce powerful social values of nature. These practices are embedded within important aspirations of some citizens for the environmental and economic future of not only Palawan but also the Philippines more broadly. I have argued, however, that as domestic tourism has transformed the ways in which a "wondrous nature" can be recognized, accessed, and made pleasurable, the resulting practices have often reproduced, rather than challenged, the local disjuncture that ecotourism is embedded within on central Palawan Island.

Acknowledgments

My thanks for the generous advice and comments from the editors of this volume and the anonymous reviewer of this chapter. The research from which this case study is taken would not have been possible without funding from the Wenner-Gren Foundation through a Dissertation Fieldwork Grant. I thank Wolfram H. Dressler, and Anna Cristina Pertierra, who have provided key guidance in developing the research that this case study is drawn from. Thanks to Will Smith for his comments on drafts of this chapter. My heartfelt thanks to those whose experiences and perspectives are the basis of this study.

Notes

1. A means that is supposedly consistent with supporting the environmental integrity of these places of nature. Although, as the following case study demonstrates, such an assertion remains highly contested on Palawan Island.
2. Palawan province includes the large Palawan Island and more than 1,700 small islands.
3. Furthermore, findings from a 1996 workshop on Ancestral Domain resource plans attended by indigenous representatives from across Palawan suggest that, at this time, attendees were adamant they did not want to encourage tourism inside Ancestral Domains (de Beer and McDermott 1996, pp. 156–57; see also Eder 1987, pp. 173–74).
4. Livelihood household survey ($n = 104$) conducted and qualified October-December 2011.

5 The term *bayanihan* is derived from rural neighbourhood practices of moving a family's entire house to a new location, and is often used in a national sense to refer to a communal coming together to achieve a particular goal. Bankoff draws on Filipino anthropologist F. Landa Jocano's extensive work on Filipino social values to suggest that the meaning of *bayanihan* "is definitely more complex than mere 'unity' or 'togetherness'—it has the connotation of shared identity and common association" (Bankoff 2007, p. 28).
6 DENR is the acronym for the Department of Natural Resources. The interviewee is referring to the contested devolution of the Park during the 1990s (see Dressler 2009).
7 However, as is apparent from comparing Sablan's (2003) account with the description included in this chapter, many of the jokes and narrations told inside the Underground River are the same.
8 Issues of accessing the Underground River have converged with a growth of businesses in the provincial-yet-urban downtown of Puerto Princesa rather than at the entry port of Sabang. Studies document how even during 1997 when the number of "nature tourists" was less than 40,000 (79 per cent domestic), the accommodation hub and tourism revenue were concentrated in downtown Puerto because the Park was considered to be an easy day trip (Goodwin 2002, p. 341).
9 All names used in this chapter are pseudonyms.
10 The woman in her sixties and her daughter were visiting from Mindanao. All the other guests were living in Metro Manila at the time of their visit.
11 Indeed, on one occasion, my Tagbanua research assistant did literally challenge the narration of a tour guide, by correcting him on local history and then taking over the narration himself.

References

Alampay, Ramon Benedicto A., and Carlos Libosada. 2005. "A Framework for Classifying Ecotourism Initiatives in the Philippines." In *Sustainable Tourism: Challenges for the Philippines*, edited by Ramon Benedicto A. Alampay, 127–60. Makati City, Philippines: The Philippine APEC Study Center Network and the Philippine Institute for Development Studies.

Alcedo, Patrick. 2014. "How Black is Black? The Indigenous *Atis* Compete at the Ati-atihan Festival." In *Dance Ethnography and Global Perspectives: Identity, Embodiment, and Culture*, edited by Linda E. Dankworth and Ann R. David, 37–57. Basingstoke: Palgrave Macmillan.

Aquino, Benigno S III. 2011. "Speech of His Excellency Benigno S. Aquino III President of the Philippines during the official launch of the Puerto Princesa Underground River Campaign." Malacañan Palace, Manila. Official Gazette, June 6. Accessed May 2, 2014. www.gov.ph/2011/06/06/speech-of-president-aquino-at-the-launch-of-the-puerto-princesa-underground-river-campaign-june-6-2011/

Austin, Rebecca L. 2003. "Environmental Movements and Fisherfolk Participation on a Coastal Frontier, Palawan Island, Philippines." PhD diss., University of Georgia, Athens, GA.

Bankoff, Gregory. 2007. "Living with Risk; Coping with Disasters: Hazard as a Frequent Life Experience in the Philippines." *Education about Asia* 12 (2): 26–9.

Broad, Robin, and John Cavanagh. 2001. *Plundering Paradise: The Struggle for the Environment in the Philippines*. Philippines: Anvil Publishing.

Brosius, Peter J. 1999. "Green Dots, Pink Hearts: Displacing Politics from the Malaysian Rain Forest." *American Anthropologist* 101 (1): 36–57.

Cannell, Fenella. 1999. *Power and Intimacy in the Christian Philippines.* Quezon City: Ateneo de Manila University Press.
Carrier, James G., and Daniel Miller, eds. 1998. *Virtualism: A New Political Economy.* Oxford: Berg.
Carrier, James G., and Donald V. L. Macleod. 2005. "Bursting the Bubble: The Socio-Cultural Context of Ecotourism." *Journal of the Royal Anthropological Institute* 11 (2): 315–34.
Carrier, James G., and Paige West, eds. 2009. *Virtualism, Governance and Practice: Vision and Execution in Environmental Conservation.* New York: Berghahn Books.
De Beer, Jenne H., and Melanie J. McDermott. 1996. *The Economic Value of Non-timber Forest Products in Southeast Asia.* Amsterdam: IUCN.
Dove, Michael R. 2006. "Indigenous People and Environmental Politics." *Annual Review of Anthropology* 35: 191–208.
Dressler, Wolfram Heinz. 2009. *Old Thoughts in New Ideas: State Conservation Measure, Development and Livelihood on Palawan Island.* Manila: Ateneo de Manila University Press.
Dressler, Wolfram Heinz. 2011. "First to Third Nature: The Rise of Capitalist Conservation on Palawan Island, the Philippines." *The Journal of Peasant Studies* 38 (3): 533–57.
Eder, James F. 1987. *On the Road to Tribal Extinction: Depopulation, Deculturation, and Adaptive Well-being among the Batak of the Philippines.* Los Angeles, CA: University of California Press.
Eder, James F.. 2008. *Migrants to the Coasts: Livelihood, Resource Management, and Global Change in the Philippines.* Belmont, CA: Cengage Learning.
Eder, James F., and Janet O. Fernandez, eds. 1996. *Palawan at the Crossroads: Development and the Environment on a Philippine Frontier.* Quezon City: Ateneo de Manila University Press.
Fabinyi, Michael. 2010. "The Intensification of Fishing and the Rise of Tourism: Competing Coastal Livelihoods in the Calamianes Islands, Philippines." *Human Ecology* 38 (3): 415–27.
Fletcher, Robert. 2014. *Romancing the Wild: Cultural Dimensions of Ecotourism.* Durham, NC: Duke University Press.
Goodwin, Harold. 2002. "Local Community Involvement in Tourism around National Parks: Opportunities and Constraints." *Current Issues in Tourism* 5 (3–4): 338–60.
Li, Tania Murray. 2002. "Engaging Simplifications: Community-Based Resource Management, Market Processes and State Agendas in Upland Southeast Asia." *World Development* 30 (2): 265–83.
Mowforth, Martin, and Ian Munt. 2009. *Tourism and Sustainability: Development, Globalisation and New Tourism in the Third World.* New York: Routledge.
Ong, Lei Tin Jackie, Donovan Storey, and John Minnery. 2011. "Beyond the Beach: Balancing Environmental and Socio-Cultural Sustainability in Boracay, The Philippines." *Tourism Geographies* 13 (4): 549–69.
Pertierra, Raul. 2002 *Txt-ing Selves: Cellphones and Philippine Modernity.* Manila: De La Salle University Press.
Philippine Information Agency. 2012. "Robredo Lauds Hagedorn, Local Gov't as PPUR Makes it to New 7 Wonders of the World." Accessed April 29, 2014. ncr.pia.gov.ph/index.php?article=261328327221.
Puerto Princesa Subterranean River National Park. 2008. *Park visitor statistics for the Puerto Princesa Subterranean River National Park.* Puerto Princesa City: PPSRNP Centro Office.
Rasch, Elisabeth Dueholm. 2014. "'Ecotourism, not Mining, in Palawan!' Territorial Narratives on the Last Frontier (Palawan, the Philippines)." In *The Ecotourism-Extraction*

Nexus: Political Economies and Rural Realities of (Un)comfortable Bedfellows, edited by Bram Büscher and Veronica Davidov, 236–54. New York: Routledge.

Rodolfo, Maria Cherry Lyn S. 2009. "Crafting Filipino Leisure: Tourism Programmes in the Philippines." In *Domestic Tourism in Asia: Diversity and Divergence*, edited by Shalini Singh, 235–51. London: Earthscan.

Sablan, Niño Mark M. 2003. "Cave of Wonders." *Philippine Daily Inquirer (Lifestyle)*, April 16. Accessed May 5, 2014. http://news.google.com/newspapers?nid=2479&dat=20030416&id=mERaAAAAIBAJ&sjid=ZSUMAAAAIBAJ&pg=2384,296635.

Santos, Tina G. 2011. "PAL to use bigger jets to boost Underground River tourism." *Philippine Daily Inquirer*, November 20. Accessed April 29, 2014. http://globalnation.inquirer.net/19057/pal-to-use-bigger-jets-to-boost-underground-river-tourism.

Seiler, Christof. 2014. *Growth in (Eco)tourism and its Effects on Livelihoods in the Philippines: A Case Study in Cabayugan, Puerto Princesa City, Palawan*, unpublished masters thesis, Department of Geography, University of Zurich.

Tsing, Anna Lowenhaupt. 1999. "Becoming a Tribal Elder and Other Green Development Fantasies." In *Transforming the Indonesian Uplands: Marginality, Power, and Production*, edited by Tania Murray Li, 159–202. Singapore: Harwood Academic Publishers.

West, Paige, and James G. Carrier. 2004. "Ecotourism and Authenticity: Getting Away from It All?" *Current Anthropology* 45 (4): 483–491.

Winter, Tim, Peggy Teo, and T. C. Chang, eds. 2009. *Asia on Tour: Exploring the Rise of Asian Tourism*. New York: Routledge.

7 The greying of greenspeak?

Environmental issues, media discourses, and consumer practices in China

Wanning Sun

Research on environmentalism in China has pointed to the connection between environmental non-governmental organizations (ENGOs) and new media and online technologies, in enabling Internet- and web-based collective actions and mobilization (Liu 2011; Dong 2013; Xu 2014). In a highly influential and frequently cited work, which considers the role of transnational ENGOs, the mass media and environmental activism via the Internet, Guobin Yang and Craig Calhoun (2007) trace the formation and circulation in China of "greenspeak". They use the term in a positive light; it has nothing to do with the "greenwash" that prevails in some critical environmental studies. The scholars argue that the greenspeak discourse, contrary to the Maoist discourse of taming and conquering nature, warns of the dangers of irresponsible human behavior toward nature and calls for public action to help protect the environment. Greenspeak appeals to and is practised by students, media professionals, intellectuals, and other socioeconomic elites in urban China. In the same work, Yang and Calhoun also argue that web-enabled environmentalism contributes to the formation of civil society and the emergence of a "green public sphere".

Acutely aware of the fraught nature of the debate surrounding the concept of the public sphere both outside and inside the Chinese context, Yang and Calhoun are careful to point out that they adopt a more "relaxed" notion of the public sphere, taking the term to refer loosely to "social space" or "public space". With this proviso in place, the authors simply define their use of the public sphere to mean a social space that consists of "discourses, publics engaged in communication, and the media of communication" (Yang and Calhoun 2007, p. 214). The authors pointed to a "fledging green public sphere" in China, which they see as including the active participation of state-controlled media as well as commercial media. This is because, they suggest, the Chinese government supported media coverage of environmental issues in the first place; commercial media had gained more freedom as a result of reforms; and many media professionals themselves were active environmentalists. Yang and Calhoun's view is somewhat reinforced in an analysis of 10 Chinese newspapers' coverage of environmental issues from 2008 to 2011 (Tong 2014). Adopting a quantitative framing method, the study finds that Chinese journalists, enjoying more autonomy in covering environmental problems than other issues, demonstrate a critical reflective outlook in their coverage of environmental risks.

In the past few years, especially since the frequent appearance of smog in many Chinese cities since January 2013, the harm and risk posed by environmental problems are no longer local issues concerning a hitherto unheard of river or preventing a remote endangered species from extinction. Today, environmental risk has become much more national in scale, more in-your-face in nature, and takes the form of widespread public risk, to which everyone is vulnerable. When Chinese journalist Chai Jing posted her 2-hour documentary *Under the Dome* online in March 2015, it drew hundreds of millions of viewers (Yuan 2015). So, if the public has become more conscious than ever of the environmental risk they are living with, has this increased awareness translated into a higher level of green activism and more rigorous public debates on environmental issues? Is the "critical reflective outlook" of environmental reporting enhanced by the recent exacerbation of China's environmental problems?

Set in the three related contexts of the state news media, lifestyle television programs, and the realm of consumer behavior and the market, this chapter addresses these questions by examining how environmentalism intersects with politics at a number of levels. It first considers the politics of the party-state, and examines how political constraints result in the government's playing a role that is at best ineffectual and at worst censorious. This is followed by a discussion of how environmental issues are dealt with in the space of lifestyle consumer advice, a media genre that is responsive to both political sensitivity and the regime of ratings in the media industry. This is by implication an analysis of the cultural politics of representation, aiming to identify major ways in which certain forms of lifestyle politics are endorsed, encouraged and cast as desirable. The last part outlines the political-economic factors underpinning the commodification of the concept of "green" in a competitive consumer market.

State media and the party-state

Despite its serious environmental problems, China has in fact impressed the world with a number of environmental achievements. In recent years, its government has published a series of policies and plans aimed at addressing environmental problems, including, among many, a plan to cut carbon emissions, reduce the production of cement and steel, invest in cleaner and more sustainable energy, and treat contaminated waterways and farmlands (Martina et al. 2014). Intentions and objectives, however, are one thing; political will and the administrative capacity to enforce these policies quite another. While state media are tireless when it comes to announcing green government policies and plans, they are often shy of explicitly saying how effective these measures are, given that the central government is up against big polluting industries and growth-driven local governments. For instance, reducing China's over-dependence on coal as the staple source of energy has been on the government's agenda for more than a decade, but instead of seeing a lowered coal consumption, the share of coal in the nation's energy mix has risen from 68 to 72 per cent (Chen 2014).

As the most important actor in shaping the past, present, and future of China's environment, the Chinese government has an indispensable role in the formation of a truly green public sphere. Unlike its counterparts in liberal-democratic countries, the Chinese government, operating under one-party rule, does not need to be concerned with making popular decisions in the name of jobs and economic growth in order to win votes and stay in office. At the same time, precisely because it operates under one-party rule and its political legitimacy does not come from democratic elections, the need to establish and maintain political legitimacy is constant and paramount. From the point of view of the party-state, the government's capacity to engage in "stability maintenance" (*weiwen*) through sustained economic growth is key to its sustained claim of political legitimacy. The preoccupation with maintaining stability dominates the history of rule of the Chinese Communist Party, and the current regime led by Xi Jinping and Li Keqiang is no exception. Stability—or the threat of instability—has provided a justification for oppression, censorship, and inaction on the part of the media. Having taken on a life of its own, stability maintenance is not just a political aspiration; it is a powerful assemblage of discourses, policies, processes, and institutions.

Yang and Calhoun point out that for ENGOs to operate effectively in China, they have to appear non-political and therefore non-threatening to the political regime. Indeed, as Peter Ho also points out, a key strategy of survival of the ENGOs in China thus far has been the "depoliticization of environmental politics" (Ho 2007, p. 195). A decade ago it may still have been possible to represent environmental issues as non-political issues, to a certain extent. Recent environmental disasters in China, however, particularly the lingering smog in major cities, mean that social stability, the political legitimacy of the party, and people's health and well-being all have become perilously entwined. In the past, the government's dilemma between economic growth and environmental protection may have been a theoretical issue concerning only policy makers. No longer: The increasing prevalence of smog in the country's urban centers has led ordinary people to question its causes and consequences and the price of their government's relentless drive for economic growth. This development has one serious implication: News coverage of environmental issues is becoming more and more sensitive in the political sense.

A survey of how key state media outlets such as Central Chinese Television (CCTV), the *People's Daily*, *Guangming Daily*, and *Economic Daily* covered smog in 2013 points to this sensitizing process. First, during that period, most of the perspectives and informed opinions on smog were provided by government and state-authorized scientists, and the voices of ENGOs were seldom heard. Second, most journalists engaged in various degrees of self-censorship while reporting on the smog. They avoided touching on a wide range of underlying factors, including how economic interests and power struggles were bound up with environmental issues. Nor did they touch on the complicity between government and big businesses. Third and related to the first two, the main angle in covering the smog was to "deal with the matter factually" (*jiushi lunshi*)—i.e., to give readers scientific "facts" about smog, such as its chemical components or the number of days on which it had manifested—without delving into politically sensitive interpretation of what caused the pollution, who was responsible, the extent of the risk to people's health, and what needed to be done in the future to bring about fundamental change (Jia 2014). It seems that while China's environmental journalism may have been more open to critical reflection in the past, this critical space has been diminished rather than expanded since environmental problems have assumed a national and more political dimension.

To be absolutely clear, the Chinese government is more acutely aware than ever of the risk of further environmental degradation in China, and it is sincere in its intention to fix China's environment. In November 2014, China and the United States announced a landmark agreement on carbon cuts, with China's President Xi Jinping pledging to set China's carbon emissions to fall after 2030 (The White House 2014). Some have gone so far as to point to a process of the "greening of the Chinese state", given that the Chinese government has passed a wide range of environmental laws and regulations and set up key environmental bureaucratic bodies (Ho and Vermeer 2006). However, despite the government's pro-environment rhetoric and regulations, its hands are tied by its own agenda of developing the economy, maintaining stability, and securing support and legitimacy from its population. For instance, the Chinese government has been very proactive in supporting green industries and now is a world leader in areas such as solar panel production. At the same time, the evidence suggests that such seemingly pro-environmental successes are sometimes achieved at the cost of polluted lands and rivers. For example, Chinese producers of polycrystalline silicon, a material used in key components of solar cells, are responsible for the dumping of toxic byproducts that are harmful to humans, animals, and soil (Liu 2013). China has become the world's largest and most important promoter of renewable energy (Mathews 2014a). Yet the development of renewable energy is driven less by the debate on climate change than it is motivated by the search for energy and resource security, with a view to achieving energy self-sufficiency and expanding capacity for manufacturing and building supply chains of renewable energy generation equipment (Mathews 2014b).

So, facing these constraints, how do the state media cover environmental issues? One key approach is the calendar-driven media campaign style of reporting. The commemoration of the *China Environment Centennial Journey* each year since 1993 is the most prominent example (Yang and Calhoun 2007). In this annual campaign, 14 governmental departments, in coordination with 28 national state media outlets, engage in a spate of environmentally themed reporting. Another approach is often referred to as "event-driven environmentalism", taking the form of media campaigns that often adopt a combination of military parlance (for example, metaphors of battle) and business-speak ("meeting the quota", "deficit"). This was clearly the style of media campaign for Beijing's Blue Sky Project, launched in 2008 in anticipation of the Beijing Olympic Games in 2008 (Xu 2012).

Finally, and perhaps most important, one must remember that censorship, the state media's oldest "trick of the trade", is still very much in place, especially when coverage of environmental issues threatens to reveal the complicity between the government and big businesses. In April 2014, Ma Tianjie, Greenpeace's program director in China, had this to say on *Q&A*, a current affairs panel discussion on Australian television, when he was asked about how to live with censorship:

The censorship is getting more sophisticated but we dance with it, play with it and interact with it. We held a press conference last year to challenge China's biggest coal company's practices. We had a full house. Chinese journalists came to give their support, knowing too well that they would not be allowed to report on the event. So, we used the opportunity to send the information out to mobilize netizens

(ABC 2014)

The coal company Ma was referring to was the state-owned Shenhua, the biggest coal company in the world by production volume. Greenpeace took Shenhua to task for its over-exploitation of groundwater and for the illegal dumping of toxic industrial wastewater in Erdos in Western China (Greenpeace East Asia 2014). Ma's comments point to ENGOs' capacity to engage in media tactics, but they also make clear a number of sobering facts. First, they reveal the Dr. Jekyll-and-Mr. Hyde nature of the Chinese government on the issue of environment. The tangled web of political and economic interests involving both the government and big businesses represents the biggest obstacle to the environmental cause in China. Second, although green NGOs might devise ways of "dancing with" censorship, the fact remains that, for state media, especially in relation to polluting practices involving state-owned businesses, censorship—rather than active endorsement and support of greenspeak—is the *de rigueur* response. In light of this, it is hardly surprising that *Under the Dome* was taken off from China's main video sites such as Youku and Tencent soon after it became a "smash-hit" (Beaumont-Thomas 2015). While it may be true that ENGOs in China to some extent practice "embedded activism", characterized by their informal, non-confrontational partnership with the government (Ho 2006), recent research on the use of social media by local ENGOs in China suggests that such DIY grassroots activism is limited, "temporary and fragile", and has to navigate complex and subtle relationships with the government (Xu 2014, p. 1374).

Consumer lifestyle advice

Focusing on controversial media formats and genres such as news—as I have done so far—tells us what happens when political needs and market initiatives clash, posing a potential threat to stability, but this is only half of the picture. The other half, which runs the risk of being obscured by this focus, is equally if not more important: It has to do with how the party-state authorities and the market work together to ensure that the stability maintenance machine functions smoothly. Contrary to what some may expect, the party-state and its media policy favor diversity in terms of audience, function, medium, and format. This is because diversity along these lines is considered not only desirable in terms of content appeal but also, more important, a more diverse content is deemed by the government to be more conducive to stability maintenance (Sun 2015). This commitment to diversity was affirmed in the outgoing Party Chairman Hu Jintao's work report to the 18th Party Congress in 2012, when he says that "we must ensure that that our social and cultural life is diverse and plentiful", and that "our cultural products must become more abundant and diverse" (Hu 2012). Just as balance and equilibrium in terms of the number of species is needed to ensure ecological soundness in the natural world, policy statements and top leaders' instructions make it clear that they see the key to maintaining China's ideological ecology in the media to be a balance and equilibrium of various forces—social, cultural, economic, and political.

Lifestyle television programs, by the nature of the genre and format, specialize in giving everyday practical and viable life advice to consumers, and as such, in terms of genre, function, and format, they are an important "species" in the general ecology of the Chinese media. Among a long list of recommendations on what the Party must do in the future, Chairman Hu mentioned the need for the Party to "guide our people to engage in cultural practices in which they can express themselves, educate themselves, and provide services to themselves" (Hu 2012). Lifestyle media embody precisely this kind of cultural practice. Although lifestyle media genres in China often prominently feature "state-authorized" experts (Farquhar and Zhang 2012), these genres are generally considered to be politically uncontroversial and economically lucrative cultural products that provide practical information and services to consumers. Ranging from CCTV 2's renovation show *Transforming Spaces* to its makeover show *Shopping for Fashion*, to Shanghai Television's Channel Young *Fashion Guide*, from local Bengbu Television's *At Your Service* to Zhejiang TV's *Woman Who Likes to Help*, a plethora of lifestyle programs that combine information with entertainment and employ a diversity of formats deliver to viewers, on a regular basis, much-needed knowledge about how to survive the economic and social challenges thrown up by economic reforms (Xu 2007, 2009; Sun 2012). While they appear to be non-political on the surface, these programs are nevertheless highly effective in teaching people a wide range of skills and a set of new attitudes—in the realms of health care and "life nurturance" (*yangsheng*); mental, psychological, and emotional well-being; familial and interpersonal relationships; personal finance, travel, and everyday living—which are necessary to survive the turbulences caused by the transition from socialism to a neo-liberal market economy.

Admittedly, lifestyle programs are not the place to ask probing questions and engage in in-depth investigation into the causes and effects of environmental damage. Nor is lifestyle advice likely to become the primary site to engage in campaigns aimed at raising public awareness and advocating citizen involvement in environmentalist activities. Having said this, it is also true that, as the staple diet of most television viewers in China, lifestyle programs present themselves as a potentially valuable site from which to advocate a greener way of life. As Yang and Calhoun rightly observe, to practice environmentalism is to adopt a new understanding of the meaning of life, a new moral vision, and a new personhood (2007, p. 215). And lifestyle television programs, dedicated to teaching viewers "desirable" ways of living, are constituted by many popular categories of makeover, self-transformation, and overhaul of the self, body, and soul. Critiques of these cultural forms reveal that as a popular media and cultural expression, lifestyle television provides a justification as well as moral support for the transition from a state-regulated life to a self-managed way of living (Lewis 2008a, 2011). At the same time, there is also evidence (Lewis 2008b, 2012; Bonner 2011) to suggest that it could be a much more useful site to guide consumers to become more environmentally responsible citizens. Indeed, lifestyle programs in the Global North, especially in food television, are increasingly dealing with issues to do with environmentalism and ethical consumption (Lewis 2008b). So, questions naturally arise pertaining to the Chinese case: How are environmental issues constructed in lifestyle programs on Chinese television, and what kind of strategies and solutions are proposed? Equally important, if, as is discussed earlier, environmental news is more likely to be censored than promoted due to its perceived capacity to trigger social instability, to what extent can lifestyle television present itself as an alternative discursive space to promote genuinely green messages?

It has to be said that programs with an explicit green focus are few and far between, but this does not mean that we should rule out lifestyle television programs as a potentially effective discursive space. One example that testifies to this potential is a 2010 episode of Channel Young's wedding show (*Xingshang Hunli*), which points to some real possibilities in relation to environmental pedagogies. Preceded by a few episodes of weddings, featuring for instance a European wedding and a traditional Chinese wedding, the episode in question features a "Low Carbon Wedding". Rather than in a fleet of stretch limousines, the bride, groom, bridesmaids, and best men all arrive at the wedding riding bicycles. Guests receive invitation cards made from recycled milk cartons and a subway ticket that incentivizes them to take public transport to the wedding. The host interviews the bride and groom on the design of their wedding clothes—all made from recycled material but looking stylish and glamorous. Guests are shown as being suitably impressed with the novel ideas behind the design, presentation, and green ethos of the event. They say they have learned a lot from this event and that they are going to think about how they will organize their own weddings.

The newlyweds are featured on the show as much for their individualistic consumption practices as for their environmental activism. Nevertheless, the show points to the potential usefulness of the lifestyle media in promulgating a new ethical position, a different moral vision, and an alternative way of life. To be sure, many consumer-oriented television programs do make gestures toward introducing green ways of living. *Transforming Spaces* (*Jiaohuan Kongjian*) on CCTV 2 (China Central Television) is a renovation show that adopts the typical format of a renovation show and combines the genres of reality TV, competition and makeover. As part of the show, each episode has a segment entitled "Turning Oldies into Goodies" (*Jiuwu Gaizao*), in which Teams A and B are given the task of turning a discarded consumer item into something useful. An episode in March 2014, for instance, gave contestants the task of finding innovative ways of recycling an empty tea tin. Team A turned a few tins into a number of flower pots for fake flowers, whereas Team B made a toy train with connecting carriages. Although one may wonder how useful flower pots for fake flowers are or how durable a toy train made of a few tins can be, the message behind this show was unmistakable: Recycling is a worthy consumption practice.

Unlike Channel Young's *Weddings*, however, many lifestyle programs that do touch on green topics and themes do not actively push a pro-environment discourse. Instead, the focus of these programs is often the consumers' body and health. Narratives are mostly geared toward the question of how individuals can stay healthy or even beautiful in a polluted environment or how they can protect themselves from unsafe food, water, and toxic air. These shows betray a fatalist and defeatist view of individuals' capacity to save the Earth, yet at the same time they emphasize the need for individuals to develop coping mechanisms, in particular the need to strengthen the body, which is increasingly at risk and under attack. The health of the individual body, rather than the health of the environment, forms the central concern of such lifestyle advice.

In other words, rather than positively promoting what actions can be taken collectively to work toward a greener environment or to adopt an environmentally responsible lifestyle in one's own consumption practices, lifestyle programs mostly function as a "survival kit" for viewers eager to learn how to live optimally in an environment that is no longer "green". Cosmetic and beauty advice aside, this "how to survive the environmental risk" theme has many narrative variants, ranging from coping with air and water pollution and staying healthy, or detecting counterfeit food products and staying safe, to renovating one's apartment without inhaling too many chemical vapors. These types of advice can be found in a variety of lifestyle shows, including shows on cooking, renovation, fashion, and travel. However, it is in the programs on health and well-being, which make up a significant proportion of the lifestyle advice programs on local and provincial television, that a connection between environmental issues and health risk is most explicitly made. For instance, *Zero Distance to Health*, a local program on Bengbu Television in Anhui Province in eastern China regularly presents consumer warnings and advice on a wide range of products. An episode in early 2011, for instance, tells viewers that a significant proportion of toys for sale in the shops pose health risks of one kind or another. The program outlines—textbook-style and complete with charts and tables—the risk to children's health associated with toys on account of unacceptably high levels of chemicals and noise or a lack of child-proofing in the design, and so on. It suggests that consumers look for clues that identify unsafe toys, including color, smell, design, and labeling. In its didactic style, the show also presents the latest "scientific findings" relating to the potential health risks of purchasing and using certain domestic appliances, of renovating the apartment, or simply of everyday activities such as breathing air, drinking water, and eating food. The widely agreed assumption behind these narratives is that individuals cannot do much to change the environment they live in; all they can do is change the way they live their lives so that they maximize their chance of survival.

If more "parochial" local television stations such as Bengbu TV approach environmental issues by providing viewers with basic knowledge aimed at self-protection, are high-end consumer advice shows on national or metropolitan channels more "enlightened", and do they approach these issues from a less self-serving point of view? A general survey of the content of some such programs suggests perhaps not. *Popular Eats* (*Renqi Meishi*) on Shanghai's Channel Young, the only channel in China dedicated to lifestyle television, regularly features tips on how to *bu* (replenish) the body to strengthen it against external invasions of germs, bacteria, and viruses. Broadcasting from Monday to Friday at 7:00 p.m., the show is the most popular consumer guide on where and what to eat in Shanghai. On March 5, 2014, an episode of *Popular Eats* takes consumers to a restaurant that specializes in seahorse soup. The host gives a microphone to the chef, who proceeds to tell viewers about the medicinal value of seahorses as a tonic. Conspicuously missing from the conversation is the fact that a number of seahorse species have long been listed by environmental protection bodies as threatened and endangered, largely due to unsustainable harvesting, and that China, with its long-standing tradition of consuming seahorses for their supposed medicinal value, constitutes the biggest market for seahorses.

Environmental issues provide a new prism through which individuals negotiate their respective sense of who they are and how they should live their lives as citizens and consumers. These examples from lifestyle shows on Chinese television point to a cacophony of moral and ethical voices in contestation and negotiation. At the same time, even though it is impossible to generalize across the board, it does seem that self-protecting and self-preserving discourses in popular lifestyle media, especially on topics of *yangsheng* (nurturing life)—the most popular topic in lifestyle programs, which attract the biggest audience group on Chinese television—cast into doubt the reach and efficacy of greenspeak in China. Lifestyle advice makes up the bulk of China's television content, and the shows command high ratings in comparison with news and current affairs. Yet despite its potential to present itself as an environmentally friendly pedagogic space in the media, lifestyle advice as we currently know it is more charged with the discursive task of assisting individuals in their self-governing efforts aimed at self-protection and less burdened with introducing consumption practices associated with environmental messages and ethical consumption. In the absence of the party-state's intervention, market forces—through the regime of ratings—play a crucial role in determining and shaping lifestyle content. Consequently, environmentalist messages have a chance to get through only when it is believed that they may boost ratings.

Commodifying the concept of green

Yang and Calhoun identify the key dimensions of a green public sphere as consisting of "an environmental discourse or greenspeak; publics that produce and consume greenspeak; and media used for producing and circulating greenspeak" (2007, p. 212). If we are to assess the extent to which such a green public sphere exists, it is not enough just to look at ways in which the media produce narratives and discourses. We also need to ask to what extent the green concept has infiltrated the market and how it has informed people's consumption practices. Equally important, we need to make careful distinction between "greenspeak" and "greenwash". While the former refers to green narratives that have genuine environmentalist messages to promote, the latter describes deceptive marketing strategies that use green discourses to promote products and services.

Ethical and sustainable consumption is becoming a major issue of public debate in many countries in the Global North. In China, too, whether and how consumers respond to green messages are questions that concerns market researchers. Many findings point to the fact that the concept of "greenness" helps sell products. One study (Chang 2011) finds that, due to a number of factors including perceived higher prices, perceived lower quality, and perceived effectiveness, consumers vary in their attitude toward green products and their willingness to buy them, even if they are consistently concerned about the environment. Another study (Zhao et al. 2014) of consumer behavior in Qingdao City, eastern China, which surveyed 500 respondents in four districts of the city, finds that most consumers know that being green is politically correct and good for the health and, in some cases, lowers energy bills. However, the same survey also finds that, in general, Chinese consumers are not inclined to pay more to purchase appliances that are environmentally friendly but do not bring immediate personal benefit. Even more worryingly, this study suggests that consumers are not prepared to change their habits in order to reduce their use of natural resources such as water. What does motivate them, however, is the economic benefit of making some money from selling recyclables such as old newspapers and cans (Zhao et al. 2014). Having said that, other research (for example, Chan 2004) suggests that consumers do respond to advertising that has a green appeal. A controlled experiment conducted in China suggests that, regardless of the level of consumer environmental concern, for low-involvement products an ad with green appeal, compared to a similar one without green appeal, elicits a more favorable consumer response (Kong and Zhang 2013).

Despite this variable engagement with green issues in urban China, a "green economy" or market consisting of the production and consumption of organic, fresh, and "all-natural" food is starting to take off (Zhou 2011). As on lifestyle shows, personal health and risk are prominent in determining green consumption practices. Apart from equipping themselves with air purifiers and face masks, people are also turning to ways of safeguarding food safety. Online shopping for organic produce is on the rise. Just as in Hong Kong (see chapter 12 in this volume on Hong Kong), a handful of urban individuals in Beijing have taken to renting farmland on the outskirts of the city to grow their own vegetables, a practice that has captured the imagination of the Chinese population. Food, beverages, and cosmetic products that their manufacturers claim are natural, hence "green", are in vogue, and urban residents are becoming more interested in buying their vegetables direct from farmers' markets (Xiao 2014).

The concept of green not only helps sell everyday products, it is also exploited to sell cultural products such as television programs. In an increasingly competitive media environment, the television market has embraced the concept of green as a branding and packaging strategy. Travel TV is a good case in point. Originally known as Hainan TV (the television station of Hainan Province), the channel, in order to acquire a nationally competitive edge in the increasingly competitive market, went through a process of rebranding and emerged in 2002 as the Travel Channel, the only designated travel channel in China (Sun and Chio 2012). At the start of the year, the channel launched its new green look with a new station logo and a revamped program schedule. In order to drive home the association between the Travel Channel and the concept of green media, the station's logo appeared in stark monochrome green. At 6:00 p.m. on January 3, 2010, for 1 hour the channel changed the backdrop of the whole program to green instead of a default color (Li 2012).

Despite this green repackaging, the channel continues to offer a smorgasbord of travel shows, fashion, recreational shows, variety shows, and lifestyle programs featuring— often prominently—the highly unsustainable sport of golf as one of its promoted sports. The channel's official website makes clear that its three priorities are travel, fashion, and golf. In other words, the notion of "green" is exploited as a marketing ploy, a product differentiation tactic and a branding exercise, rather than representing a real commitment to environmental concerns. A careful perusal of the programs produced by this supposedly green channel reveals little evidence of it's being part of the "green public sphere". One may be tempted to conclude that by wrapping itself literally in a green cloak, the channel is in fact responsible for promoting a wide range of consumption and recreational activities—for example golfing—that seem to put strain on rather than protect and preserve the environment.

The competitive television market has also forced other channels to milk the appeal of "going" green, which has had the adverse effect of watering down the green message. On May 1, 2010, Qinghai Satellite TV launched *Low Carbon Everyday* (Tiantian Ditan), the first television program in China dedicated to the environment. After the Climate Change Summit in Copenhagen in 2009 and the Party Congress in March 2010, "low carbon" became a catchphrase in urban China, synonymous with a new and more ethical way of life. Cashing in on the symbolic value of the term, *Low Carbon Everyday* was broadcast at 18:55 every day, lasting 5 minutes. Despite its brevity, the program quickly attracted high ratings due to its daily dose of environmentally friendly advice and information that consumers could easily understand and even act on. A perusal of the content produced on this program in the first year or so reveals a genuine and consistent commitment to promoting green messages. For instance, Episode 166, "Low-carbon Domestic Appliances", introduces new furniture and household appliances that are made from paper and encourages viewers to experiment with making their own furniture out of recycled paper. Episode 167, "Recycling Your Garbage", introduces a few ways in which domestic garbage can be turned into garden soil, renewable energy, and reconstituted plastic building material. Episode 168, "Taking a Low-carbon Shower", advises consumers on ways of saving water, saying that long showers are not only unnecessary for cleaning purposes, they are also bad for the skin. The episode also demonstrates to viewers how to save water if they follow a different shower routine. Episode 177, "Low-carbon Fashion", demonstrates convincingly to viewers that expensive, fashionable clothes require much more energy to make and urges viewers to be aware of this factor when clothes-shopping.

Ironically, if protecting the environment was its original objective, the program may have become a victim of its own success. A year or so after launching the show, Golden Eagle Media, the creative design and planning team, affiliated with the successful Hunan Satellite TV that was behind *Low Carbon Everyday*, decided that the popularity of the program could be exploited to achieve further profit.

In August 2011, the 5-minute program was extended to half an hour each day, while still labeled China's first television program dedicated to green themes. A juxtaposition of the content before and after the format change, however, reveals a much more noticeable dilution of the green content and padding with much non-green content. Now packed with celebrities, light-hearted news about trends in consumer practices, and recreational activities, green elements in the show are retained albeit to a much lesser extent. On March 17, 2014, the program features a flower exhibition in a city in Jiangsu; a school that has started to hire young male teachers for primary school children; a high-tech hands-free suitcase designed by university students that can follow its owner around; an example of artificially manufactured sunshine designed by architects of high-rise buildings in Sydney; and a forecast predicting that Africa will be the biggest polluter in the world by 2030. While some of these "news" items are clearly related to environmental protection or at least have some green content, one is left wondering how the inclusion of others—hiring young male teachers for primary school or designing a hands-free suitcase—can be justified. More relevant to the discussion here is that while marketing strategies aimed at product enhancement and product differentiation may have been effective at increasing the ratings of programs, they seem to have done less to promote and sustain a genuine green discourse. There is little evidence to suggest that such advertising challenges consumers' reluctance to change their consumption habits for the sake of a greener environment. Nor is there much evidence to suggest that the green (re)packaging of consumer advice programs aims to guide consumers toward more environmentally conscious and responsible consumption practices. What we have witnessed here instead are conscious efforts to exploit the green concept and capitalize on existing green credentials. Much akin to Toyota's marketing campaign to promote its hybrid car, which "works to obfuscate sustainability as an actionable agenda" (de Burgh-Woodman and King 2013, p. 163), these market strategies contribute mostly to the adverse effect of "greenwashing" or what I call the "greying" of green discourse and in doing so, diminish—rather than enable—the prospects of a vibrant greenspeak.

Conclusion

This discussion has unfolded in three disparate yet related contexts: the state news media, lifestyle television programs, and the realm of consumer behavior and the market. While we have witnessed the "growing politicization of life and lifestyle practices" in the global North (Lewis and Potter 2011, p. 5), this has not yet occurred in China, at least not on a large and sustainable scale. Instead, we have seen the politicization of environmental news in the state news media, which has led to unprecedented levels of control in the name of maintaining stability. Environmental issues are now more subject to censorship and propaganda than before. We therefore are confronted with a paradoxical scenario. On the one hand, the public has become more conscious than ever of the environmental risk they are living with. On the other hand, green activism and rigorous public debates on environmental issues have much less space to maneuver than they did a decade ago. This is indeed ironic and poignant. Despite the obvious problems usually associated with one-party authoritarian regimes, they do in theory have a crucial advantage over liberal-democratic societies: They are more capable of deploying the state apparatus to mobilize, enforce and implement environmental measures. As this discussion shows, however, the Chinese state's involvement in environmental causes seems to take the form of tokenistic and superficial campaigns and coverage. It is fair to conclude that, so far, the party-state has passed up a crucial opportunity to be a global leader in these issues.

In its attempts to tackle environmental issues, the Chinese Communist Party is often held to ransom by the very market forces it has unleashed. At the same time, it is clear that the potential of lifestyle media to be "generative of modes of popular civic politics" and to speak to "progressive modes of citizenship and activism", which have been tapped elsewhere (Lewis 2008b, 227), is yet to be realized. So far, the main incentive of marketizing the concept of green seems to be an economic bottom line. As we can see from lifestyle and consumer advice media, green-themed content is produced more with the practical aim of improving consumers' health on an individual basis and less as a moral and ethical imperative to save the Earth or improve the conditions of human life.

This chapter has argued that in order to arrive at a clear understanding of the scope and reach of greenspeak in China, we need to consider China's media and communication as an ideological-ecological system whose function and purpose is to maintain and ensure the social stability and political legitimacy of the party-state. Of course, the use of the term *ecological* is metaphoric, implying a comparison of various media forms and genres to species of life forms. An ideological-ecological system denotes a complex relationship and interaction between various media forms, genres, and practices in the Chinese media and communication sector. This approach entails looking at how environmental issues are talked about in the mainstream media—including the state media and the commercial mainstream—in conjunction with what is referred to as "greenspeak". This discussion points to the possible shrinking of the green public sphere in China—if it ever existed—and the greying of greenspeak. While this conclusion is not as upbeat as one may wish, achieving a more accurate and realistic assessment of the impact and size of a genuine green public sphere may well be a first important step toward effective environmental action.

References

Australian Broadcasting Corporation. 2014. *Q & A*, April 7.

Beaumont-Thomas, Ben. 2015. "Smash-Hit Chinese Pollution Doc Under the Dome Taken Offline by Government." *The Guardian*, March 9. Accessed May 5, 2015. http://www.theguardian.com/film/2015/mar/09/chinese-pollution-documentary-under-the-dome-taken-offline-government.

Bonner, Frances. 2011. "Lifestyle Television: Gardening and the Good Life." In *Ethical Consumption: A Critical Introduction*, edited by Tania Lewis and Emily Potter, 231–43. London: Routledge.

Chan, Ricky Y. K. 2004. "Consumer Responses to Environmental Advertising in China." *Marketing Intelligence & Planning* 22 (4): 427–37.

Chang, Chingching. 2011. "Feeling Ambivalent about Going Green: Implications for Green Advertising Processing." *Journal of Advertising* 40 (4): 19–32.

Chen, Shu. 2014. "GDP 7.5 vs. PM 2.5: we don't want poisoned GDP; we want clean air" ("GDP 7.5 vs. PM 2.5: bu yao you du GDP, yao hao qongqi"). *Xin Zhou Kan*, no. 410, 46–47.

De Burgh-Woodman, Hélène, and Dylan King. 2013. "Sustainability and the Human/Nature Connection: A Critical Discourse Analysis of Being 'Symbolically' Sustainable." *Consumption Markets & Culture* 16 (2): 145–68.

Dong, Dong. 2013. "Legitimating Journalistic Authority under the State's Shadow: A Case Study of the Environmental Press Award in China." *Chinese Journal of Communication* 6 (4): 397–418.

Farquhar, Judith, and Qicheng Zhang. 2012. *Ten Thousand Things: Nurturing Life in Contemporary Beijing*. New York: Zone Books.

Greenpeace East Asia. 2014. "World's Biggest Coal Company Shenhua to Stop Exploiting Groundwater in China." April 8. Accessed April 26, 2014. http://www.greenpeace.org/eastasia/press/releases/climate-energy/2014/shenhua-coal-china-water.

Ho, Peter. 2006 "Trajectories for Greening in China: Theory and Practice." In *China's Limits to Growth: Greening State and Society*, edited by Peter Ho and Eduard B. Vermeer, 1–26. Oxford: Wiley-Blackwell.

Ho, Peter. 2007. "Embedded Activism and Political Change in a Semiauthoritarian Context." *China Information* 21 (2): 187–209.

Ho, Peter, and Eduard B. Vermeer, eds. 2006. *China's Limits to Growth: Greening State and Society*. Oxford: Wiley-Blackwell.

Hu Jintao. 2012. "Report to the 18th Party Congress." Ciaxin Online, November 8. Accessed January 20, 2014. http://china.caixin.com/2012-11-08/100458021_all.html.

Jia, Guanghui. 2014. "An Analysis of the Public Nature of News reporting on Smog in China" ("Zhongguo wumai yiti chuanbo de gonggongxing bianxi"). *China Media Report* 13 (2): 38–46.

Kong, Ying, and Aihua Zhang. 2013. "Consumer Response to Green Advertising: The Influence of Product Involvement." *Asian Journal of Communication* 23 (4): 428–47.

Lewis, Tania. 2008a. *Smart Living: Lifestyle Media and Popular Expertise*. New York: Peter Lang.

Lewis, Tania. 2008b. "'Transforming Citizens?' Green Politics and Ethical Consumption on Lifestyle Television." *Continuum: Journal of Media & Cultural Studies* 22 (2): 227–40.

Lewis, Tania. 2011. "Making Over Culture? Lifestyle Television and Contemporary Pedagogies of Selfhood in Singapore." *Communication, Politics & Culture* 44 (1): 21–32.

Lewis, Tania. 2012. "'There Grows the Neighbourhood': Green Citizenship, Creativity and Life Politics on Eco-TV." *International Journal of Cultural Studies* 15 (3): 315–26.

Lewis, Tania, and Emily Potter. 2011. "Introducing Ethical Consumption." In *Ethical Consumption: A Critical Introduction*, edited by Tania Lewis and Emily Potter, 1–23. London: Routledge.

Li, Xiang. 2012. "A Brief Discussion of the Role of the Environmental Channel in the Constitution of China's Green Cultural Sector" ("Xiaoyi dianshi huanbao pingdao zai woguo luse wenhua chanye goujian zhong de zuoyong"). *Xinwen Zhishi* (Journalistic Knowledge) 2: 40–2.

Liu, Jingfang. 2011. "Picturing a Green Virtual Public Space for Social Change: A Study of Internet Activism and Web-Based Environmental Collective Actions in China." *China Journal of Communication* 4 (2): 137–66.

Liu, Yingling. 2013. "The Dirty Side of a 'Green' Industry." World Watch Institute. Accessed May 5, 2014. http://www.worldwatch.org/node/5650.
Martina, Michael, Li Hui, David Stanway, and Stian Reklev. 2014. "China to 'Declare War' on Pollution, Premier Says." *Reuters*, March 4. Accessed April 28, 2014. http://www.reuters.com/article/2014/03/05/us-china-parliament-pollution-idUSBREA2405W20140305.
Mathews, John. 2014a. "China's Genuine Green Revolution." *The Australian*, April 16.
Mathews, John. 2014b. "The Realpolitik behind China's Renewables Push." *The Australian*, April 22.
Sun, Wanning. 2012. "Localizing Chinese Media: A Geographic Turn in Media and Communication Research." In *Mapping Media in China: Region, Province, Locality*, edited by Wanning Sun and Jenny Chio, 13–27. Abingdon, UK: Routledge.
Sun, Wanning. 2015. "From Poisonous Weeds to Endangered Species: *Shenguo* TV, Media Ecology and Stability Maintenance." *Journal of Current Chinese Affairs* 44 (2): 17–37.
Sun, Wanning, and Jenny Chio. 2012. "Introduction." In *Mapping Media in China: Region, Province, Locality*, edited by Wanning Sun and Jenny Chio, 3–12. Abingdon, UK: Routledge.
The White House. 2014. "Fact Sheet: U.S.-China joint Announcement on Climate Change and Clean Energy Cooperation." The White House, Office of the Press Secretary. Accessed November 12, 2014. http://www.whitehouse.gov/the-press-office/2014/11/11/fact-sheet-us-china-joint-announcement-climate-change-and-clean-energy-c.
Tong, Jingrong. 2014. "Environmental Risks in Newspaper Coverage: A Framing Analysis of Investigative Reports on Environmental Problems in 10 Chinese Newspapers." *Environmental Communication* 8 (3): 345–67.
Xiao, Mingchao. 2014. "The 2013 China Consumer Report: The Outlook for 2014" ("2013 Zhongguo Xiaofei Baogao, Cong 2013 Kan 2014"). *New Weekly* (*Xin Zhou Kan*) 410: 38–41.
Xu, Janice Hua. 2007. "Brand-New Lifestyle: Consumer-Oriented Programmes on Chinese Television." *Media, Culture & Society* 29 (3): 363–76.
Xu, Janice Hua. 2009. "Building a Chinese 'Middle Class': Consumer Education and Identity Construction," In *TV China*, edited by Ying Zhu and Chris Berry, 150–68. Bloomington, IN: Indiana University Press.
Xu, Janice Hua. 2012. "Online News Report of Air Quality Issues in Beijing." *Telematics and Informatics* 29 (4): 400–17.
Xu, Janice Hua. 2014. "Communicating the Right to Know: Social Media in the Do-It-Yourself Air Quality Testing Campaign in Chinese Cities." *International Journal of Communication* 8: 1373–393.
Yang, Guobin, and Craig Calhoun. 2007. "Media, Civil Society, and the Rise of a Green Public Sphere in China." *China Information* 21 (2): 211–36.
Yuan, Ren. 2015. "Under the Dome: Will This Film Be China's Environmental Awakening?" *The Guardian*, March 5. Accessed May 5, 2015. http://www.theguardian.com/commentisfree/2015/mar/05/under-the-dome-china-pollution-chai-jing.
Zhao, Hhui-hui, Qian Gao, Yao-ping Wu, Yuan Wang, and Xiao-dong Zhu. 2014. "What Affects Green Consumer Behavior in China? A Case Study from Qingdao." *Journal of Cleaner Production* 63: 143–51. Accessed April 28, 2014. doi:/10.1016/j.jclepro.2013.05.021.
Zhou, Jie. 2011. "Green Food and Organic Food." *Minsheng Weekly* (Minshen Zhoukan) 13: 37–8.

8 Building a green community
Grassroots air quality monitoring in urban China

Janice Hua Xu

Introduction

Among Chinese urban residents there have been increasing public concerns about how air pollution affects human health, as many wear masks outdoors on smoggy days or purchase home air-purifying devices. Mass media and government websites have been publicly announcing air quality data of Beijing and other major metropolitan areas on a regular basis. When Beijing was preparing for the 2008 Olympics, the city launched a multi-year "Blue Sky Project," taking measures such as relocating factories, strengthening public transportation, and tightening vehicle emission standards while publicly counting the number of "Blue Sky Days" (Xu 2012). Yet the air quality data announced by the Beijing Municipal Environmental Protection Bureau (BMEPB) was met with skepticism from many residents and international visitors, particularly when the Bureau announced a day as meeting the criteria of Blue Sky Days but the public witnessed smog conditions.

The concern over air quality has led to individual-initiated regular monitoring activities, for instance, an online "Beijing Blue-Sky Visual Diary" posted at ditan360.com. It was created by an office worker, Lu Weiwei, and her friend, with photographs of the city's sky for 365 days in a row at different neighborhoods. By reviewing the photos, they determined Beijing had just 180 blue sky days during that time period, which differs from the official statistics that Beijing had 285 blue sky days. The BMEPB responded that its own definition of blue sky meant air quality reaching or exceeding certain levels based on the monitoring of pollutants, which include air-related particulate matter, sulphur dioxide, and nitrate dioxide, even if it is a rainy, snowy, or cloudy day (Chen 2011).

Similar monitoring activities using the Internet as a publishing outlet have been initiated by urban citizens taking daily photos of nearby landmark locations. For instance, one resident living across from Beijng TV Station took daily photos of the tower, shared them among his social media circles, invited concerned individuals to contribute their own photos to the site, and even expand it to include data from other large cities. One citizen in Nanjing with an online name "Grey-Yellow Turnip" not only took daily photos of the city but also posted comparisons of new white cotton face masks and those used for one day, to show the contrast in colors.

While individual-initiated monitoring activities are helpful in awareness raising and questioning the authenticity of official data, they usually rely on methods that are associated with human senses and are limited in their scope of influence. In comparison, grassroots monitoring activities organized by nongovernmental organizations (NGOs) are more likely to have a stronger impact and potentially affect official monitoring process or policy making. This is due to the availability of resources such as equipment and experienced volunteers as well as their communication networks and access to outside support. With the expansion of environmental concern and activism in China, newly formed NGOs in recent years have been engaged in politically sensitive issues, such as anti-dam campaigns and advocacy for pollution victims (Matsuzawa 2012). Their activities have expanded from education and volunteering to mass protests and civil litigations, sometimes leading to confrontations with local authorities and large corporations.

This chapter examines emerging forms of grassroots air quality monitoring in major cities in China since 2011 that have occurred in response to widespread concerns regarding urban air pollution. In particular, it reports on NGO-organized air quality monitoring and blogging activities related to $PM_{2.5}$, an airborne particulate matter less than 2.5 micrometers in size, the results of which often challenge announced data from government environmental agencies. This chapter explores the information-sharing, awareness-raising, and mobilization aspects of these initiatives through data gathered from personal interviews, online diaries, and microblogging of activists. By analyzing their different ways of self-organizing and member recruitment, both online and on the ground, the chapter also examines how a green community takes shape and grows during the age of the Internet.

Community-based environmental monitoring

Community-based monitoring (CBM) initiatives by nonprofessionals and citizen groups concerned about the environment have been growing worldwide, not only in developed countries such as the United States and Canada but also in developing countries such as India (Conrad and Hilchey 2011). In many cases, these grassroots efforts have helped decision makers and NGOs enhance their ability to monitor and manage natural resources, track species at risk, and conserve protected areas, contributing relevant information and actions to solving environmental problems. The growth of CBM activities in recent years is often due to an increase in public knowledge and concern about anthropogenic impacts on natural ecosystems and a lack of, or inadequate and incomplete, data and monitoring initiatives by professional scientists and government agencies (Conrad and Daoust 2008). Key scholars have argued that local environmental knowledge and local capacity to conduct environmental monitoring and measurement are an essential part of sustainable development, as they involve the people who are most affected by environmental change and contain signals derived from local systems of observation, practice, and indigenous knowledge (Conrad and Hilchey 2011). However, there is disagreement about whether social or locally based knowledge and citizen science projects conducted by non-professionals are more effective than expert knowledge, when facing environmental problems; thus questions remain about the role that local people and researchers might play in the monitoring process (Hambly 1996).

Some researchers suggest that CBM is mostly likely to appear in economically advantaged countries that have "higher standards of living and an age and/or class structure that assures an adequate supply of potential volunteers" (Pfeffer and Wagenet 2007, p. 235). As a form of community science, defined as an interaction between professionals and lay people (Carr 2004), in developed countries it is contributing to the democratization of environmental decision making by offering avenues for citizens to make meaningful inputs into environmental management. On the other hand, CBM activities can be understood in the framework of grassroots environmental action, which refers to the ways ordinary people participate in the management of their environment, including a wide range of actions people take on the local level to manage and protect their natural resources, with the potential to help reverse, arrest, or prevent environmental decline (Ghai and Vivian 2014). In Asian countries without a liberal democracy, environmentalist activities initiated at the grassroots level can occur when they are motivated, encouraged, and supported by outside actors such as the state or international organizations. They can also occur in situations where the people must "formulate their plans and conduct their activities in spite of the neglect, resistance or even active opposition of external forces" (Ghai and Vivian 2014, p. 1). In many cases, grassroots movement organizations have a choice with regard to the modes through which they engage the state—"bypassing, challenging, pressuring, and supporting the state" (Breyman 1993, p. 147).

As a CBM case with wide influence, Chinese urban citizen air quality monitoring activities from 2011 to 2012 attempted to variously bypass, challenge, and pressure the state due to a sense of its lack of transparency or accuracy on $PM_{2.5}$. In this context, this chapter poses a number of questions and discusses the issues they raise: What are the communication mechanisms of involving citizens to volunteer in monitoring activities? What is the relationship of CBM with state environmental agencies? Can citizen-collected data be used not only for environmental awareness raising but also to promote policy change?

Grassroots environmental monitoring in China

CBM relies on the consistent efforts of volunteers with green awareness, including attitudes, beliefs, and perceptions, in order to understand the nature and source of environmental problems. Scholars found in a comparative study that there is a reasonably coherent sense of generalized environmental awareness among Chinese citizens similar to that found with North American respondents, especially among well-educated urban residents (Xiao, Dunlap, and Hong 2013). Among China's environmentalists, there is a shared identity—a sense of socio-environmental responsibility, a combination of social responsibilities and environmental care (Xie 2011)—which is related to the tradition of Chinese intellectuals being concerned about the fate of the nation and its people. Among the general public, media campaigns that encourage urban citizens to adopt a low-carbon lifestyle, use more public transportation, and drive cars less often have been appealing to public consciousness on environmental issues. Meanwhile, the rhetoric and practices of China's "community building" (*shequ jianshe*) initiatives since the late 1990s aimed at reorganizing urban middle-class neighborhoods also encouraged responsible consumption and individual behaviors that promote a "harmonious" community (Tomba 2009). Community-wide activities organized by neighborhood committees to "beautify community environment" have included practices such as planting trees, classifying garbage, and restricting use of plastic shopping bags. Although as Lewis and Potter (2011) point out, the discourse of ethical consumption is not necessarily marked by a coherent set of shared politics or values, these practices of care, solidarity, and collective concern are meaningful for a lifestyle choice that is not necessarily wholly defined by consumer culture.

Traditionally, grassroots environmental monitoring in China takes the form of individual citizens' reporting pollution offenders who fail to implement national environmental laws and regulations, especially when they are directly affected by the problem in their local environment. The 1996 *State Council Decision Concerning Certain Environmental Protection Issues* encourages public reporting on, and exposing of, violations of environmental protection laws and regulations. Since the late 1990s, new participatory mechanisms have been gradually adopted: for instance, the public hearing component of the Environmental Impact Assessment Law as well as regulations related to public dissemination of environmental information (Wu 2009). Individuals can complain about pollution incidents to local agencies directly or use telephone hot lines, mass media, and even public protests in some cases. Occasionally, local environmental agencies even offer cash rewards to citizens who provide solid evidence about pollution sources. However, the recourse available to individuals is limited to reactions to existing pollution problems, as there are few opportunities to challenge plans or for preemptive actions and lobbying prior to developments that might lead to pollution (Schwartz 2004). In this context, it is likely that as Hsin-Huang Michael Hsiao (1999) suggests, grassroots environmental actions stem often from short-sighted "victim consciousness" that focuses on grievances in contrast to long-term "environmental consciousness."

The existing complaint system, which allows Chinese urban citizens to report environmental problems to local authorities and get feedback, has many areas that need improvement (Van Rooij 2006; Tilt 2007). Warwick and Ortolano found in a qualitative analysis of Shanghai Municipal Government's environmental complaints system that it is useful for uncovering information not previously known to the Environmental Protection Bureau (EPB) about some self-evident pollution emissions from industrial enterprises, thus serving as "an important, yet somewhat unreliable, source of information about the many environmental problems not otherwise detected by regulators" (2007, p. 237). As citizens do not recognize many violations, especially those not identifiable by the physical senses, Warwick and Ortolano suggest that increasing the public's environmental awareness and access to information would further enhance the effectiveness of the current system.

However, as noted above, individuals sometimes bypass state agencies and conduct alternative grassroots environmental monitoring by posting information online and sharing their monitoring data with other netizens. Though restricted by government censorship, the Internet has been instrumental in "not-in-my-backyard" activism in China for public participation in environmental matters, which often involve contentious tactics that exert considerable pressure on local officials to open participatory channels and adopt more inclusive decision-making processes (Johnson 2010). Through case studies among homeowners in different southern cities such as Xiamen, Huang and Yip (2012) describe the functional significance of the Internet to collective action as an information-disclosure platform and a discussion platform, serving also as a mobilization structure and a facilitator in locating external allies. Microblogging provides an important online platform because it can conveniently and inexpensively foster public online issue-networks beyond geographical boundaries (Yang 2013; Huang and Sun 2014). It is also found among Chinese citizens that extensive use of smartphones and mobile tweeting were positive predictors of engagement in online civic discourse (Wei 2014). With its low cost, popularity among young people, and flexibility, microblogging has been used by many local environmental activists to publicize their agendas and gain supporters for their work.

While the levels of environmental awareness among citizens are uneven, there has been increasing attention paid to the public voice in city environmental management, though Chinese government officials and researchers are still struggling with the concept of the public's right to participate and the processes this might involve (Moore and Warren 2006). In particular, Martens (2006) sees opportunities and potentials for involvement by Chinese citizens and consumers in environmental management in five key environmental issues: protection of nature and bio-diversity; local control of environmental pollution; construction of green company images; establishment of sustainable household practices; and participation in international conventions and treaties. Individuals could participate through various groups that are semi-formal or informal in nature, such as consumer groups, homeowner committees, student organizations, local automobile clubs, or hobby groups such as hiking clubs, which can be formed online. They can also get involved through activities organized by their work units, environmental NGOs, or other grassroots groups.

As environmental activism emerges as one of the earliest and most active areas of civil society in modern China, grassroots organizations have become capable of "effectively mobilizing resources, appealing to citizens' newly perceived or desired identities, and building up a modest level of counter-expertise against state-dominated information" (Ho 2007, p. 189). As demonstrated in the campaigns to preserve snub-nosed monkeys in Yunnan province and Tibetan antelope (Hildebrandt and Turner 2009; Matsuzawa 2012), there has been increasing networking between grassroots NGOs and journalists, government-sponsored NGOs, international NGOs, and local people affected by developmental projects. The activists have also been using rights-based discourses that emphasize individual property rights and consumer rights to raise environmental awareness among the public.

Community-based air quality monitoring activities in urban China

Chinese environmental NGOs became involved publicly in air quality monitoring after Beijing's official air quality measurement became controversial. Its method was considered inconsistent with international standards, as it excluded the level of the pollutant $PM_{2.5}$. This type of particulate is more toxic than PM_{10} components, such as dirt, dust, smoke, mold, and pollen, and is small enough to directly enter the lungs and even the bloodstream, with serious health effects on people with heart or lung disease, older adults, and children (Consulate General of the United States, Shanghai China 2013). Since 2008, the U.S. Embassy in Beijing has been tracking and releasing air quality data, issuing hourly air quality readings on a Twitter account @BeijingAir using the U.S. EPA standard as its measure. Later, its consulates in major cities, such as Guangzhou and Shanghai, also started posting measurement results. The discrepancy between the U.S. and Chinese data has stirred intense discussions among urban residents and bloggers.

In summer 2011, Beijing-based NGO Daerwen Nature Quest Agency initiated a grassroots air quality testing campaign focusing on $PM_{2.5}$ levels, urging the government to measure and announce its levels. On its website, members of the organization post test results taken at various locations in Beijing, along with the weather conditions, equipment used, and names of participants. The group offered any city resident the opportunity to borrow the equipment, learn how to use it, and post their "air quality diaries" on the Daerwen website.

Within weeks, similar activities appeared in other large cities, including Wuhan, Chongqing, and Nanjing. Environmental NGO leaders organized existing members and newly recruited volunteers to measure $PM_{2.5}$ pollution level at different neighborhoods and regularly post air quality logs online, using hand-held devices donated or lent by equipment manufacturers or purchased through fundraising.

For this research project, the author collected data in 2012 through web analysis and interviews of the following groups: Daerwen Nature Quest Agency based in Beijing; the Wuhan branch of Friends of Nature; Yueqing Green Volunteers Association based in Wenzhou; Shanghai Citizen Measurement Group; and Chongqing Youth Environmental Exchange Center. Among the five groups, Daerwen started posting $PM_{2.5}$ data first, in September 2011, though some measurement activities started in July. It is the largest of the five groups, but its air-quality testing posts were less frequent than the others. The Chongqing NGO was the last to join the action in May 2012. All of the groups except for Daerwen have only one to two full-time staff, working primarily with volunteer teams to conduct measurements.

Citizen expertise versus official agencies

The NGOs announced on their websites and through microblogging that the purpose and significance of their air quality measurement activities was to provide test results regularly to the public as an alternative source of information because official data may be unavailable or unreliable. For instance, Daerwen Nature

Quest Agency explains in its website that although it is "not an authoritative agency with specialized measurement qualification," it uses specialized measurement equipment and is "responsible for the authenticity of the test results" (Darwen Nature Quest 2015). The site attached the World Health Organization's recommendation for $PM_{2.5}$ levels as well as a draft Chinese air quality standard under discussion by lawmakers for reference purpose. Its website also posted articles on the "killer" effect of $PM_{2.5}$ on human health and the importance of its inclusion in air quality evaluations.

A representative of Friends of Nature in Wuhan states that there are three purposes for their air testing activities—to provide to the public a long-lasting alternative source of information; to have a better understanding of air pollution through long-term observation and to publicize knowledge and methods to prevent pollution; and to participate in nation-wide air testing activities and let more citizens understand the truth of China's air quality (August 9, 2012, telephone interview).

The leader of Shanghai Citizen Measurement Group explains that the goal of unofficial air testing is to demonstrate a position about public access to information, even though it may not be highly accurate, as there is a difference between nonprofessional testers and professionals:

> Grassroots testing is about the public's right to know. Eventually we hope that the government or professional institutions will have accurate data announced. We can achieve this through our pressure or influence . . . If unofficial testing can exist for 10 years, perhaps it will become really professional
> (August 14, 2012, telephone interview)

Most of the activists update the test results every day, some several times a day, all on a volunteer basis. Some of the posts are accompanied by photos and charts, and some have long paragraphs of background information. In the city of Wuhan in central China, the local branch of Friends of Nature plays a key role in testing, with no full-time staff but about 70 volunteer members, nearly half of them school teachers. Five members were responsible for the regular air quality–testing activities, while others participated from time to time. Aside from posting test results in "Wuhan Air Diary" from March 2012, they also compare their results with official data and add local weather information and photos to illustrate visibility. Gathering and posting the information online requires approximately half an hour to one hour per day, depending on the level of experience. Those with computer or data processing background upload information faster. The Wuhan NGO leader describes how he works on the air quality diary every day:

> I do monitoring three times a day, in the morning before going to work, in the afternoon before cooking dinner, and before going to sleep at night. I spend an hour every day in acquisition, data processing, mapping, and publishing. If there is an unusual weather condition, such as fog or haze, I would follow closely and release real-time data repeatedly
> (August 9, 2012, telephone interview)

In Shanghai, where the daily air quality postings are briefer, it takes an experienced volunteer only a few minutes to measure and upload the results on a typical day. These activities have influenced netizens' opinions as well as the policies of Chinese environmental agencies, forcing some of them to take steps to measure and announce the levels of $PM_{2.5}$, particularly in cities where the U.S. Consulates' air quality twitter messages made the issue highly visible.

The NGOs that received equipment sponsorship (Shanghai, Guangzhou, Wenzhou, and Wuhan) from Daerwen Nature Quest Agency all used a slogan, "I Gauge Air Quality for My Motherland," in their websites or team names, inspired by a propaganda phrase during the Great Leap Forward mass mobilization movement in the 1950s. According to the Daerwen representative (August 2012, pers. comm.), this slogan first appeared as the title of an article in the newspaper *Southern Weekend* (Feng and Lu 2011) about these activists and was adopted by the NGOs in other cities, who came up with slogans such as "I Gauge Air Quality for Wuhan." The article helped bring public attention to the grassroots air quality testing activities, as it highlighted the controversy over whether $PM_{2.5}$ should be adopted as part of official testing standards. Although the activity of collecting and posting air quality data can be seen as subversive, members of the movement portray themselves as nature lovers and concerned citizens, instead of political dissidents, contributing to the collective good with scientific tools.

Gathering support: Online and offline

As most members of the Chinese public had never heard of the term $PM_{2.5}$ before, in the early days of building support, activists used social media to form Internet discussion threads, arrange group meetings, recruit new members locally, and raise funds through online transactions. All of the key NGO groups also use microblogging sites to enable continuous publication of test results and to reach out to local residents in the area concerned. These sites sometimes also function as platforms for raising questions and having dialogue with local government agencies, particularly when severe pollution conditions affect visibility and outdoor activities. Some NGO leaders also periodically write on their personal blogging sites, detailing their personal journeys of air monitoring and announcing lectures, gatherings, or fundraising events. Online Weibo "fans" (followers) of the bloggers grew increasingly aware of the air pollution levels in their cities and expressed dissatisfaction with official environmental agencies and city bureaucrats through discussion threads. Some of them, including many college students, started to participate in the announced offline events and joined air-testing trips. With a range of personal and web networking efforts, the NGOs have collaborated with bicycle clubs, coffee shops, libraries, newspapers, and corporations.

The NGOs thus use social media not only to announce and comment on test results but also to attract public interest and build relationships with various groups vital to their agenda—audience, volunteers, donors, local collaborators and, in some cases, city environmental agencies. They often post group gathering invitations, volunteer recruiting announcements, and donation appeals for equipment purchase. Social media and e-mails are used to attract participants to meet offline to demonstrate the do-it-yourself testing process and to advertise lectures, picnics, short tours, fundraising events and, in the case of Shanghai, vegetable shopping trips. In the first meeting of the group "I Gauge Air Quality for Wuhan," held in March 2012, there were 29 participants, including members of the NGO, online QQ (an instant messaging program) group members, volunteers, and representatives of college environmental groups, according to the NGO blog. The meeting also included representatives of partner groups—from the local media, a bicycle association, the Energy Saving Industry Network, and Wuhan EPB—marking the often broad makeup of these groups.

Equipment acquisition has posed one of the biggest challenges but the NGOs have been very creative and entrepreneurial in their fundraising activities. Initially Daerwen Nature Quest Agency offered some testing equipment to collaborating NGOs outside Beijing, although most of the groups involved acquired their equipment later through their own fundraising activities. Daerwen also provided a bank account number to a few smaller NGOs, as an activist explained, making it possible for them to raise funds legally, because China has strict restrictions on organizational fundraising. As the largest NGO among the five researched, Daerwen has a public environmental education center, called the Nature University, which holds weekly activities in the environmental class and outdoor sites.

NGOs have also used online venues to raise funds. To raise funds for a set of equipment that costs 25,000 yuan (1 yuan = 0.16 U.S. dollars), Friends of Nature in Wuhan appealed to netizens by asking for donations in the amount of 25 yuan or its multiples. As recorded in the NGO's Sina blog site Airwuhan, in January and February of 2012, the NGO received online donations from 22 individuals, 9,678 yuan in total, as well as offline donations of 8,785 yuan through fundraising events.

In Wenzhou, the Green Volunteer Association of Yueqing City, a small NGO of two staff members, used microblogging to appeal for donations and interest-free loans to acquire equipment. Its most successful fundraising practice was to sell oranges to netizens around the Spring Festival of 2012, announcing that all profits from the sale would support the air testing project. A coffee shop owned by a volunteer was used as the pickup spot for the orders. The NGO sold more than 1,300 boxes of oranges at the price of 60 yuan each, most of them online, and raised more than 20,000 yuan to pay off what they owed for the equipment.

Meanwhile, the Wenzhou NGO created multiple events to get average citizens interested in the $PM_{2.5}$ issue, instead of publishing testing results daily, believing that merely posting results online would not draw public attention or help people understand the issue. The NGO initiated a project called "$PM_{2.5}$ Air Museum," encouraging its Weibo followers to carry testing equipment when taking any trip and to bring back a bottle containing the air and a piece of paper with the testing results to the NGO. They were also asked to post their results on their individual microblogs, to reach their friends and blog followers. The NGO aimed to spread the information about $PM_{2.5}$ to 100 local residents in the second half of 2012. The NGO leader believes that these activities have raised awareness on preserving the blue sky and white cloud of the area, leading to strong opposition among netizens to a plan to build a cement factory there.

In Chongqing, the NGO recruited participants of the air quality tests online through advertising at a volunteer registration network called Loving Heart Savings Bank, which has files of individuals willing to volunteer for various forms of activities. Volunteers have three types of $PM_{2.5}$-related duties: One group does routine testing and results posting; one group works on special testing events, such as a full-day air quality measurement at Chongqing Zoo; and one group works on science education on the Internet, writing posts on Weibo under "#IamPM2.5" and other subjects. Volunteers post test results online in their personal microblogs, and a daily summary chart appears in the evening hours on the group's site @ChongqingPM2.5. The volunteers have their own online QQ discussion group and microblogging site while activities offline include regular meetings and special events. In addition to measuring air quality data, the volunteers, many of them college students, also monitor and compile long-term data and analyze monthly trends of the testing results. The group conducted a survey among city residents about their knowledge of $PM_{2.5}$ as well as their major environmental concerns.

Making an impact

Non-official monitoring can suddenly become the center of public attention when the air condition in a city deteriorates significantly and impacts people's daily routines. On June 11, 2012, when serious smog in Wuhan led to a yellowish sky, a smoky smell, and low visibility, rumors spread about a chlorine leak from Qingshan Chemical Plant and a Wuhan Steel Company boiler explosion. Online posts also indicated that many residents reported feeling sick and showed symptoms of poisoning. Friends of Nature posted hourly air test results, finding $PM_{2.5}$ level more than 10 times higher than normal, and they urged the Wuhan EPB to "explain the cause, take responsive actions and dissipate public fear." The blogging posts were followed and resent by many netizens on that day, reflecting anger toward the sluggish actions of municipal environmental agencies. Later, an official announcement appeared at the Wuhan government website to dispel rumors, explaining that straw burning in the neighboring provinces of Anhui and Hebei was the main source of the smog (Luan 2012). According to Wuhan police blogging @PingAnWuhan, network police conducted an investigation and detained two individuals for fabricating rumors online.

At the early stage of the monitoring movement, the volunteers were filling a void in the official air quality announcements, pressuring the government to measure $PM_{2.5}$. In 2012, more and more city environmental agencies modified their standards and started broadcasting $PM_{2.5}$ results, but the activists still believed it was crucial to continue with their own tests, stressing their identity as DIY testers distant from official agencies. The Wuhan NGO representative expressed confidence in his handheld equipment when comparing his own results with the government data:

Our aim is not to try to be expert, but to have our presence. We only hope that other than the official channels, there are nonofficial sources providing measurement data . . . Our equipment costs 25,000 yuan each. Theirs cost 12 million yuan, standing in one location called Central China Region Air Measurement Super Station. They held two open house days and invited us, trying to overwhelm us so we would stop, but on the contrary it strengthened our confidence, because the data we got that day were very similar

(August 9, 2012, telephone interview)

Regardless of the quality of the data, the self-testing movement has had a visible impact on environmental education and awareness raising and, in some cases, lobbying. EPBs in some cities were pressured by the activists to add new $PM_{2.5}$ measurement locations in densely populated neighborhoods or industrial areas, which were previously not measured because of expected poor air quality while some data that were previously unannounced became available on official websites: for instance, in May 2012, when Wuhan EPB complied with a request by Friends of Nature to publicize $PM_{2.5}$ measurement data after the agency set up multiple monitoring stations around the city.

In February 2012, China released a new ambient air quality standard, which sets limits for the first time on $PM_{2.5}$. The new standards take effect nationwide in 2016, but major cities such as Beijing and provincial capitals are required to implement the standards earlier, from the beginning of 2013. Provincial-level environmental agencies publicize monitoring results regularly, recommending that residents should wear masks and avoid outdoor activities when the indexes are too high. Some have also created $PM_{2.5}$ cell phone apps to offer mobile access to data to citizens.

Meanwhile, some activists expressed caution in the interviews on whether their CBM activities should expand in scale, explaining that their current goal is not to draw a big crowd, which might lead to authority interventions, but to have a continued presence. This is particularly true for participants in large cities such as Shanghai, where the police put pressure on them by monitoring their efforts and making frequent phone calls to discourage them.

Among the NGO leaders, there were questions about whether they should present themselves to the public as environmental information monitors or advocates and educators. Although some emphasize the importance of the existence of nonofficial testing data, others consider daily postings less significant than enlightening the public on the meanings of the data and raising awareness on local environmental protection measures.

Some activists were wary of media attention and potential government interference with their activities. For instance, the Chongqing NGO originally posted their own test results and the results of the U.S. Consulate, but later they stopped posting the U.S. data to avoid a confrontational stance with the local government, described as "strong-handed" in the interview. This NGO also expressed concern about the time demand of maintaining an Internet presence with a large follower base. Skipping posting the U.S. data also made it easier for volunteers to do the uploading. The NGO is making efforts to train volunteers to maintain the equipment and standardize the measurement and uploading procedures.

Communication channels and relationship building

As the activists point out, the strengths of the CBM air quality testing activities are its mobility, ability to offer frequent updates, and perceived distance from authorities who often lack public trust. These qualities are highly compatible with the features of social media. Microblogging enables the instant dissemination of short fragments of information, thus offering constant updates on air quality at locations of interest to the residents in different urban neighborhoods. The interactive and flexible features of social media also allow scientific information to be communicated easily to concerned citizens with a personal touch. The five small NGOs manage to enhance and consolidate their presence through regular posting of air test result announcements, coexisting with or challenging official data. Social media have played a key role in various aspects of the CBM campaigns, from advocacy and raising awareness to building capacity for the grassroots NGOs in complicated political conditions.

Meanwhile, the relationship-building role of microblogging is supported through a combination of online and offline activities, which allows for different levels and forms of citizen involvement, facilitating and reinforcing commitment to the group and nurturing interpersonal relationships. The initial interest in local air quality and distrust of authorities attracted many online followers, with some of them gradually became willing to support the organizers by answering NGO calls for volunteering, donating, or learning to do the measurement process themselves. Though it may not lead necessarily to stable and/or lasting practices, social media can be seen as a new tool for NGO collaboration and networking across different geographic regions. Across different cities, a collective identity has emerged among the volunteers as defenders of the right of the public to know, a concern of broad resonance among urban Chinese residents across the country.

For NGOs, mainstream media may not be the most effective channel to reach out to their audiences, even though activists often raise media attention with their actions. Most of the NGO leaders in the air quality measurement movement prefer to take a "low-key" stance so that the issue-related activities that concern them can be sustained on a manageable scale, and they were not actively seeking media coverage that might put unwanted labels on them or draw extra attention from the authorities. The issue of air quality was already a politically contentious issue, given the international attention on the subject from the start of Beijing's bid for the 2008 Olympics as well as the contrasting results of the Chinese environmental agencies and the U.S. Embassy. The controversy probably enhanced the visibility of the NGO's work while at the same time subjecting them to more surveillance, which can take various forms and intensity in different cities. Thus their choice of communication methods and tools, in addition to technical or financial restraints, reflects the local survival strategies of grassroots groups.

Conclusion: A tentative community

By the end of 2013, an online "Community Air Monitoring" network was formed, which consisted of measurement data from 13 cities in different parts of China provided by NGOs and individual volunteers (Xue 2013). According to the organizer of the network, Liu Jun from the Wuhan branch of Friends of Nature, while there were more self-testers interested in participation, the issues of data management, equipment maintenance, and funding sources challenged its further growth. The Network coexists with a "National Environmental Air Monitoring Network" that publishes data online issued by the government.

CBM activities in China embody a rich diversity of emerging initiatives and practices that contribute to the growth of environmental activism and environmental awareness. To overcome their lack of resources, NGOs draw public attention to tangible, pragmatic goals that are usually related to the well-being of local citizens. Thus they establish legitimacy, raise public awareness, and at the same time strive for support from all possible collaborators (which at times may include Western environmental groups) to sustain their needs in terms of financial, technical, manpower, and publicity. While the organization structures are somewhat fluid, the issue-centered activities can be highly effective with the persistent and effective coordination and leadership of core members of the locally based groups. These goals enable the formation of a temporary collective identity among individuals and groups, dispersed in time and space, to take collective actions with a definite agenda, circumventing restrictions against co-presence, such as a street rally, even though online activities might be also monitored and censored by the authorities to various extents.

In China, grassroots environmentalist activism thus far has demonstrated its own characteristics, which are related to the cultural heritage and sociopolitical conditions of the country. Among many Chinese citizens, there is a desire for a better understanding of the changes to their environment and the risks of urban pollution and of different levels of interest in participating in collective activities for a green community. As a successful example of CMB, the air quality testing activities can be seen as turning citizens' private lifestyle choices such as following official air quality reports and choosing low-emission automobiles into forms of civic action linked to collective awareness raising and information sharing. NGOs are developing new methods to encourage their online audiences to take action, turning them from blog followers to volunteers. A fluid green community is formed as volunteers take both online and offline roles—learning the skills of using equipment, acquiring pollution data in public places, and posting information through microblogging to share with netizens. The Internet is used not only as a mobilization tool for grassroots groups but also as a space for collectively producing and publishing alternative information.

CBM activities in China also centrally involve the issue of how to manage relationships with official institutions. For activists, the process of expanding the movement and building coalitions unavoidably involves negotiating with public institutions of some sort, such as libraries, universities, news media, or city environmental agencies. If there are corporate sponsors involved, they might also have an intricate relationship with the government. The outcomes at different areas might vary immensely, depending on the political will and capacities of the specific NGOs as well as their past relationship with local agencies. While they may have an influence on local environmental policy, it is equally possible for activist causes to be absorbed or incorporated into the agendas of official institutions, challenging their links to grassroots movements. This is particularly relevant for environmental groups, as the NGO organizers are becoming more and more effective at monitoring hazards and raising awareness of citizens' rights but face much tougher hurdles in preventing and reducing pollution now and in the future.

References

Breyman, Steve. 1993. "Knowledge as Power: Ecology Movements and Global Environmental Problems." In *The State and Social Power in Global Environmental Politics*, edited by Ronnie D. Lipschutz and Ken Conca, 124–57. New York: Columbia University Press.

Carr, Anna J. L. 2004. "Why Do We All Need Community Science?" *Society and Natural Resources: An International Journal* 17 (9): 841–49.

Chen, Zifan. 2011. "Beijing's blue-sky diary." *China Dialogue*, February 28. Accessed July 17, 2015. https://www.chinadialogue.net/article/show/single/en/4134-Beijing-s-blue-sky-diary

Conrad, Cathy C., and Krista G. Hilchey. 2011. "A Review of Citizen Science and Community-Based Environmental Monitoring: Issues and Opportunities." *Environmental Monitoring and Assessment* 176 (1-4): 273–91.

Conrad, Catherine T., and Tyson Daoust. 2008. "Community-Based Monitoring Frameworks: Increasing the Effectiveness of Environmental Stewardship." *Environmental Management* 41 (3): 358–66.

Consulate General of the United States, Shanghai China. 2013. "U.S. Consulate Shanghai Air Quality Monitor." Accessed July 17, 2015. http://shanghai.usembassy-china.org.cn/airmonitor.html.

Darwen Nature Quest. 2015. "Introduction." Accessed July 17, 2015. http://www.bjep.org.cn/pages/Index/40-85.

Feng, Jie, and Zongshu Lu. 2011. "I gauge air quality for my motherland" (Wo Wei Zuguo Ce Kongqi). *Southern Weekend (Nanfang Zhoumo)*, October 28. Accessed July 17, 2015. http://www.infzm.com/content/64281.

Ghai, Dharam, and Jessica M. Vivian. 2014. "Introduction." In *Grassroots Environmental Action: People's Participation in Sustainable Development*, edited by Dharam Ghai and Jessica M. Vivian, 1–19. London and New York: Routledge.

Hambly, Helen. 1996. "Grassroots Indicators: Measuring and Monitoring Environmental Change at the Local Level." *ILEIA Newsletter* 12 (3): 14–5.

Hildebrandt, Timothy, and Jennifer L. Turner. 2009. "Green Activism? Reassessing the Role of Environmental NGOs in China." In *State and Society Responses to Social Welfare Needs in China: Serving the People*, edited by Jonathan Schwartz and Shawn Shieh, 89–110. London and New York: Routledge.

Ho, Peter. 2007. "Embedded Activism and Political Change in a Semiauthoritarian Context." *China Information* 21 (2), 187–209.

Hsiao, Hsin-Huang Michael. 1999. "Environmental Movements in Taiwan." In *Asia's Environmental Movements: Comparative Perspectives*, edited by Yok-shiu F. Lee and Alvin Y. So, 31–54. New York: ME Sharpe.

Huang, Ronggui, and Ngai-ming Yip. 2012. "Internet and Activism in Urban China: A Case Study of Protests in Xiamen and Panyu." *Journal of Comparative Asian Development* 11 (2): 201–23.

Huang, Ronggui, and Xiaoyi Sun. 2014. "Weibo Network, Information Diffusion and Implications for Collective Action in China." *Information, Communication & Society* 17 (1): 86–104.

Johnson, Thomas. 2010. "Environmentalism and NIMBYism in China: Promoting a Rules-Based Approach to Public Participation." *Environmental Politics* 19 (3): 430–48.

Lewis, Tania, and Emily Potter, eds. 2011. *Ethical consumption: A Critical Introduction*. London and New York: Routledge.

Luan, Chao. 2012. "Straw Burning Blamed for Grey Haze in Central China." *Xinhuanet*, June 11, 2012. Accessed July 17, 2015. http://news.xinhuanet.com/english/china/2012-06/11/c_131645729.htm

Martens, Susan. 2006. "Public Participation with Chinese Characteristics: Citizen Consumers in China's Environmental Management." *Environmental Politics* 15 (2): 211–30.

Matsuzawa, Setsuko. 2012. "Citizen Environmental Activism in China: Legitimacy, Alliances, and Rights-based Discourses." *ASIA Network Exchange: A Journal for Asian Studies in the Liberal Arts* 19 (2): 81–91.

Moore, Allison, and Adria Warren. 2006. "Legal Advocacy in Environmental Public Participation in China: Raising the Stakes and Strengthening Stakeholders." *China Environment Series* 8: 3–23.

Pfeffer, Max J., and Linda P. Wagenet. 2007. "Volunteer Environmental Monitoring, Knowledge Creation and Citizen-Scientist Interaction." In *The SAGE Handbook of Environment and Society*, edited by Jules Pretty et al., 235–49. London: SAGE Publications.

Schwartz, Jonathan. 2004. "Environmental NGOs in China: Roles and Limits." *Pacific Affairs* 77 (1): 28–49.

Tilt, Bryan. 2007. "The Political Ecology of Pollution Enforcement in China: A Case from Sichuan's Rural Industrial Sector." *The China Quarterly* 192: 915–32.

Tomba, Luigi. 2009. "Of Quality, Harmony, and Community: Civilization and the Middle Class in Urban China." *Positions* 17 (3): 591–616.

Van Rooij, Benjamin. 2006. "Implementation of Chinese Environmental Law: Regular Enforcement and Political Campaigns." *Development and Change* 37 (1): 57–74.

Warwick, Mara, and Leonard Ortolano. 2007. "Benefits and Costs of Shanghai's Environmental Citizen Complaints System." *China Information* 21 (2): 237–68.

Wei, Ran. 2014. "Texting, Tweeting, and Talking: Effects of Smartphone Use on Engagement in Civic Discourse in China." *Mobile Media & Communication* 2 (1): 3–19.

Wu, Fengshi. 2009. "Environmental Politics in China: An Issue Area in Review." *Journal of Chinese Political Science* 14 (4): 383–406.

Xiao, Chenyang, Riley R. Dunlap, and Dayong Hong. 2013. "The Nature and Bases of Environmental Concern among Chinese Citizens." *Social Science Quarterly* 94 (3): 672–90.

Xie, Lei. 2011. "China's Environmental Activism in the Age of Globalization." *AAP: Asian Politics & Policy* 3 (2): 207–24.

Xu, Janice Hua. 2012. "Online News Reports of Air Quality Issues in Beijing." *Telematics and Informatics* 29 (4): 409–17.

Xue, Lei. 2013. "Assemble in the name of $PM_{2.5}$." (Yi $PM_{2.5}$ de mingyi jihe). *Beijing Youth Daily*, November 11. Accessed July 17, 2015. http://epaper.ynet.com/html/2013-11/11/content_23194.htm?div=-1.

Yang, Guobin. 2013. *The Power of the Internet in China: Citizen Activism Online*. New York: Columbia University Press.

9 *Keitai mizu*

A mobile game reflection in a post-3/11 Tokyo, Japan

Larissa Hjorth and Fumitoshi Kato

Introduction

When Lisa Nakamura (2002) dubbed the city of Tokyo as the Western default setting for science fiction, she was signaling to the city's intricate, multiple, and hidden cartographies. When we think about the cartographies of Tokyo, we tend to think about the electronic spaces of Akihabara or the intricacies of the city's rail system. Behind the backdrop of Tokyo's image as a futurist megacity is a complex urban environment that is renegotiating many issues to do with energy and sustainability especially after the earthquake, tsunami, and Fukushima nuclear plant disaster known as 3/11. One such cartography is that of water—underneath Tokyo's twenty-first-century modernity evidenced through skyscrapers, neon signs, and mobile media is a plethora of rivers and streams. While at first the connection between twenty-first-century mobile media and the historical importance of water may seem abstract, it is through the marriage of these two modern and traditional features of Japanese culture that we can connect to Japanese environmentalism.

It is the relationship between media, water, and place—as a vehicle for understanding environmentalism—that the project *Shibuya: Underground Streams* sought to explore. A collaboration between the Australian Research Council Linkage project Spatial Dialogues and the BOAT PEOPLE Association *Shibuya: Underground Streams* brought together Australian and Japanese artists to reflect upon the relationship between art, screen culture and the environment (especially climate change). Through a series of video projections, sound performances, installations, and mobile games in a shipping container in a Shibuya park in June 2014, *Underground Streams* sought to provide a space in which everyday commuters in the busy area of Shibuya could take time to reflect upon their environment, climate change, and especially hidden streams. In particular, one of the mobile game elements, *keitai mizu* (mobile water), sought to highlight the significant role mobile media have played in restructuring narratives in and around the environment and its relationship to grassroots movements in Japan.

This chapter explores the role of artistic interventions into the everyday as a tool for rethinking entanglements between Asian cities, climate change, and the environment. With the trauma of 3/11 still haunting Tokyo, *Underground*

Streams sought to provide ways in which the environment could be reflected upon as well as affording a space for dialogue. Through discussing the site-specific mobile game, *keitai mizu* and its deployment by a group of university students, this chapter considers how camera phones and moblogs (mobile blogs) operate not only as a space for personal journals but also as a way for instigating reflection upon the environment. *Keitai mizu* renders game players into investigators by using the camera phone and Twitter as part of the discovery process in uncovering the natural water streams under the urban cartographies.

In order to examine the role mobile media might play in providing alternative ways for narrating environmentalism in contemporary post-3/11 Tokyo, this chapter explores three areas. First, the chapter contextualizes the rise of mobile media and moblogs in Japan and how this can help to reinvent the environment and practices of place. Second, we outline the shifting political landscape in and around environmentalism in Japan. Third, the chapter turns to the case study of *keitai mizu* as a way in which to reprioritize the place of the environment through water cartographies.

Visualizing a sense of place: Camera phone practices, moblogs, and place

Camera phone practices have become an integral part of everyday life. No experience is too banal to photograph and share; rather, as Ilpo Koskinen (2007) and Søren Mørk Petersen (2009) have argued, camera phone practices are ordered by banality. In their everydayness, they reflect and amplify the rhythm and movements across places, spaces, and temporalities. Camera phones practice shape, and are shaped by, different modes for conceptualizing place (Ito 2003; Ito and Okabe 2005).

In second-generation camera phones, apps such as Instagram, geo-tagging—and thus locative media—almost becomes default. These apps play an active role in how places are conceptualized, mapped, and experienced (Ozkul 2015). With camera phone geo-tagging, the temporal and spatial dimensions of places get overlaid with the social and electronic. Through apps such as Instagram, geo-tagging outlines the "geographical and temporal identification of a media artifact" that "suppresses temporal, vertical structures in favor of spatial connectivities" (Hochman and Manovich 2013).

Location-based services (LBS) are changing how we visualize intimate cartographies though shifting camera phone practices within the app ecology. With LBS, Jason Farman suggests the digital map is "a social network that engages users as embodied interactors rather than disembodied voyeurs" (2010, p. 869). The combination of digital maps and their augmented reality are not purely visual (Farman 2010; Lapenta 2011), they are, as Pink suggests, about "emplaced visuality" (2011). Camera phone practices are key to representing and experiencing places as playful with co-present others. In this way, camera phone photo taking and sharing can be viewed as part of ambient play as well as intimate co-presence.

Mobile apps and photo sharing offer key ways of exploring the everyday urban landscape as a site of environmental contestation. Through apps such as Instagram and Twitter, intimates within everyday practices can connect co-presently. A picture of a single coffee cup can tacitly signal to someone elsewhere feelings of longing and co-presence. Through the combination of picture, geo-tagging and text, such messages can provide ambient ways for intimates to stay co-present throughout the day. The combination of image, geo-tag, and text can also allow users to construct their own narratives about place, mobility, and the environment that challenge conventional stories. Through multiple shared visual, textual, and geo-locative narratives, these apps can provide us with a more complex picture of the urban as a site for contestation.

With the growth in mobile apps, we are also witnessing the blurring between the intimate and the public. While in Western culture the intimate and public were seen as diametrically opposed through binaries such as public versus private space, mobile media apps further render the intimate *public* and public *intimate* (Hjorth and Arnold 2013). This sees an amplification of what Lauren Berlant defined as "intimate publics"—that is, intimacy has taken on new geographies and forms of mobility, most notably as a kind of "publicness" (1998, p. 281).

However, in a digital material environment, intimate relations are not simply performed in pairs or bounded groups; rather, they traverse the online and offline; in that, they are also performed in physical public worlds but in electronic privacy (for example, when someone privately sends a friend a camera phone image of him- or herself in a café), and in an electronic public that is geographically private (for example, when we read personal messages posted to us in a publicly facing Facebook page or on Twitter, while in the private space of our homes). In each different culture, mobile media are shaped, and shaped by, the existing rituals and practices. Specifically in Japan, mobile media have played a key role in expanding rituals in and around intimacy (Ito and Okabe 2005). For example, in a culture where sharing one's feelings face-to-face is not encouraged, mobile media have allowed for intimacies to be spoken without the embarrassment or shame.

With mobile media entangling the public with the intimate in new ways, this means they can play key roles in representing how we think about the environment and issues around sustainability. Social media such as mixi and LINE have been demonstrative of the role of media to reflect offline intimacies and debates, while media such as Twitter provides an avenue for Japan's growing grassroots politics (Gill, Steger, and Slater 2013).

Increasingly within the educational space, the role of mobile media is being configured to express this growing user agency. Tools such as moblogs can help with "flipped" classrooms by making students active in their learning processes. Within moblog spaces, the process of uploading photographs can see the distinction between one's private and public domains of activities begin to blur. For more constant users of the moblogs, this uploading can contribute to shape and reshape one's readiness to engage in the process of face-to-face communication with community members. It may also expand our tempo-spatial images of a "classroom," for example, and thereby generates a sense of togetherness even when a member's presence is not available (Kato 2014).

Such moblogs can be understood as a "place" for one's face-work as part of everyday life modes of presentation (Goffman 1967). The notion of face refers to an image of self-delineation in terms of approved social attributes. Through the process of taking and posting a photo, an individual attempts to understand his or her personhood within an organizational setting. In posting a photo, a member is constructing and maintaining the relationships with others. An individual's postings are not only displaying to other members what he or she has seen but also, he or she is displaying about him- or herself and his or her understandings about the relationships with other members.

From the standpoint of developing a qualitative research method, a camera phone can be understood as a new "gear" for conducting field studies, because it enables us to record and compile diverse standpoints as a set of photos. Especially, it can capture a series of micro-moments embedded within an individual's day-to-day activities. Particularly, it enables researchers to collect and compile images of the local community. Once selected and uploaded to social media, visual images and sharing of them may enhance our awareness about the resources of the community. Photos compiled can be examined in terms of understanding the characteristics of the local community, and more interestingly, they lead us to speculate upon multiple viewpoints of ourselves. Shared images may connect people together, functioning as a "community builder" and thus adding to the conversations and narratives in and around environment.

The relevance of mobile media to environmental concerns was particularly highlighted by the experiences after 3/11 Earthquake in the Tohoku region of Japan (Gil, Steger, and Slater 2013). The key role played by mobile media in the context of this particular environmental disaster can be understood as a major turning point in terms of recognizing the functions and capacities of mobile communications. While phone lines were not functioning properly directly after the Earthquake, Hjorth and Kim for instance discovered that social media—such as twitter and Facebook—were very much "alive" and thus utilized to share disaster information at hand (Hjorth and Kim 2011).

For example, it was reported that many people working in the Tohoku region and central business district of Tokyo had to either give up going home or to walk home while many of the public transportation systems were not working. The term *kitaku-nanmin* ("returner refugees") was coined and used to describe the ones who had difficulties in getting back home. It was reported that on the very day of the disaster, approximately 5.1 million people could not reach home. This phenomenon amounts to about 28 per cent of the people who were outside their home at the time of the disaster.

Of those who decided to walk home, they often shared information virtually about ongoing changes in the status of trains and buses, changing their travel routes accordingly. The event also demonstrated the strengths of the ties generated through the use of social media via smartphones. Through this experience, many Japanese citizens created new accounts on social media in order to be prepared for future possible disaster situations. After the 3/11 incident, the "perpetual contact" (Katz and Aakhus 2002) of mobile phone–facilitated social media became a key part in many millions of Japanese lives as a way to provide a sense of constant connectedness with physically separated but electronically co-present family and friends. As we discuss in the next section, the agency of mobile media practices to rearticulate the role of place and the environment have their history in Japanese environmentalism.

Locating the environment: Japan and environmentalism

The significant role mobile media have played in restructuring narratives in and around the environment and their relationship to grassroots movements in Japan cannot be underestimated (Gill, Steger, and Slater 2013). In order to understand these shifts, one needs to understand Japanese environmentalism—a phenomenon that has a history beginning within the Meiji Period (a period marked by great industrialism) and marked by two key stages after 1960s urbanization (Ministry of Foreign Affairs in Japan 2010). The first Japanese environmental movement emerged in the 1970s exemplified by the Minamata and the Love Canal incidents. Together with rapid motorization, air pollution via photochemical smog became one of the major environmental issues. People soon came to recognize that wrongdoers were not only companies but also played a role. The second stage of environmentalism— as represented by anti-development and ecological movements in the 1980s and 1990s—focused upon the relationship between ecology and lifestyle.

In the 1990s, pushing back against the rapid industrialization and urbanization of the 1970s and 1980s, local grassroots and community-based environmental movements dubbed the *Jyumin-Undo* (local residents campaign) emerged (Mitsuda 1996). Writing a few years after the landmark *United Nations Conference on Environment and Development* or Rio Earth Summit of 1992, Jonathan Taylor argues that from the early 1990s, "Japan has attempted to position itself rhetorically as a global environmental leader". However, for Taylor, this position was underscored by the reality of the "Japanese model of development" as "linked to Asia's continuing environmental crises" (1999, p. 535). And yet the traditional notion of *mottainai* ("what a waste")—while repressed up until the 1980s economic bubble burst—has continued to play a key role in everyday Japanese life (Masters 2008). In 2000, The Basic Law for Establishing the Recycling-based Society came into effect—establishing Japan as a "recycling-based society". Given Japanese tendencies toward mass production, consumption, and disposal, the Law aims to shift the cultural emphasis toward a reduction of environmental loading.

While grassroots, community-driven environmental groups have grown over the past three decades, it is in the wake of 3/11 that we see new forms of environmentalism that involve new forms of protest and engagement entangled with the digital (Gill, Steger, and Slater 2013). As David H. Slater (2011) observes in his analysis of post-3/11, prior

> ... the threat of nuclear radiation and critiques of the nuclear industry have been skillfully politicized in ways that have led to the largest set of demonstrations in Japan (with the exception of Okinawa) since the US-Japan security treaty protests of the 1960s and 1970s. These protests have been based in Tokyo,

utilizing urban networks of activists who have provided the digital framework for organization that has brought together an older generation of anti-nuclear activists, young families, hip urbanites, office workers and union protesters.

After 3/11, women (and especially mothers) have become the driving voice for anti-nuclear protests in Japanese society and policy. Through digital media, they spread their stories of agency and grassroots politics. As Slater observes,

> Women, and in particular, mothers, have been quite active in radiation measurement, calls for contaminated soil removal, and efforts to secure safe food since the early months of the crisis. Today, perhaps more than any other group, they have emerged as particularly effective anti-nuke spokespersons." This phenomenon has been dubbed as the "Women from Fukushima Against Nukes" (*Genptasu iranai Fukushima kara no onnatachi*).

In a joint article with Nishimura Keiko and Love Kindstrand, Slater (2011) highlights the pivotal role social media has played in new forms of environmental activism after 3/11. As they note,

> The fervor, organization and momentum that culminated in the events that occurred up to and around the September 19, 2011 march of 60,000 people in Tokyo, the largest such gathering since the 1970s AMPO campaign against the Japan–U.S. Security Treaty, were seen by many of us as examples of the unexpected power of social media to provide alternative narratives that could give rise to significant political action
>
> (2011, n.p)

Indeed, the ambient, intimate, and co-present characteristics of social media have afforded young and old with new ways in which to express and engage with politics. Social media such as Twitter, Instagram, and Line are viewed as both political and personal (Hjorth and Arnold 2013). It is this engagement with politics and especially green issues that our case study *keitai mizu* explores—demonstrating how a game can be a vehicle for not just critical but also practical engagement with media, people, and the environment within everyday entanglements.

Keitai mizu: A site-specific mobile game

> When the earthquake occurred, I was alone in my room playing a monster hunter PSP game. Exactly at the time, I was fighting with a monster who makes an earthquake so that I didn't realize that an actual, offline quake had occurred. Only after beating down the monster, I realized something different around me. A fish tank had overflowed and books had fallen down. Initially I was not really shocked by the earthquake itself, but felt frustration with the aftermath—the power failure, panic buying, nuclear accident, and such

stuff. During this time I stayed inside with a friend and continued to play the monster hunter game. But the game was no longer entertaining

("Toshi", 25 Japanese male, interview)

The quote from "Toshi" sees him playing a haptic game during the 2011 Tokyo earthquake, tsunami, and earthquake disaster known as 3/11. Affective and personal technologies such as social and mobile media make us rethink old psychological models of emotion. In times of trauma, mobile media are increasingly becoming a vehicle for material and immaterial textures and contours of grief. Everybody deals with crisis in different ways, and this individualism is being amplified within mobile media just as it is creating new avenues for accessing a sense of community, support, and help.

Toshi's immersion within the PSP game was so deep that he mistook the quake vibrations for the monster's movements within his game. In the moments after he realized the horror of the real-life event, he desperately tried to contact friends and family to no avail. In the days after 3/11 and as multiple and conflicting news reports emerged across mass and social media, Toshi with a friend used the game to hide from the pain and confusion. Later, it emerged that the national broadcaster, NHK, had deliberately withheld important information about the Fukushima reactor under the instructions of the government.

Toshi—like millions of other Japanese—shifted their trust toward mobile media such as Twitter and LBS such as Foursquare and Instagram to help them not only to gain a sense of intimate publics but also to have a sense of perpetual co-presence with their family and friends. What becomes apparent in conversation with Toshi is that his gameplay is about intentional escapism, particularly when the world is too traumatic and confusing. The picture that begins to emerge is one whereby there are multiple forms of presence and engagement around mobile gaming that need to be accounted for beyond the clumsy notion of casual.

As noted elsewhere, mobile games are often problematically categorized as casual games (Hjorth 2009). However, as Keogh notes, "a casual game does not simply offer an easier or more shallow experience than a traditional videogame, but an experience that is more flexible with the player's time, more easily incorporated into the player's everyday life" (Keogh 2014, p. 269). It is this flexibility and ease of incorporation, especially when adapted to mobile social media games or involving the insinuation of game elements into an application or service, that so thoroughly instills mobile games into the routines and habits of our social lives. One way to understand mobile games beyond the problematic label of casual is through ambient play and intimate co-presence. This is especially the case with camera phone practices that often accompany and play an unofficial role in mobile gaming. One example is China's Foursquare equivalent, *Jiepang*, whereby players deployed unofficial camera phone practices so much that the company rebranded its application to make camera phone taking and sharing an integral part of its social experience of place (Hjorth and Gu 2011).

Given the important role played by camera phone practices in the ambient and co-present experience of place through digital cartographies, the site-specific mobile game *keitai mizu* was motivated by the question "How could we harness Twitter and camera phone apps to make a game that reflected upon the environment in new ways?" It was in a post-3/11 context that *Shibuya: Underground Streams* was born. Through a series of video, sound, game, and sculptural narratives, *Shibuya: Underground Streams* sought to make the general public in Tokyo consider the underground streams making up much of Tokyo.

In particular, the project focused upon one of the busiest places in the world, Shibuya. By placing a shipping container in a park over the month of June 2013, the project sought to explore the idea of cartographies—water, emotional, social, playful, psychological, historical, and geographic. Given that Tokyo is made up of numerous little rivers underneath all the trains and roads, we wanted to make audiences aware that they are literally perpetually *walking on water* (Figure 9.1).

We asked Japanese and Australian artists to make a series of abstract and representational works of water creatures that were then placed around the park. The project sought to disrupt dichotomies between art and non-art, water and non-water, game and non-game, player and ethnographer. Players had 15 minutes to hunt for photos and share online various *native-only* water-related creatures and objects that had been placed around the site. They then "captured" the art with their camera phones and shared it online via Twitter or Instagram. Winners only sent pictures of the native species to the *keitaimizu* Twitter account (Figure 9.2). The game deployed both old (geocaching) and new (Twitter and Instagram) media to turn players into ethnographers.

The game space was blurred across online and offline spaces, with Instagram and Twitter enabling co-present friends to share the experiences and images. Through the process of game play, participants became more mindful of the local water species as well as reflective upon the fact that the city is made up of numerous little rivers underneath all the trains and roads. We wanted to make audiences aware that they are literally perpetually *walking on water* (Figure 9.1).We wanted participants to think about the ways in which place can be mapped in different ways and provide multiple histories and geographies (Carter 2010; Verhoeff 2013; Wilmott 2012). Maps are performative—We shape maps as they shape us.

Keitai mizu attempted to challenge boundaries between official and unofficial game spaces by blurring them with different modes of play (Figures 9.3; 9.4; 9.5;

Figure 9.1 Shibuya: underground streams

Figure 9.2 *Keitai mizu* (mobile water) game

Figure 9.3 *Keitai mizu* players

Figure 9.4 Co-present and ambient play examples of *keitai mizu*

138 *Larissa Hjorth and Fumitoshi Kato*

Figure 9.5 Co-present and ambient play examples of *keitai mizu*

Figure 9.6 Co-present and ambient play examples of *keitai mizu*

9.6). In particular, camera phone practices partake in new haptic visualities that bring emotional and social dimensions of place and play to the official game play space and drive the motivation for use. By deploying camera phone practices as part of the mobile game, players can develop the melodramatic elements—the affective and emotional dimensions—to engage friends into the play of being mobile.

Through the playful use of Instagram geo-tagging whereby numerous images of artefacts were assembled upon the website, players were able to see other players' guesses (what they thought were the native animals) and their location through geo-tagging. This created a sense of emplacement but also displacement as other players searched for some art objects that were either mistaken for rubbish in the park or too small to see (some artworks, such as Yasuko Toyoshima, were semi-transparent creatures only 5 cm long). The *Spatial Dialogues* website became a series of emplaced visualities of the park through each of the players' interpretations. The mapping of the park and its underground streams became a series of Instagram clues. Players needed to pay attention to the environment as an assemblage of the visible and invisible.

Part of the enjoyment of the project was not only the entanglements between the methods and its transmission but also how the project lived on in different ways that saw the participants taking the key role. For example, when one student group came through to play, one of the other students took it upon herself to document their experiences and responses and turn it into a short film that she then uploaded onto Vimeo. This video was one of the few artifacts of transmission left after the ephemeral work had ceased. Moreover, traces of the play could be found in participants' Twitter accounts, creating new nodes for co-present entanglement.

Conclusion: Visualizing the environment and ambient play

In this paper, we have proposed an understanding of mobile media as playing an important part in rethinking the environment and a sense of belonging. Through the case study of *keitai mizu*, we deployed Instagram and Twitter as quotidian media to reconsider the entanglement between being connected to the environment and intimate co-presence and ambient play within the everyday. This example allows us to think through the ways in which art and mobile media might provide alternative ways for understanding and talking about environmentalism by asking players to reflect upon their natural environment camouflaged within urban cartographies. Rather than mobile media just contributing to the growing problems around e-waste, it can be a vehicle for collaboration, agency, and politics.

Through the discussion of *keitai mizu*, we have sought to provide poetic ways in which players can become investigators in understanding their everyday environments in new ways. As we have argued, camera phone practices contribute to the various performative cartography cultures emerging in an age of smartphones. Camera phone images and sharing, especially through geo-tagging, create new ways in which place can be depicted through overlays between the electronic and social, geographic, and emotional. They can connect the political to the personal in new ways that can provide insight into alternative understandings of being "green".

References

Berlant, Lauren. 1998. "Intimacy: A Special Issue," *Critical Inquiry* 24 2 (Winter): 281–88.
Carter, Paul. 2010. *The Road to Botany Bay: An Exploration of Landscape and History*. Minneapolis, MN: University of Minnesota Press.

Farman, Jason. 2010. "Mapping The Digital Empire: Google Earth and the Process of Postmodern Cartography." *New Media & Society* 12 (6): 869–88.
Gill, Tom, Brigitte Steger, and David H. Slater. 2013. *Japan Copes with Calamity*. New York: Peter Lang.
Goffman, Erving. 1967. *Interaction Ritual: Essays in Face-to-Face Behavior*. New York: Pantheon Books.
Hjorth, Larissa. 2009. *Mobile Media in the Asia-Pacific*. London: Routledge.
Hjorth, Larissa, and Kay Gu. 2011. "The Place of Emplaced Visualities: A Case Study of Smartphone Visuality and Location-Based Social Media in Shanghai, China." *Continuum: Journal of Media and Cultural Studies* 26 (5): 699–713.
Hjorth, Larissa, and Kyoung-hwa Yonnie Kim. 2011. "The Mourning After: A Case Study of Social Media in the 3.11 Earthquake Disaster in Japan." *Television & New Media* 12 (6): 552–59.
Hjorth, Larissa, and Michael Arnold. 2013. *Online@AsiaPacific: Mobile, Social and Locative Media in the Asia-Pacific*. London: Routledge.
Hochman, Nadav, and Lev Manovich. 2013. "Zooming into an Instagram City: Reading the Local through Social Media." *First Monday* 18 (7). Accessed September 28, 2013. http://dx.doi.org/10.5210/fm.v18i7.4711.
Ito, Mizuko. 2003. "Mobiles and the Appropriation of Place." *Receiver*, no. 8. Accessed December 10, 2005. http://academic.evergreen.edu/curricular/evs/readings/itoShort.pdf
Ito, Mizuko, and Daisuke Okabe. 2005. "Intimate Visual Co-Presence". Paper presented at *Ubicomp*, Takanawa Prince Hotel, Tokyo, Japan, September 11–14. Accessed June 28, 2006. http://www.itofisher.com/mito/.
Kato, Fumitoshi. 2014. "Learning with Mobile Phones." In *The Routledge Companion to Mobile Media,* edited by Gerard Goggin and Larissa Hjorth, 236–44. New York: Routledge.
Katz, James E., and Mark Aakhus, eds. 2002. *Perpetual Contact: Mobile Communication, Private Talk, Public Performance*. Cambridge: Cambridge University Press.
Keogh, Brendan. 2014. "Paying Attention to *Angry Birds:* Rearticulating Hybrid Worlds and Embodied Play through Casual iPhone Games." In *The Routledge Companion to Mobile Media*, edited by Gerard Goggin and Larissa Hjorth, 267–75. New York: Routledge.
Koskinen, Ilpo. 2007. "Managing Banality in Mobile Multimedia." In *The Social Construction and Usage of Communication Technologies: European and Asian Experiences*, edited by Raul Pertierra, 48–60. Singapore: Singapore University Press.
Lapenta, Francesco. 2011. "Geomedia: On Location-Based Media, the Changing Status of Collective Image Production and the Emergence of Social Navigation Systems." *Visual Studies* 26 (1): 14–24.
Masters, Coco. 2008. "The Japanese Way." *Time Magazine*, April 17. Accessed August 10, 2014. http://content.time.com/time/specials/2007/article/0,28804,1730759_1734222_1734215,00.html
Ministry of Foreign Affairs in Japan. 2010. Japan's Initiative to Cope with Global Environmental Problems. Accessed August 10, 2014. http://www.mofa.go.jp/policy/environment/pdfs/jp_initiative_pamph.pdf
Mitsuda, Hisayoshi. 1996. "Surging Environmentalism in Japan: Back to the Root." Presented at the 9th World Congress of Rural Sociology, Bucharest, July 22–26. http://archives.bukkyo-u.ac.jp/rp-contents/SO/0030/SO00300R119.pdf
Mørk Petersen, Søren. 2009. "Common Banality: The Affective Character of Photo Sharing, Everyday Life and Produsage Cultures." PhD diss., IT-University of Copenhagen.

Nakamura, Lisa. 2002. *Cybertypes: Race, Ethnicity, and Identity on the Internet.* London: Routledge.

Ozkul, Didem. 2015. "Transforming Cities, Transforming Locations: Locative Media and Sense of Place." In *Mobility and Locative Media: Mobile Communication in Hybrid Spaces*, edited by Adriana de Souza e Silva and Mimi Sheller, 101–16. New York: Routledge.

Pink, Sarah. 2011. "Sensory Digital Photography: Re-thinking "Moving" and the Image." *Visual Studies* 26 (1): 4–13.

Slater, David H. 2011. "Fukushima Women against Nuclear Power: Finding a Voice from Tohoku." *Japan Focus*, November 9. Accessed September 20, 2014. http://www.japanfocus.org/events/view/117.

Slater, David H., Nishimura Keiko, and Love Kindstrand. 2011. "Social Media, Information and Political Activism in Japan's 3.11 Crisis." *Japan Focus*. Accessed June 15, 2014. http://www.japanfocus.org/-Nishimura-Keiko/3762.

Taylor, Jonathan. 1999. 'Japan's Global Environmentalism: Rhetoric and Reality." *Political Geography* 18 (5): 535–62.

Verhoeff, Nanna. 2013. *Mobile Screens: The Visual Regime of Navigation.* Amsterdam: Amsterdam University Press.

Wilmott, Clancy. 2012. "Cartographic City: Mobile Mapping as a Contemporary Urban Practice." *Refractory: A Journal of Entertainment Media,* December 28. Accessed June 15, 2014. http://refractory.unimelb.edu.au/2012/12/28/wilmott/

10 Living co-ops in Korea

Sustainable living, communal labor, and social economy

Sun Jung

On December 1, 2012, The Cooperative Association Fundamental Law took effect in South Korea (hereafter Korea). Over the next 100 days, 137 cooperative associations were registered in Seoul alone (with more than 500 registered nationwide). To encourage these cooperative associations (hereafter co-ops), the City of Seoul announced that it would increase its number of co-ops to 8,000 by 2022, making up 5 per cent of the gross regional domestic product (Park So-Hui 2013). This drastic change reflects Mayor Park Won-Soon's background as founder and manager of the Hope Institute, a think tank designed to promote grassroots solutions to social, educational, environmental and political problems. One key activity of the Hope Institute has been a citizen-driven campaign to revitalize cooperative associations, groups that were struggling for survival in Korea's conglomerate-led neoliberal market economy, faced as they were also with issues including the polarization of wealth, increased youth unemployment, and the broader collapse of small and medium enterprises (in other words, activities all linked to the idea of a social economy). The three major candidates for the 2012 presidential election—Moon Jae-In, An Cheol-Soo, and Park Geun-Hye—all promised a "welfare nation" and a "sustainable society" along with a focus on developing a "social economy."

The boom in co-ops is a good example of Korea's rapidly changing socio-political climate today. Along with other groups, living cooperative associations (생활협동조합, 生活協同組合 , せいかつきょうどうくみあ) lie at the center of a phenomenon that mirrors the desires of Korea's contemporary middle class for sustainable, green lifestyles. These middle-class urban consumers who voluntarily participate in direct trading with rural producers have also become a driving force in this alternative food supply chain. Modeled on Western co-ops (particularly the Legacoop in Bologna, Italy), these local co-ops seek to become part of a global movement that fights against rural poverty, respects the environment, and practices food safety. Korea's living co-ops embody the rising social economy and a growth in the public awareness of sustainable living, a consequence of rapid globalization and economic neoliberalization widely practiced in the global marketplace. At the same time, the emerging living co-ops in Korea are also closely related to the *guinong/guichon* ("moving back to village") phenomenon, reflecting the nostalgic desires of urban middle-class citizens toward a cooperative

Living co-ops in Korea 143

community where they as both producers and consumers practice community-based cooperative labor (traditionally known as *dure*). The community they desire is imagined, however, as most of these urban consumers have never experienced these communal laboring operations in reality. With its emphasis on community values and cooperation, this *dure* movement also lies in direct opposition to the neoliberal economic paradigm.

This phenomenon is, of course, not unique to Korea. Many Asian countries are increasingly faced with the harsh sharp inequalities resulting from the polarization of wealth and the effects of a footprint that is increasingly negative toward the environment. In response to this, state governments, civic groups, and the media have seized on the urban sustainability frameworks to address these growing social and environmental problems. These efforts are evident in social media–empowered civic movements, urban community restoration projects, a range of media representations of green lifestyles, and the often-heated discourses about the social economy across the region. The push for environmental and social sustainability often directly contradicts the push by influential urban business coalitions for corporations, cities, and countries to be more economically competitive with their regional and global rivals. The interaction between urban sustainability and economic development discourses raises questions around current entrepreneurial strategies (mainly practiced by major multinational enterprises (MNEs)) and invites an exploration of the implications of integrating concepts (and practices) such as sustainability and social justice within urban economic development policy. In the case of Korea, such interactions manifest through the emerging living co-op movement and a restoration of the notion of *dure* (collaborative community sentiments). Community enterprise environmental coalitions that incorporate the states' broader vision of sustainability and social equity present alternatives to existing socioeconomic coalitions (predominantly driven by the globally dominant neoliberal capitalist system). They suggest a new type of sustainable lifestyle built upon a pro-community sentiment and environmental health.

Research into neoliberalism and neoliberal social systems in Asia has been undertaken by a range of researchers in both cultural studies and the social sciences (Ong 2006; Hadiz 2006; Rodan and Hewison 2006; Chang, Fine, and Weiss 2012; Park, Hill, and Saito 2012; Anagnost, Arai, and Ren 2013). In this work, however, social practices that react against this system and the social economies that exist as an alternative in the region are under-discussed. In recent years, a number of Korean-language books have discussed local co-ops as a mode of social economy, community restoration, and environment-friendly farming (for example, Park Won-Soon, the mayor of Seoul, and his various books on community-driven social enterprise and the sharing economy). Despite this, there is no in-depth academic discussion on the current boom in living co-ops in Korea in relation to sustainable lifestyle (especially in English). A handful of existing studies written in English on Korean co-ops primarily deal with agricultural co-ops, in particular relation to their development, policy-making processes, and social impacts (especially in food markets). This chapter, therefore, seeks to explore Korea's living co-ops and associated emerging green lifestyles by focusing on the cosmopolitan desires of the urban middle class toward environmentally friendly, sustainable living as well as the nostalgic desires that drive them toward cooperative communities. It also examines how this emerging civic movement reflects broader Korean society's demand for a new socioeconomic paradigm—the social economy—which can ideally provide an antidote to the accumulation of neoliberal economic fatigue.

Sustainable living and emerging social enterprises in Korea

Sustainability and sustainable development came to global prominence when the World Commission on Environment and Development published its 1987 report, "Our Common Future" (commonly referred to as The Brundtland Report). Since then, sustainability discourse has addressed social equity alongside its original site of interest, environmental well-being. When considering the inseparability of environmental quality and human equality, Julian Agyeman constructed what he called a Just Sustainability Paradigm: "from global to local, human inequality is bad for environmental quality . . . the dominant wilderness, greening and natural resource focus [of the existing notion of 'environment'] now includes urban disinvestment, racism, homes, jobs, neighborhoods and communities" (2008, p. 152). Sustainability, therefore, does not simply refer to a "green" or "environmental" concern (although these aspects of sustainability are unquestionably essential); rather, a truly sustainable society must ensure a better quality of life for all its citizens, where "wider questions of social needs and welfare and economic opportunity are integrally related to environmental limits imposed by supporting ecosystems (Agyeman, Bullard, and Evans 2002, p. 78). Recent trends in Korea toward social enterprise (and the associated living co-op boom) mirror this very philosophy of "just sustainability".

The term *social enterprise* was first coined by Joseph Banks (1972), who proposed that business organizations should use managerial skills to address and resolve social problems. In recent years, this has become a global phenomenon as a result of the growing needs of expanding marginalized communities, the increased dominance of multinational corporations, and the withdrawal of the State from public service and provisions (Drayton and Greiner cited in Yue 2012). Many individuals or groups of individuals with similar interests—driven largely by passion and a strong vision to challenge the existing economic system—established their own companies or organizations to provide products and services to the market through which they could make a positive social impact. Studying the transformation of social movements and civil society in contemporary Japan, Broadbent and Barrett (2005) observed how the voluntary involvement and participation of Japanese citizens in these types of groups demonstrated a vigorous interest in issues that were of a general benefit to society (such as the reduction of global warming since the mid-1990s). This has also been the case in other Asian countries over recent years, which have witnessed a surge in social movements and nongovernmental organizations on issues including the environment, sustainable living, and social well-being and equity. This has coincided with the rise of an urban, well-educated, and prosperous middle class in the region as well as the emergence of social media community networks.

The Social Enterprise Promotion Act was recently enacted in Korea, and broader institutional support is now available. After Park Won-Soon was elected as the mayor in October 2011, the Seoul government introduced supporting policies and launched several innovative campaigns. In early 2012, the city government set up a division dedicated to nurturing social enterprises in Korea. A social enterprise certification system was introduced to promote social enterprises, and a total of $5.9 million was earmarked to support the business development of social enterprises. Other city initiatives included promoting 50 innovative social enterprises to solve social issues, opening an online shopping mall to sell products manufactured by social enterprises, organizing a co-ops festival, nurturing social start-ups that offer jobs for the disadvantaged, selecting exemplary enterprises to receive assistance in accessing domestic and overseas sales channels, reviving villages in the city, and creating co-ops run by local communities (Park 2012, p. 51). Park also founded a pioneering social enterprise called The Beautiful Store in 2002, which can be considered Korea's first social enterprise. The Beautiful Store's original slogan was "One person's trash is another's treasure" and is one of the first small, nonprofit organizations in the country. The store's recycle-and-reuse campaign helped spread the culture of sharing and recycling as a way to establish a sustainable economic ecosystem. It also incorporated the fair-trade movement early on, setting up a subsidiary called The Beautiful Coffee (Park 2012, p. 50).

The emergence of this alternative economic structure may be a natural consequence of globalization and the technological developments that have brought numerous crises in neoliberal Korea. Due to the increasingly competitive nature of the global economy, multinational corporations maintain their profits by relying on unsustainable forms of production. The enormous financial gains that are being made by those fortunate enough to benefit from these neoliberal economic policies come with "large social and ecological costs in terms of higher pollution levels, greater resource exploitation, less protection for workers and massive social and cultural dislocation" (Agyeman, Bullard, and Evans 2002, p. 79). This exploitative economic system does not, however, guarantee continued success in generating socioeconomic competitiveness, and the "social reproduction" factor has become increasingly significant. Social reproduction refers to "strategies for conserving open-space, reducing commute times, delivering public transport, providing affordable housing, improving access to services (such as healthcare), and creating and preserving good wage-earning jobs for those not holding one of the city-region's 'signature' jobs" (Krueger and Savage 2007, p. 215). In this context, by reinforcing the notion of social reproduction, social enterprises maintain continuous competitiveness of both society and the nation as a whole. They are experimental and offer an alternative way of doing business that utilizes corporate efficiency and productivity to put people first, advance local communities, and enhance the public interest. They grow out of the basic human need to live in harmony and community with others.

Booming co-ops in Korea and the use of alternative media

According to the International Co-operative Alliance (ICA), "a co-operative is an autonomous association of persons united voluntarily to meet their common economic, social, and cultural needs and aspirations through a jointly-owned and democratically-controlled enterprise" (2013).[1] In response to growing socio-political turmoil, economic stagnation and the social insecurity that future generations face in terms of jobs, essential social services and even just meeting their basic needs, the International Co-operative Alliance (ICA) has identified four key issues that cooperatives can address: environmental degradation and resource depletion; an unstable financial sector and increasing income inequality; a growing global governance gap; and a seemingly disenfranchised younger generation (ICA 2013). Its basic philosophy resonates with the concerns of many Koreans over recent years.

The key issues in the 2012 Korean presidential election centered around notions of a "welfare nation" and a "sustainable society" along with a focus on developing a "social economy." Even before the election, there had been a series of citizen campaigns both on- and offline reinforcing these socio-political themes, reflecting the widespread public interest in contemporary Korea in community-based grassroots-driven small enterprise, where people seek creativity, cooperativeness, justice, sociality, and sustainability rather than commercial competition. The value of the latter has become emblematic of the existing neoliberal capitalist climate, predominantly led by large multinational corporations. Korean citizens have strongly and urgently demanded a higher quality of life that is epitomized in the notions of "sustainable living" and a "welfare nation." However, President Park Guen-Hye's new state government was not able to meet these demands. Taking office in early 2013, there were high expectations of President Park, and she met with much resentment in September of the same year when she backtracked on the big welfare pledges that helped bring her to power (Arirang 2013).[2] Former Korean Minister of the Environment and podcaster Yoon Yeo-Joon stated, "in this current neoliberal climate where capitalist (or market) power overpowered state power, civil power is the only force that can help the state to win its inherent role back to serve the people" (Yoon 2013). Various grassroots-driven socio-cultural movements such as social enterprises, co-ops, and alternative media have emerged to drive the demanded social changes that it is widely felt the political system is incapable of implementing.

During 2011 and 2012, countless social media–driven current affairs podcasts were launched as a result of government interference in the existing mainstream media. The former Lee Myung-Bak government attempted to control the media by parachuting in presidential cronies to run the country's most prominent media outlets and to implement increased censorship (*The Economist* 2012). Consequently, Korea "declined from Free to Partly Free to reflect an increase in official censorship, particularly of online content, as well as the government's attempt to influence media outlets' news and information content" (Freedom House 2011). This oppressive scenario drove the boom in alternative media, particularly current affairs podcasts such as *Podcast Yoon Yeo-Joon*, *Iteolnam*, and *Nakkomsu* (aka *Naneun Kkomsuda* or *I'm a Weasel*). The latter is a satirical weekly podcast focusing on current political, economic, and social events within Korea.³ It presents an irreverent but penetrating presentation and analysis of prevailing (and sometimes overlooked) issues, and this has garnered fanatical nationwide popularity that has resulted in it being the most downloaded podcast in the News and Politics section on iTunes globally as of 19 October 2011. As a pioneer of the new political media shaping Korean politics, it raised the question of whether the advent of social networking, blogs, and other avenues of information dissemination (in short, alternative media) may change the political landscape in Korea, and reinforce just social sustainability. Following this, media co-ops such as *Pressian* have since been launched, promulgating the philosophies of both just sustainability of the local media environment and social enterprises.

These grassroots-driven alternative media activities in turn facilitate the current steep rise of co-ops, as social networks are similarly based on mutual recognition and sharing similar interests and visions. In their book *Understanding Alternative Media*, Bailey, Cammaerts, and Carpentier suggest four different conceptual approaches to describe alternative media: serving a community; alternative media as an alternative to mainstream media; linking alternative media to civil society; and alternative media as rhizome (2008). In regard to the fourth point, they indicate that the complexity and illusiveness of alternative media have now become defining elements. Alternative media not only functions "as an instrument giving voice to a group of people related to a specific issue but also become a medium for rearticulating impartiality and neutrality and grouping people and organizations already active in different types of struggle for equality" (Bailey, Cammaerts, and Carpentier 2008, p. 29). This approach highlights the fluidity and contingency of community media organizations where alternative media can question and destabilize public and commercial media organizations, while their elusiveness in turn guarantees them a degree of independence as it makes them hard to control in terms of legislation (Bailey et al. 2008, p. 29). In Korea's oppressive media environment, ordinary citizens welcomed alternative media that challenged the monolithic views of state-controlled media and allowed alternative voices.

In the case of Korea's co-ops, alternative media outlets such as online community radio are used to serve communities directly. A close link between these co-ops and the podcasts allows alternative voices, which in turn helps to promote the offline co-op movement. For example, *Gongjongongsaeng* is a podcast that is dedicated to co-ops and social economy, which discusses information and new trends in co-op movements.⁴ One of the weekly regular spots of YTN's *Fresh Economy* (which also provides a podcast service) introduced a broad range of co-ops that were able to promote their projects and operations to listeners, simultaneously adding to their audiences' knowledge of co-ops. *Iteolnam* covered various co-op-related issues, such as the launch of media co-op *Pressian* in episode 344. After a couple of years, however, many leading podcasts—including *Nakkomsu* and *Iteolnam*—had to shut down due to complex socio-politico-economic reasons. The seizure of these many once-leading-podcasts aptly demonstrates the limitations of grassroots-driven alternative media and their relationship with civil movements. It is evident that socio-political structural problems of a state (such as authoritarian government control) are easily dispersed among such loosely organized groups of activists, resulting in critical barriers in the construction of new forms of socio-political action.

Dure and nostalgic desires toward imagined Ma-eul

Just 1 year after The Cooperative Association Fundamental Law took effect, the number of registered cooperative associations in Korea had reached 3,597 (Korea Cooperatives 2014). The *Dure* living co-op in Sungmisan *ma-eul* is one of the earlier models and one of the most dynamically functioning living co-ops in Korea. Seongmisan *ma-eul* is a community based around shared ideals located in the center of Seoul, which engages people from a wide area including Seongsan-dong, Seogyo-dong, and Mangwon-dong (in Mapo-gu).[5] *Ma-eul* in Korean refers to "village" or "community," and the term predominantly applies to those in rural areas. *Dong* or *dongne* is often used to describe neighborhood in urban settings. Thus, the term *ma-eul* itself already implies urban middle-class people's longing for a rural community and the traditional village. Seongmisan *ma-eul* was first established by neighbors who united for communal child care in 1994. This kind of cooperative child care system was the first of its kind in contemporary Korea. Communal child care subsequently led to starting other kinds of cooperative community organizations and businesses, such as Seongmisan school (an alternative school), cafés, regional recycling ventures, town theatre, radio station, and the *Dure* living co-op. The *ma-eul* brought back the concept of communalism that had been long forgotten in the seemingly indifferent cosmopolitan city of Seoul. The *Dure* living co-op was launched in 2001 and has since become the center of the *ma-eul* socially, politically, economically, culturally, and psychologically. In addition to supplying safe and environmentally friendly food to *ma-eul* consumers via a direct link to producers, it also functions as a driving force behind the initial "community building" of Sungmisan *ma-eul* (Lee 2012). It was the first living co-op in Korea that linked and resided within a particular community (Lee 2012). The *Dure* co-op also ran after-school programs for children, another key way that it sought to connect to the community.

The term *dure* originated from a communal laboring operation that has been practiced since the primitive era, particularly in rice farming (Joo 2006). As the process of rice farming is high-maintenance and a large amount of labor is required at every stage of cultivation, mutual cooperation was essential. While small *dure* consists of six to eight members, larger *dure* includes entire villages. Under the leadership of the chosen leader or *Haengsoo,* there were various committee members to facilitate operations (Joo 2006). In the past, most traditional village or neighborhood organizations in Asia had a close hierarchical structure where patriarchal chiefs were steered by political patrons into predominantly conservative and mono-directional avenues. Even the successful environmental protest movements during the 1960s and 1970s had to gain support from notable local figures such as chiefs, elders, and other elites who wielded enormous power and socio-political control within communities (Broadbent 2003). Nevertheless, in recent years, it has become evident that new forms of associations have arisen, evolving out of the mutual interests of ordinary citizens. Today's co-ops offer a clear example of this: Even though they inherit the basic philosophies of *dure*, in contrast to older-style community organizations, these new co-ops are composed of individuals who are willing to pursue their shared socio-politico-economic interests within a largely horizontal structure reliant upon trust-based relationships with strangers and people outside their immediate social circle. These new ways of network building are dramatically enhanced by social media technologies in the current Web 2.0 environment, and with the growth of the urban middle-class, social movements have been very active on the local political front and constantly address concerns about consumer interests, consumer rights, education issues, and environmental well-being.

The activities of the living co-op *Hansalim*, for example, illustrate the increasing concerns with the environment, food safety, and direct trade between farmers and consumers. In Korean, "*han*" means "great, one and whole," and it also refers to all living things on earth. "*Salim*" has two meanings: It is the domestic work that takes care of their houses, families, and children and also means "to revive" and "to give life." Thus, *Hansalim* is a compound of these two words, meaning "save all living things." Founded in 1986, *Hansalm* is now the biggest living co-op in Korea, with 168 offline stores as of March 2014. *Hansalim* is a co-op where producer communities in rural areas and consumer members in urban areas cooperate, trading environmentally friendly organic products directly through its own distribution system without any commission-based sales. Product prices are determined by consultation between producers and consumers, independent from the market's price system.[6] To maximize the efficiency of these operations, members rely on social media: Through their blog bulletin boards or Twitter postings, members of *Hansalim* share their thoughts and ideas with other members, allowing everyone's experiences to be reflected in their operation processes within rather a horizontal social network.[7] They also run an online shopping mall where consumers in urban areas can easily purchase fresh food products directly and have them delivered from local farms, and through its mobile application, users can access co-op-related news and information (such as recipes using *Hansalim* products).[8]

On their website, a research report illustrates how high school students' changing diets— where they consume only an organic vegetarian menu prepared with *Hansalim* products—have created "miraculous results."[9] According to the report, all of the 25 voluntary participants lost an average of 3 kg after 2 months, and their cholesterol levels also notably dropped, while antioxidant nutrient levels increased. Stress levels were also reported to have decreased. The website links to the "*Hansalim* Food Life Education Centre" blog, which offers a range of educational programs where co-op members (and/or any participant) can learn about food safety, environmentally friendly diets, and fresh local food consumption for children, families, communities, and farmers. *Hansalim* emphasizes the significance of decreasing "food mileage" by consuming local food.[10] According to Korea Agro-Fisheries & Food Trade Corporation, through the existing distribution channel with major super market chains, consumers pay five times more for a radish compared to its primary cost (cited in Han 2013). *Hansalim* has a 76 per cent return of its profit price back to the producer (Hansalim 2011). As a social economy system, most profits are returned to the producers themselves (bar expenses linked to organizational operation costs), which is a strikingly different scenario from that of the large supermarket chains who take anywhere from 50 per cent 70 peer cent of the producers' profits (Hansalim 2011). A decrease in food mileage impacts direct trading between producers and consumers, meaning consumers pay a more just price for products.

It is now common for urban middle-class Koreans to consume seasonal food products from overseas producers through the established international distribution networks associated with hypermarkets and "super super markets."[11] According to Statistics Korea, the total revenue of hypermarkets reached $33.7 billion in 2013, a figure that has tripled over the past 10 years (Statistics Korea 2013a). These *jaebeol*-owned market chains aggressively target local consumers who once used privately owned small marts or traditional neighborhood markets. A variety of products from across the world and competitive prices attracted consumers, eventually driving small markets out of businesses. Such vicious business practices soon demolished the fiscal ecosystem of the local food distribution industry when small local shop owners lost their means of support, while consumers paid overblown distribution costs to conglomerates. As a consequence, producers earn less profit. In this situation, the public awareness of the need to rebuild the economic ecosystem and consumer demand for sustainable living triggered the current boom in living co-ops. *Hansalim* emphasizes how consuming local food by known producers through direct trading rejuvenates the local food industry and eventually enhances social sustainability, allowing both minor suppliers (for example, farmers and small neighborhood shop owners) to all survive.

In addition to the issues around food safety and local food consumption, the revitalization of communities—*ma-eul*—is another top priority for many living co-ops including *Dure* and *Hansalim*. These co-ops attempt to rebuild cooperative *ma-eul* sentiments and traditional *ma-eul* cultures. Joo Kang-Hyeon argues that human society has a strong yearning for community (2006, p. 7), explaining in part the active attempts of many urban middle-class citizens in Korea to move to rural areas (a process known as the *guinong/guichon* or "moving back to farming/village" phenomenon). The number of urban dwellers moving to rural areas has steadily increased in recent years—a phenomenon attributed mainly to a desire to be away from urban life and to pursue eco-friendly lifestyles with an emphasis on wellbeing. According to Statistics Korea, the number of people leaving cities for farms has constantly increased over the recent few years (17,464 in 2011; 19,657 in 2012; 18,825 in 2013; Statistics Korea 2013b). Almost half of the urban households that moved to farming in 2013 were from Seoul and its vicinities. This movement benefits the economy by creating jobs in agriculture, galvanizing rural communities, and distributing resources more efficiently on the national level (Asia News

Network 2013). It is now not uncommon to find producers (farmers) associated with living co-ops such as *Dure* and *Hansalim* who are *guinong* population: For example, Chae Jin-Hui, a producer/supplier of bracken for *Hansalim* is a *guinong* farmer who used to be a *Hansalim* consumer living in Seoul.[12]

A majority of this *guinong/guichon* population has an urban middle-class background: They are often well-educated and relatively young compared to the existing aged village population. By adopting advanced agricultural technologies, they are often actively involved in the living co-op movement as a producer group and have become a key driving force behind revitalizing the cooperative community. Significantly, in terms of the word "*gui*" ("returning"), it is worth noting that most of these *guinong* populations have never engaged in *nong* (farming) or lived in *chon* (village) before. The terminology of "returning" then implies nostalgic desires toward *imagined* sentiments or practices that they have never actually experienced, yet they are feeling they imagine that traditional *ma-eul* must have had: These include a sense of cooperation, fellowship, mutual assistance, and caring. By performing *guinong/guichon*, they attempt to reestablish forgotten virtues that actually have never existed in their lifetimes. By attempting to restore cooperative community sentiments and values, these contemporary middle-class consumers/producers contribute toward the construction of sustainable modes of living as well as rebuilding the financial ecosystem underpinning the local food supply chain.

Conclusion

Justice and equity issues must be incorporated into the core of social sustainability practices where social minority groups (defined in terms of race, class, and gender) must be considered in depth. The class and social inequalities experienced by many ordinary citizens (both producers and consumers) within Korea's neoliberal capitalist system often manifest in the ways that individuals suffer social exclusion, unequal wealth redistribution, and inequitable access to environmentally friendly goods. In the example of living co-ops in Korea, members are usually farmers/fishers in rural areas or factory workers in small and medium-sized towns and often suffer social inequalities under the *jaebeol*-dominated food supply system in Korea. The other side of this is the middle-class urban consumers who, to a certain degree, too often suffer social exclusions and economic pressures under extremely competition-driven neoliberal capitalist system in Korea's many city spaces.

The boom in living co-ops is a barometer of what many contemporary Korean citizens from rural citizens and factory workers to the precarious middle classes are yearning for—environmentally as well as socially sustainable living. This new movement raises a range of questions: What kind of socio-political elements lead members of living co-ops to participate in cooperative social enterprises? How do their decisions enable them to create new job opportunities and horizontal work environments, which to a certain degree deconstruct the existing neoliberal capitalist structure and (re)establish sustainable social structures? How does this new movement signify an emerging shift toward sustainable lifestyles in the region more broadly, implying as it does both cosmopolitan as well as nostalgic desires of many middle-class Korean citizens today? Focusing on these issues, this chapter has examined the interaction between Korea's specific socio-politico-cultural contexts and grassroots practices as a key context driving the rise in living co-ops and the construction of a sustainable living movement in Korea. In this context, it is evident that creating and participating in living co-ops empowers members, enabling social inclusion, equity, and environmental well-being through the delivery of sustainable development.

Notes

1 The values cooperatives uphold are self-help, self-responsibility, democracy, equality, equity, and solidarity, while the seven principles voluntary and open membership, democratic member control, member economic participation, autonomy and independence, education, training and information, co-operation among co-operatives, and concern for community (International Co-operative Alliance 2013).
2 President Park scaled down "pension payouts for the elderly and delay planned college tuition subsidies by 1 year until 2015 due to a revenue shortfall—flagship pledges that won her support from young and old voters during the presidential elections last year" (Arirang 2013).
3 See http://radio.ddanzi.com/radio. The four main presenters include Kim Ou-Joon (president, Ddanzi media group); Joo Jin-Woo (investigative journalist, newsweekly SisaIN), Kim Yong-Min (producer/political critic); and Jeong Bong-Joo (politician/writer).
4 See http://www.podbbang.com/ch/6409.
5 The term "*gu*" refers to city's administrative district or precinct while "*dong*" refers to the subdivided area under *gu*.
6 *Hansalim* producers own their own farms or processing facilities, and all products are delivered from production sites to consumers directly through the distribution center. Every New Year, *Hansalim* members gather together for a meeting, where they decide how big an amount of crops will be cultivated where, by whom, and with how much of the price. In the market, the instability of the price of agriculture products is frequent according to the situation of the climate or supply and demand. But *Hansalim* distributes the products at the stable price promised at the meeting (Hansalim 2011).
7 See https://twitter.com/hansalim1986.
8 See http://shop.hansalim.or.kr and https://play.google.com/store/apps/details?id=com.anchor.hansalim.
9 See http://hansalimnews.tistory.com/55.
10 Food mileage (or food miles) is a term that refers to the distance that food is transported from the time of its production through distribution until it arrives on the consumers' dining table. According to the National Institute of Environmental Research, Korea's average food mileage per person is 7,085 tkm, almost 10 times higher than France (cited in Cho 2013).
11 "Hypermarket" refers to big-sized super markets that are mostly *jaebeol*-owned super market chains, for example, E Mart, Lotte Mart, and Home Plus. "Super super market" refers to those corporate-owned supermarkets that are bigger than privately owned local marts or convenient stores and smaller than hypermarkets, which includes GS Supermarket, Lotte Mart, Kims Club Mart, Home Plus Express, and E Mart Everyday.
12 See http://www.hansalim.or.kr/?p=12598.

References

Agyeman, Julian. 2008. "Toward a 'Just' Sustainability?" *Continuum: Journal of Media & Cultural Studies* 22 (6): 751–56.

Agyeman, Julian, Robert D. Bullard, and Bob Evans. 2002. "Exploring the Nexus: Bringing Together Sustainability, Environmental Justice and Equity." *Space and Polity* 6 (1): 77–90.

Anagnost, Ann, Andrea Arai, and Hai Ren, eds. 2013. *Global Futures in East Asia: Youth, Nation, and the New Economy in Uncertain Times*. Palo Alto, CA: Stanford University Press.

Arirang. 2013. "President won's Scaling Down of Welfare Pledge: Analysis." *Arirang News*, September 26. Accessed March 2, 2014. http://www.arirang.co.kr/news/News_View.asp?nseq=151647.

Asia News Network. 2013. "Balancing S. Korea's population distribution," ANN. 3 September. Accessed March 2, 2014. http://www.asianewsnet.net/Balancing-S-Koreas-population-distribution-51120.html.

Bailey, Olga Guedes, Bart Cammaerts, and Nico Carpentier. 2008. *Understanding Alternative Media*. New York: Open University Press.

Banks, Joseph. 1972. *The Sociology of Social Movements*. London: Macmillan.

Broadbent, Jeffrey. 2003. "Movement in Context: Thick Networks and Japanese Environmental Protest." In *Social Movements and Networks: Relational Approaches to Collective Action*, edited by Mario Diani and Doug McAdam, 204–32. New York: Oxford University Press.

Broadbent, Jeffrey, and Brendan F. D. Barrett. 2005. "The Transformation of Social Movements and Civil Society." In *Ecological Modernization and Japan*, edited by Brendan F. D. Barrett, 66–87. London and New York: Routledge.

Chang, Kyung-Sup, Ben Fine, and Linda Weiss, eds. 2012. *Developmental Politics in Transition: the Neoliberal Era and Beyond*. New York: Palgrave Macmillan.

Cho, Soo-Gyeong. 2013. "Have Thought of Food Mileage of Your Dinner Tonight?" *Media Today*, May 5. Accessed March 2, 2014. http://images.mediatoday.co.kr/news/articleView.html?idxno=109232

Freedom House. 2011. "Freedom of the Press: South Korea." Accessed August 5, 2014. http://www.freedomhouse.org/report/freedom-press/2011/south-korea

Hadiz, Vedi R., ed. 2006. *Empire and Neoliberalism in Asia*. New York: Routledge.

Han, Jin. 2013. "Preparing *Chuseok* Dinner Table with Healthy Food." *JoongAng Ilbo*, September 10. Accessed August 5, 2014. http://article.joins.com/news/article/article.asp?total_id=12567487&cloc=olink|article|default

Hansalim. 2011. *Meaningful Daily Action*. Accessed March 2, 2014. http://eng.hansalim.or.kr/wp-content/themes/eng/download/hansalim_brochure_eng.pdf.

International Co-operative Alliance. 2013. "Co-operative Identity, Values and Principles." Accessed March 2, 2014. http://ica.coop/en/what-co-op/co-operative-identity-values-principles

Joo, Kang-Hyeon. 2006. *Dure: History of Farmers*. Paju: DeulNyeok.

Korea Cooperatives. 2014. "Korea Cooperatives." Accessed January 31, 2014. http://www.coop.go.kr/COOP/main.do.

Krueger, Rob, and Lydia Savage. 2007. "City-Regions and social Reproduction: A 'Place' for Sustainable Development?" *International Journal of Urban and Regional Research* 31 (1): 215–23.

Lee Gyu-Won. 2012. "Seongmisan ma-eul Interview Analysis." In *Seongmisan ma-eul Research Report*, 1–74. Seoul: Saram-gwa Ma-eul.

Ong, Aihwa. 2006. *Neoliberalism as Exception: Mutations in Citizenship and Sovereignty*. Durham, NC: Duke University Press.

Park, Bae-Gyoon, Richard Child Hill, and Asato Saito, eds. 2012. *Locating Neoliberalism in East Asia: Neoliberalizing Spaces in Developmental States*. West Sussex: Wiley-Blackwell.

Park, So-Hui. 2013. "Park Won-Soon, 'Within 10 Years, Aim to Increase The Number of Co-ops to 8,000." *OhmyNews*, February 13. Accessed March 15, 2014. http://www.ohmynews.com/NWS_Web/View/at_pg.aspx?CNTN_CD=A0001834110

Park, Won-Soon. 2012. "When Dreams Come True: Reflections on 'Social Economy' in Korea." *Global Asia* 7 (4): 48–52.

Rodan, Garry, and Kevin Hewison, eds. 2006. *Neoliberalism and Conflict in Asia after 9/11*. London & New York: Routledge.

Statistics Korea. 2013a. *Revenues of Big Markets in 16 Cities*. Accessed March 2, 2014. http://kosis.kr/wnsearch/totalSearch.jsp.

Statistics Korea. 2013b. "Statistics of Return to Farming." Accessed March 2, 2014. http://kosis.kr/statisticsList/statisticsList_01List.jsp?vwcd=MT_ZTITLE&parmTabId=M_0 1_01#SubCont.

The Economist. 2012. "No News is Bad News." *The Economist*, March 3. Accessed March 15, 2014. http://www.economist.com/node/21549008

World Commission on Environment and Development. 1987. *Our Common Future*. . Accessed September 23, 2014. http://www.un-documents.net/wced-ocf.htm

Yoon, Yeo-Joon. 2013. "Tax Havens and the Truth of Financial Capital." *Podcast Yoon Yeo-Joon*, May 30. Accessed October 8, 2015. http://www.podbbang.com/ch/5598.

Yue, Audrey. 2012. "We're the Gay Company, as Gay as it Gets." In *Queer Singapore*, edited by Audrey Yue and Jun Zubillaga-Pow, 197–212. Hong Kong: Hong Kong University Press.

11 Urban farming in Tokyo
Toward an urban-rural hybrid city

Toru Terada, Makoto Yokohari, and Mamoru Amemiya

Why agro-activities?

The Brooklyn Grange, situated in the middle of Brooklyn, New York, is an approximately 1-ha rooftop farm overlooking the Manhattan skyline that produces 23 tons of organic produce annually (Brooklyn Grange 2014). Meanwhile, far removed from New York, situated in Nerima ward in the Asian metropolis of Tokyo, the popularity of *Taiken Noen* (Hands-on Farming), where participants grow produce while receiving instruction from farmers, continues to increase. Urban residents grow vegetables in the 1,300 or so plots on 12 farms in Nerima Ward, comprising a combined area of approximately 5 ha (Nerima Ward 2009).

At present, such agro-activities or urban farming are increasingly being incorporated into urban lifestyles around the world (Viljoen 2005; Hou, Johnson, and Lawson 2009; Gorgolewski, Komisar, and Nasr 2011; Tracey 2011). These forms of productive gardening differ from conventional "agriculture" engaged in by farmers for the purpose of crop production on large-scale farms but entail agricultural production activities that are primarily carried out by non-farmer urban residents with emphasis not only on production but also value in terms of health, environmental conservation, and social participation. It has been pointed out that this simultaneous interest in such activities around the world is underlain by a number of universal benefits of urban farming that contribute to the resolution of various problems facing large cities (Guitart, Pickering, and Byrne 2012). For example, the social benefits of such activities include environmental education for children and young people, improved food security, revitalization of the local community, engaging the elderly as productive citizens, and crime reduction (Okvat and Zautra 2011; Bendt, Barthel, and Colding 2013). The economic benefits include revitalization of the local economy through the direct sales of produce at produce stands, the supply of affordable foods, beneficial impacts on family finances resulting from self-production, and the offering of employment opportunities (Blair, Giesecke, and Sherman 1991; Voicu and Been 2008; Ladner 2011). The ecological benefits include improvement of urban flooding (flooding due to local runoff) through the maintenance of permeable land and urban ecosystems through habitat creation, urban soil improvement through the cultivation of vacant lots, and awareness of food systems ecology (Goddard, Dougill, and Benton 2010; Aubry et al. 2012; Yadav, Duckworth, and Grewal 2012).

These agro-activities function as a common prescription for the typical ailments suffered by many cities, such as increased environmental burden resulting from excess concentration of population, weakening of the local community resulting from the concentration of individuals without any previous social ties, deterioration of the biological environment due to the concentration of man-made structures, and discrimination and social exclusion in multi-ethnic countries. We can interpret the simultaneous increase in the popularity of urban agriculture in New York, Tokyo, and many other large cities around the world as a marker of the universal appeal of such practices. At the same time, the various agro-activities that have arisen in cities around the world are often inflected by relatively unique local and national cultural, social, political, and economic concerns.

In this chapter, using urban-agriculture's polar characteristics of universality and uniqueness as key concepts, we develop a broad view of agro-activities in Japan and the urban spaces in which they take place. It might appear that local uniqueness and the culture from which it originates is something ephemeral and difficult to grasp. However, it is also something that is manifested in part in the behavior and values of the people living in that society. As such, in the first part of this chapter, we focus on the way in which urban farming in Tokyo has become associated with "classic but novel" concepts, values and practices related to work and lifestyle in Japan's modern society, concepts of play-work that can be seen as complex manifestations of both global shifts in urban living and uniquely Japanese values and lifestyles. Next, we examine how this is related to the practice of urban agro-activities in present-day Japan and thereby seek to identify the unique qualities of urban farming in Japan (Figure 11.1). In the second half of the chapter, we explore the urban spaces in which these urban agro-activities are carried out. How has modern city planning, which could be said to represent a universal model for urban space, been implemented in Japan, and what has been the consequence? In addition, what are the present-day challenges facing city planning, and how are these related to urban agro-activities? Finally, we propose a future direction for Tokyo based on agro-activities.

Intermingled work and play

Among Asian countries, Japan is an advanced post-industrial society, undergoing certain ideological shifts in relation to industrialism, environmentalism, and working and living practices. The Japanese-style employment system of the past, as a general rule, promised lifetime employment and seniority-based promotion. In return for these guarantees, employees accepted long working hours. This employment system was able to support Japan's rapid economic growth in the post–World War II period by emphasizing quantitative expansion (Kawaguchi and Ueno 2013). However, in a contemporary Japan in which people's needs have diversified and happiness is not necessarily defined solely on the basis of economic satisfaction, the erstwhile employment model under this employment system still functions but is considered a thing of the past. Within Japanese society, there is a growing emphasis on quality of life and on being able to design one's own lifestyle,

Figure 11.1 A consequence of agro-activities found in Kashiwa City, a dormitory community in Tokyo metropolitan area

Photo by Toru Terada

not as a "company man (or woman)" but rather as an "independent individual" (Japan Cabinet Office 2007; Kohsaka 2010; Workshift Solutions 2015). These new lifestyles entail greater free time made possible by flexible work arrangements such as telecommuting, discretionary work, Small Office Home Office, and work sharing that can be spent participating in family or community activities or seeking eventual self-reliance by amassing personal experience, for example, by repeatedly changing jobs and participating in overseas volunteer activities during between-job periods (Chikirin 2013; Yoneda 2013). In the context of such flexible work arrangements, it is possible for individuals to not be tied to a single company or job category but, rather, to hold several jobs simultaneously. The idea of parallel careers developed by Peter Drucker, whereby an individual engages in work other than their main job, if not to the degree of being an actual side business, has been discussed by the Japanese media and is gradually taking root in Japanese society (Yanagiuchi 2013; Social Marketing Japan 2014). While it would be a stretch to say that the majority of individuals and companies presently agree to and actually implement this style of working, we would argue that it is likely to be a driving force behind the wave of social transformation that is to come.

Let us consider this style of working from the standpoint of life-work balance. Can we really escape the Japanese-style employment system of the past simply by reducing the amount of time spent on "work" and by increasing the amount of time spent on "life"—by, for example, establishing a system of extended leave (vacation) similar to Europe and North America and maximizing time spent on "life"? The present-day Japanese social system does not presume extended leave from work. For a moment, setting aside the fact that a very radical restructuring of society would be necessary to actually implement such a system, even if an extended leave system were hypothetically to be established, it is unlikely that Japanese people, who up to this point have placed greater emphasis on the work side of the equation, could easily switch to enjoying the new life that they had gained. Is it, then, simply a matter of familiarity? Will people just get used to this new balance over time? It is probably not that simple. More fundamentally, it remains questionable whether the approach of drawing a rigorous distinction between work and life would be achievable given Japanese cultural and historical background.

Shuichi Kito, a Japanese sociologist, analyzed the livelihoods in Japanese villages that were observed prior to the rapid economic growth period and identified the existence of "play-work (*Asobi-Shigoto*)" in which livelihood and play were indivisibly intertwined (Kito 1996). Kito categorized economic activities such as rice cultivation and hunting that were performed to secure food on a daily basis as "livelihood" and cultural and playful activities as its opposite, "play". However, human activities cannot be so rigorously divided into these two categories. Rather, they can be considered play-work, in which work and play are indivisibly intertwined and which lies somewhere on the spectrum between the two extremes of livelihood and play. For example, when children collect wild plants or mushrooms or catch fish in the river, these activities comprise a substantial element of play. At the same time, insofar as the harvest or yield obtained through these activities ends up on the dinner table, they are meaningful in terms of livelihood. Similarly, rice cultivation and hunting are not exclusively economic activities. They undoubtedly comprise elements that could be classified as play—for example, ceremonial meaning. Kito argued that it is in this play-work in which livelihood and play are indivisibly intertwined that the richness of human activity can be found and that the idea of play-work should be utilized in modern society as a type of work theory (Kito 1996).

In the context of modern Japan, in which industries are starting to shrink, it can be said that new socioeconomic opportunities lie in escaping the large-scale industrial system and returning to a more balanced holistic system that incorporates a personal sense of embodied living. In a time such as the present, in which we need to escape the existing value system, play can be said to be a wellspring of the creative ability required to achieve this transformation. We would argue that play-work in which play and work are indivisibly intertwined will once again be valued as one of the new styles of working. This is the result of, on the one hand, regret regarding the fact that play and work have become antithetical concepts akin to "freedom" and "obligation" as a result of the declining sense of community and permeation of capitalism in society and, at the same time, a search and challenge to find a new path to indivisibly mix work and play in the modern context.

How then does the shift to play-work link to questions of urban agriculture? As we have suggested, a new value system regarding work aimed at nurturing "independent individuals" rather than "company men (or women)" is gradually permeating in Japanese society. As an idea aligned with these ways of thinking, in recent years in Japan, the concept of "half-farmer-half-X", developed by a Japanese writer Naoki Shiomi, has begun to receive attention. "Half-farmer-half-X" refers to a new lifestyle in which individuals engage in small-scale farming (agro-activities) while, at the same time, engaging in work (X) that represents true value to the individual (Shiomi 2003). The possibilities for X are extremely diverse, ranging from half-farmer–half-artist to half-farmer–half-NPO worker or half-farmer-half-community business owner. Meanwhile, among the various potential Xs one might embrace, the other half of one's lifestyle is based in agro-activities. Agro-activities, in this case, represent play-work that indivisibly integrates both an element of *livelihood* as an activity aimed at securing of nutrients (food) for human sustenance and an element of *play* as an activity that enables one to attain a sense of mental satisfaction by interacting with nature. Given that half of one's income is earned through X, it is not necessary to rely on "agriculture" as a predominantly economic activity, while the converse is also true. Given that some level of food can be secured through agro-activities, it is neither necessary to rely solely on X for income required for survival nor is it necessary to engage excessively in X, by working long hours and so on, exclusively for the purpose of securing life. In the context of half-farmer-half-X, agro-activities represent play-work for the purpose of attaining personal emotional satisfaction *and* serve as a foundation for and guarantee required to realize "worthwhile" work (X).

While city-based agriculture in Japan can simply appear to be recreational activities for urban residents, as we have suggested, such practices can also be read as an expression of both a new attitude toward work in present-day Japan and historical forms of play-work. Such activities are aligned with the Japanese tendency to merge opposing concepts such as labor and leisure and as such are deeply connected with Japan's unique culture. Thus, while urban farming in Japan and elsewhere can be understood in terms of a growing engagement with everyday environmentalism and lifestyle-based civic values (Lewis 2015), such practices also have a particular social, cultural, and historical resonance in the Japanese context.

Japanese urban-rural cities

Tokyo has a unique cityscape, comprising both urban and agricultural environments due to the rapid migration of the rural population to the city center and lax land-use regulation. This unique characteristic of Tokyo's population and landscape allows the development of an eco-lifestyle, such as the half-farmer-half-X, play-work hybrid. The mixed land use in Tokyo blurs the boundary between urban land and agricultural land. In fact, a more detailed look reveals that farms are peppered throughout the city (Figure 11.2). This landscape feature results in the formation of a heterogenic environment consisting of a mixture of urban and agricultural usage that does not exhibit the same kind of clear perimeter and division typically observed in Western cities, whereby the area within the perimeter is clearly urban while outer areas are clearly agricultural or rural (Yokohari et al. 2000).

What kind of process, then, led to the formation of this intermingling of city and farms? Tokyo began to expand in population in the latter half of the nineteenth century. Experiencing the end of more than 250 years of isolation and the formation

Figure 11.2 Urban fabrics intermixed with small farmlands in Nerima Ward, Tokyo.
Source: Aerial photo taken in 2012 by Geospatial Information Authority of Japan

of a new government after the fall of the *Bakufu* (Samurai feudal government), Japan rapidly adopted modern and Western policies with the aim of catching up to the Western powers. Urban centers experienced industrialization approximately 100 years behind their counterparts in Western countries. Factories began to concentrate in locations such as Tokyo harbor and river mouths with good access to transportation, and people began to flood in from rural areas to satisfy the demand of these factories for labor. During the rapid economic growth period after the end of World War II, large numbers of workers, riding the wave of capitalism, flooded into the Tokyo metropolitan area. This resulted in the exclusive concentration of the population in Tokyo and a rapid expansion of the city boundary. The surrounding farm villages, formerly the site of primary production, were overrun by the expanding city, fed by the amassing of secondary industries. These secondary industries spawned demand for service industries related to business operations and management and the like, leading to the concentration of tertiary industries. As a result, the population flowing into the city increased further, causing even greater expansion of the city. With urban planning unable to adequately prepare city infrastructure in advance of the too-rapid expansion of the city, it was extremely difficult to create a well-planned city. Although a number of large-scale new towns were established, they were insufficient to absorb the entirety of the increasing population. For this reason, urban sprawl occurred in various locations, resulting in a mixture of farm villages and disordered, small-scale development and ultimately in the creation of the landscape of intermingled city and farms typically seen in aerial photos of Tokyo suburbs.

Of course, land usage regulations such as Tokyo Greenbelt Plan and zonings by Japanese city planning act were established to limit the uncontrolled expansion of the city. However, except for the establishment of several parks in a section of the planned greenbelt area, the greenbelt project could not be implemented primarily due to a lack of funds to acquire land. This led to the need to rely primarily on regulation of private land usage and an inability to financially compensate private land owners for restricting their rights to develop their property (Yokohari et al. 2000; Watanabe et al. 2008). Similarly, zoning has not resulted in adequate control of land usage. Although land within the city has been divided into areas zoned for urbanization promotion and areas zoned for urbanization control, because the desires of farmers were respected, substantial farmland is included in areas zoned for urbanization and, due to insufficient development regulations, small-scale development has penetrated into areas zoned for urbanization control (Sorensen 2001). Today, the expansive urban sprawl in Japanese suburbs is regarded as a symbol of the failure of Japan's modern urban planning, insofar as it has been modeled after examples in Western countries (Yokohari et al. 2000).

With regard to the formation of urban space in the age of modernism, the geographer Augustin Berque commented that the uniqueness of a specific place is reduced by the universality of abstract space (Berque 1993). In the case of the Tokyo metropolitan area, although the aim was to realize the modernist model of a universal city through modern urban planning, the intermingling of city and farms can be understood as a manifestation of the union between universality and uniqueness.

From the standpoint of attempting to realize a Western-style land use regime, the intermingling of city and farms could be considered a failure of modern urban planning. However, to conceive of modern urban planning as offering universal solutions is clearly problematic. As of 2005, Japan's overall population had already begun to decline, and it is anticipated that the long-term trend is for most of the Japanese cities to become smaller (National Institute of Population and Social Security Research 2014). The destiny of cities, which up to this point had fundamentally been to expand, has changed dramatically. We have thus entered an unprecedented era in terms of the history of urban planning in Japan. If we are to face this new trend of shrinking cities head on, we must naturally, radically change our way of thinking and fundamentally revise our urban planning system. Such efforts, in fact, are already underway (Japan Society of Urban and Regional Planners 2003). The idea that clear demarcation between cities and the surrounding agricultural area is the global standard and that the achievement of such a state is the hallmark of modernization may have had currency during the period in which society was developing and cities were expanding. However, it is clear that, in the age where some cities are indeed shrinking, other alternatives are necessary. What is required is a change in our way of thinking that corresponds to societal trends, not only in terms of social factors such as style of working but also in terms of spatial factors such as land usage.

If we take the above context into consideration, it follows that we must also reevaluate the intermingling of cities and farms without prejudice. The existence of arable land near or within a city is very favorable for agro-activities. If we posit that agro-activities are a suitable lifestyle based on the new value system, then we can reevaluate the intermingling of cities and farms as being a positive circumstance for the implementation of such activities. In the same way that the antithetical concepts of play and work can be fused without contradiction in play-work, we must return to a Japanese way of thinking and consider the possibility of cities and farms coexisting without contradiction.

Revitalization of cities through agro-activities

In certain respects, the shrinking of cities may further promote mixed use of land. This is because the decline in demand for residential land accompanying the decline in population will result in the emergence of vacant lots, which, on the macro-scale, will begin in the less convenient peripheral areas of cities but, on the local scale, will occur in a disordered fashion, resulting in scattered vacant lots. In Japan, where the population is already starting to decline and the housing supply is already saturated, it is easy to imagine that, once a property becomes vacant, no new buildings will be constructed, and the property will remain vacant over the long-term. Furthermore, it is expected that the number of such vacant lots will continue to increase (Policy Research Institute for Land, Infrastructure, Transport and Tourism 2012). If such property is not used for anything and simply left abandoned, it can only contribute to a net external diseconomy and have a negative impact on the surrounding community. Detroit, which experienced an economic collapse after its population was nearly halved due to the restructuring of industry and whose abandoned lots and houses have become a hotbed of criminal activity, is a prime example of what can happen (Steinmetz 2009).

Would it not be possible to reinvent such vacant lots, which will emerge in large numbers and interspersed among urban areas, into gardens where agro-activities can be carried out? One model for the implementation of agro-activities in vacant lots is small-scale vegetable production and consumption (Grewal and Grewal 2012; Hara et al. 2013; Drake and Lawson 2014). In this model, vacant lots in a residential area would be transformed into small-scale farms, where the nearby residents would grow vegetables that they themselves would consume. In Japan, there is a concept of *Chisan-Chisho* (local production, local consumption) whereby food produced in a certain area is also consumed in that area (Kimura and Nishiyama 2007; Kurita, Yokohari, and Bolthouse 2009). In the sense that food would be produced and consumed by the same people, farming in vacant lots could be considered a "self-production, self-consumption" activity (Coyne and Knutzen 2010; Deppe 2010). In a context in which problems related to large-scale agricultural production such as pesticide residue are repeatedly taken up by media, such self-production, self-consumption also enables people to grow and consume their own produce without any worry. Furthermore, in a country such as Japan that frequently experiences natural disasters such as flooding and earthquakes, the embedding of a system in local space for producing one's own food, however small the volume may be, can be effective as a safety net when the food supply chain is temporarily interrupted due to disaster. In fact, many Tokyo residents panicked when the Great East Japan Earthquake struck on March 11, 2011, and the food supply system became temporarily paralyzed due to the excessive buying and stockpiling of foodstuffs. One reason this occurred was the anxiety stemming from the fact that the entire food supply, which serves as a basis for survival, is dependent on the monetary economy. As such, it could be argued that self-production, self-consumption would also be effective in suppressing mass panic after disasters, which is considered to be one of the greatest threats in cities.

To this end, what amount of vegetables can be expected to be produced by vacant lots that have been transformed into gardens? We attempted to generate an estimate based on Kashiwa City, Chiba Prefecture, where we have conducted long-term research. Kashiwa City is a bedroom community of Tokyo located approximately 35 kilometers from the center of Tokyo, in which the bulk of residential development occurred in the 1960s and 1970s. Total land area of the city is 114.9 km^2, and current population was 406,813 as of March 2014 (Kashiwa City 2014). Unsuccessful attempts to renew residential areas that have deteriorated since their development 40 to 50 years ago have begun to result in the emergence of abandoned houses and vacant lots (Suzuki et al. 2011). In a study we conducted, we calculated vegetable yield per unit area of land for a community agricultural farm in Chiba Prefecture (Tahara et al. 2011). Based on these results, we estimated the total vegetable production potential of the 46.4 ha of vacant lots in Kashiwa City's residential areas to be 1,815 t/yr.

What percentage of total annual vegetable consumption in Kashiwa City does this amount represent? Mean annual household vegetable consumption in Chiba Prefecture is 184.1 kg (Statistics Japan 2009). As of March 2014, the total number of households in Kashiwa City was 168,445 (Kashiwa City 2014). Based on these figures, we estimate the amount that can be potentially produced on vacant lots (1,815 t/yr) represents approximately 5.8 per cent of total vegetable consumption in Kashiwa City. This may seem like a small share; however, the goal, in the first place, is not 100 per cent self-sufficiency, and, as discussed above, there are substantial social benefits associated with self-production, self-consumption, however small the amount may be. If we consider the fact that the number of vacant lots will increase in the future as the population declines, this share may increase but certainly will not decline.

Some leading-edge practices of urban agro-activity have been seen in Kashiwa City. *Kashiniwa* (rental garden) program is a scheme operated by the city since 2010, which connects the owners of vacant lots (potential gardens) and neighborhood citizens (potential gardeners). A successful example of a *Kashiniwa* program in which a neighborhood community has successfully changed an abandoned property into a community-gathering place is *Jiyu-hiroba* (freedom-place), which comprises various vegetable gardens partitioned into small gardens for individual farmers and raised-bed type gardens for elderly gardeners and other community gardeners (Figure 11.3). With this initiative, revitalization occurred not only on the land itself but also throughout the aging neighborhood community through the restoration of social ties (Watanabe et al. 2014).

Another example is a unique garden that utilizes the pre-developed area of Kashiwa City. Urban development projects are still ongoing, albeit relatively

Figure 11.3 Revitalization of *Jiyu-hiroba* through the *Kashiniwa* program
Photo by Toru Terada and Mayumi Hosoe

slowly, in Kashiwa city even under the shadow of a shrinking economy. As such, pre-developed land in front of a station remains vacant for a long time before actual building construction starts. A private company in Kashiwa City runs the community garden named "oak farm" using such temporary vacant property in front of stations. Oak farm attracts a young generation of potential citizen farmers who have recently moved into the newly developed area. Once they become registered members of the farm through payment of a membership fee, the private company supports their exploration into agro-activities by providing tools, conveying knowledge, and giving technical advice. In this system, citizens are able to enjoy the urban agro-activity experience even they do not have any prior experience of farming (Yokohari, Amemiya, and Terada 2012).

Similar examples are increasing in recent years around Japan. Toho-Leo Co., a private company specializing in greenery, maintains rooftop gardens as rental vegetable garden for urban citizens (Toho-Leo 2015). Another example of a successful agro-activity starter project is My Farm, Inc., an entrepreneurial venture company, providing intermediate connecting services between farmers who own abandoned fields and urban citizens who want to start gardening or farming (My Farm 2015). As discussed earlier, such agro-movements have profound effects on changing the traditional values of the Japanese life-work relationship. Practitioners of the half-farmer-half-X, or play-work hybrid, are beginning to publish books that document their lifestyle, such as *Country Life in Weekends* by Miori Baba (half-farmer, half-writer); *Downshifters* by Masaru Kohsaka (half-farmer, half-Japanese bar owner); and *Sixty-Percent Annual Income and Four-Days Weekend* by Bill

Totten (Japanese citizenship holder and half-farmer, half-company president; Totten 2009; Kosaka 2010; Baba 2014). For these part-time agriculturalists, the city and its associated peri-urban areas are an essential place to maintain their "half-farmer, half-X" life. Therefore, the urban-rural mixture in cities, a unique characteristic of Tokyo's land use, once again shows its potential in providing opportunities for citizens to create unique hybrid lifestyles.

A vision of cities in Asia in the twenty-first century

As we've suggested, integrated play and work is supported by intermingled cities and farms. Cities are places of both consumption and production. There is actually a city that had already realized this future vision of Japan in which agro-activities are incorporated into society. It is Tokyo's predecessor, Edo. Edo, one of a handful of the world's megacities that had a population of more than 1 million at the beginning of the eighteenth century, was a garden city with numerous farms integrated into the city. Fujii, Yokohari, and Watanabe (2002) reconstructed the land use in Edo in the mid-nineteenth century based on historical documents and maps. They found that, at the time, a little more than 40 per cent of land in Edo was used for agriculture and that numerous farms were interspersed in the urban area radiating outward for a distance of 4 and 6 km from the Edo Castle. Local production and local consumption were thoroughly enforced, with vegetables produced on farms within the city being consumed within the city. Meanwhile, Edo maintained an outstanding sanitary environment that was unmatched by any other megacity in the world at the time, whereby human waste generated in the city was returned to the farms. Describing it in modern terms, Edo was a smart city with relatively little environmental burden and high-quality amenities. The coexistence of city and farms was a manifestation of Edo's advanced environment. In Edo, cut off from the rest of the world as a result of Japan's policy of isolation and to which the modern concept of work based in the industrial revolution was not introduced, coupled with the close proximity of places of residence and places of work, it is easy to imagine that play and work were indivisibly integrated.

However, no matter how wonderful Edo's ideology was, we who live in the twenty-first century cannot return to the pre-modern era. If we understand the city as we see it today as comprising multiple layers—starting with a foundation of the natural environment including the terrain, water system, and vegetation, superimposed by the city of Edo, which in turn is superimposed by the city of Tokyo—we should not take the reactionary approach of denying the Tokyo layer and seeking to return to the Edo layer. Rather, we should recognize and accept all of these layers and develop a new vision for the city beyond today.

With the shrinking of the city, we begin to see the various layers of the city with greater clarity, including deeper layers that have, up to this point, been overpowered by the modern metropolis of Tokyo. What is beginning to emerge is a hybrid of these various layers, manifested in the form of intermingled city and farms and agro-activities. It is in such hybrids that fuse both universality and uniqueness without contradiction that we see the greatest potential for a new vision of Asian cities in the twenty-first century.

Acknowledgments

The authors gratefully acknowledge financial support of the Grants-in-Aid for Scientific Research (Project number 247800 and 25292212) provided by the Japan Society for the Promotion of Sciences. We also thank Joanne Knew for her invaluable help and Tania Lewis for providing helpful comments and suggestions.

References

Aubry, Christine, Josélyne Ramamonjisoa, Marie-Hélène Dabat, Jacqueline Rakotoarisoa, Josette Rakotondraibe, and Lilla Rabeharisoa. 2012: "Urban Agriculture and Land Use in Cities: An Approach with the Multi-Functionality and Sustainability Concepts in the Case of Antananarivo (Madagascar)." *Land Use Policy* 29 (2): 429–39.

Baba, Miori. 2014. *Country Life in Weekends* (Shumatu ha inaka gurashi). Tokyo, Japan: Diamond, Inc.

Bendt, Pim, Stephan Barthel, and Johan Colding. 2013. "Civic Greening and Environmental Learning in Public-Access Community Gardens in Berlin." *Landscape and Urban Planning* 109 (1): 18–30.

Berque, Augustin. 1993. *Cosmology of the City—Japan, the United States and Europe City Comparison* (Toshi no kosmorogi niche beioutoshihikaku). Tokyo, Japan: Codansha Ltd.

Blair, Dorothy, Carol C. Giesecke, and Sandra Sherman. 1991. "A Dietary, Social and Economic Evaluation of the Philadelphia Urban Gardening Project." *Journal of Nutrition Education* 23 (4): 161–67.

Brooklyn Grange. 2014. "About". Accessed March 28, 2014. http://brooklyngrangefarm.com/about/

Chikirin. 2013. "Let's Think Working Style of the Future" (Mirai no hatarakikata wo kangaeyou). Tokyo, Japan: Bungeishunju Ltd.

Coyne, Kelly, and Erik Knutzen. 2010. *The Urban Homestead: Your Guide to Self-Sufficient Living in the Heart of the City*. Port Townsend: Process Media.

Deppe, Carol. 2010. *The Resilient Gardener: Food Production and Self-Resilience in Uncertain Times*. White River Junction, VT: Chelsea Green Publishing.

Drake, Luke, and Laura J. Lawson. 2014. "Validating Verdancy or Vacancy? The Relationship of Community Gardens and Vacant Lands in the U.S." *Cities* 40: 133–42.

Fujii, Minami, Makoto Yokohari, and Takashi Watanabe. 2002. "Identification of the Distribution Pattern of Farmlands in Edo." *City Planning Review Special Issue* 37: 931–36.

Goddard, Mark A., Andrew J. Dougill, and Tim G. Benton. 2010. "Scaling up from Gardens: Biodiversity Conservation in Urban Environments." *Trends in Ecology and Evolution* 25 (2): 90–8.

Gorgolewski, Mark, June Komisar, and Joe Nasr. 2011. *Carrot City: Creating Places for Urban Agriculture*. New York: The Monacelli Press.

Grewal, Sharanbir S., and Parwinder S. Grewal. 2012: "Can Cities Become Self-Reliant in Food?" *Cities* 29 (1): 1–11.

Guitart, Daniela, Catherine Pickering, and Jason Byrne. 2012. "Past Results and Future Directions in Urban Community Gardens Research." *Urban Forestry and Urban Greening* 11 (4): 364–73.

Hara, Yuji, Akinobu Murakami, Kazuaki Tsuchiya, Armando M. Palijon, and Makoto Yokohari. 2013. "A Quantitative Assessment of Vegetable Farming on Vacant Lots in

an Urban Fringe Area in Metro Manila: Can It Sustain Long-Term Local Vegetable Demand?" *Applied Geography* 41: 195–206.
Hou, Jeffrey, Julie Johnson, and Laura Lawson. 2009. *Greening Cities Growing Communities: Learning from Seattle's Urban Community Gardens*. Seattle, WA: University of Washington Press.
Japan Cabinet Office. 2007. "Changes in Individual Working Style and Values for Work" (Kojin no shokubaniokeruhatarakikatayakinrounitaisuruishiki no henka). *White Paper on National Lifestyle, 2007*. Accessed April 2, 2014. http://www.caa.go.jp/seikatsu/whitepaper/h19/10_pdf/01_honpen/pdf/07sh_0302_2.pdf.
Japan Society of Urban and Regional Planners. 2003. *New Land-use Strategy on Urban-Rural Areas in Japan* (Toshinouson no atarashiitochiriyousenryaku). Kyoto, Japan: GakugeiShuppan-Sha.
Kashiwa City. 2014. "Population Statistics." Accessed April 10, 2014. http://www.city.kashiwa.lg.jp/soshiki/020800/p000018.html.
Kawaguchi, Daiji, and Yuko Ueno. 2013. "Declining Long-Term Employment in Japan." *Journal of the Japanese and International Economies* 28: 19–36.
Kimura, Aya Hirata, and Mima Nishiyama. 2007. "The Chisan-Chisho Movement: Japanese Local Food Movement and its Challenges." *Agriculture and Human Values* 25 (1): 49–64.
Kito, Shuichi. 1996. *Rethinking Nature Protection: Environmental Ethics and Network* (Shizenhogo wo toinaosukankyourinri to nettowaku). Tokyo, Japan: Chikuma Shobo Publishers.
Kosaka, Masaru. 2010. *Life in Slowing Down: Downshifters* (Gensoku shite ikiru: Daunshihutazu). Tokyo: Gentosha.
Kurita, Hideharu, Makoto Yokohari, and Jay Bolthouse. 2009. "The Potential of Intra-Regional Supply and Demand of Agricultural Products in an Urban Fringe Area: A Case Study of Kanto Plain, Japan." *Geografisk Tidsskrift–Danish Journal of Geography* 109 (2): 147–59.
Ladner, Peter. 2011. *The Urban Food Revolution: Changing the Way We Feed Cities*. Vancouver, British Columbia: New Society Publishers.
Lewis, Tania. 2015. "'One City Block at a Time': Researching and Cultivating Green Transformations." *International Journal of Cultural Studies* 18 (3): 347–63.
My Farm. 2015. "Hands-on Garden my Farm." Accessed February 2, 2015 http://myfarmer.jp/.
National Institute of Population and Social Security Research. 2014. "Population Statistics." Accessed on April 6, 2014. http://www.ipss.go.jp/p-info/e/Population%20%20Statistics.asp.
Nerima Ward. 2009. "Nerima community building plan utilizing agriculture and farmlands" (Nerima-kuToshinougyounouchi wo ikashitamachidukuripuran). Accessed March 28, 2014. http://www.sangyo-rodo.metro.tokyo.jp/norin/nogyo/machidukuri/2modelplan/01nerima-plan.pdf.
Okvat, Heather A, and Alex J. Zautra. 2011. "Community Gardening: A Parsimonious Path to Individual, Community, and Environmental Resilience." *American Journal of Community Psychology* 47 (3-4): 374–87.
Policy Research Institute for Land, Infrastructure, Transport and Tourism. 2012. "Current Status of Open Spaces and its Potential Utilization Schemes." Accessed April 8, 2014. http://www.mlit.go.jp/pri/houkoku/gaiyou/syousai/pdf/os02.pdf.
Shiomi, Naoki. 2003. *Half-Famer Half-X as a Way of Life* (hannouhanekkusutoiuikikata). Tokyo, Japan: Sony Magazines.

Social Marketing Japan. 2014. "Monju—A Web Site for Supporting Parallel Carrier Workers." Accessed April 2, 2014. http://monju.in/.

Sorensen, André. 2001. "Building Suburbs in Japan: Continuous Unplanned Change on the Urban Fringe." *The Town Planning Review* 72 (3): 247–73.

Statistics Japan. 2009. "Household Expenditure Survey." Accessed April 10, 2014. http://www.stat.go.jp/data/kakei/5.htm.

Steinmetz, George. 2009. "Detroit: A Tale of Two Crises." *Environment and Planning D: Society and Space* 27 (5): 761–70.

Suzuki, Kohei, Mamoru Amemiya, Toru Terada, and Makoto Yokohari. 2011. "Distribution of Vacant Lots in a Tokyo Suburb and its Restoration by Gardening Activities." *Research Abstracts on Spatial Information Science CSIS DAYS 2011*, 20.

Tahara, Shinichi, Makoto Yokohari, Hideharu Kurita, and Toru Terada. 2011. "A Quantitative Assessment of Agricultural Production from Allotment Gardens." *Journal of the Japanese Institute of Landscape Architecture* 74 (5): 685–88.

Toho-Leo. 2015. "Machinaka-Saien (Garden in City)". Viewed on February 2, 2014. http://www.machinaka-saien.jp/.

Totten, Bill. 2009. *Sixty-Percent Annual Income and Four-Days Weekend* (Nenshu rokuwaridemo shukyu yokka toiu ikikata). Tokyo, Japan: Shogakukan Inc.

Tracey, David. 2011. *Urban Agriculture: Ideas and Designs for the New Food Revolution*. Vancouver, British Columbia: New Society Publishers.

Viljoen, André, ed. 2005. *CPULs: Continuous Productive Urban Landscapes*. Oxford, UK: Architectural Press.

Voicu, Ioan, and Vicki Been. 2008: "The Effect of Community Gardens on Neighboring Property Values." *Real Estate Economics* 36 (2): 241–83.

Watanabe, Takashi, Marco Amati, Kenya Endo, and Makoto Yokohari. 2008. "The Abandonment of Tokyo's Green Belt and the Search for New Discourse of Preservation In Tokyo's Suburbs." In *Urban Green Belts in the Twenty-First Century*, edited by Marco Amati, 21–36. Farnham, UK: Ashgate.

Watanabe, Yosuke, Mariko Miyamoto, Mamoru Amemiya, Toru Terada, and Makoto Yokohari. 2014. "Development Process of Publicness of a Community Garden Established by the *Kashiniwa* Program." *Journal of the Japanese Institute of Landscape Architecture* 77 (5): 713–18.

Workshift Solutions 2015. "About Workshift." Accessed February 10, 2015. http://workshift-sol.co.jp/en/.

Yadav, Priyanka, Kathy Duckworth, and Parwinder S. Grewal. 2012. "Habitat Structure Influences below Ground Biocontrol Services: A Comparison between Urban Gardens and Vacant Lots." *Landscape and Urban Planning* 104 (2): 238–44.

Yanagiuchi, Keiji. 2013. *Second Name Card to Alter our Life* (Jinseigakawarunimaime no meishi).Tokyo, Japan: Crossmedia Publishing.

Yokohari, Makoto, Kazuhiko Takeuchi, Takashi Watanabe, and Shigehiro Yokota. 2000. "Beyond Greenbelts and Zoning: A New Planning Concept for the Environment of Asian Mega-Cities." *Landscape and Urban Planning* 47 (3–4): 159–71.

Yokohari, Makoto, Mamoru Amemiya, and Toru Terada. 2012. "Concept of 'Urban Agro-Activities' for Urban Sustainability." *The Japanese Journal of Real Estate Sciences*. 26 (3): 78–84.

Yoneda, Tomohiko. 2013. *Life Design in the Era of Ours* (Bokura no jidai no raifudezain). Tokyo: Diamond, Inc.

12 Farming against real estate dominance

The Ma Shi Po community farm in Hong Kong

Ka-ming Wu

Busy and crowded streets, hundreds of people cramming together at crossroads, glass-windowed skyscrapers lined up along harbor coastlines—these are some of the images that best capture the city landscape of Hong Kong. Hong Kong is one of the world's most densely populated cities, with more than 7 million people living in a total area of only about 1,100 square kilometers. Rapid economic growth since 1970 has earned the city the honor of being one of Asia's "four little dragons". But if developmental success and urban prosperity are key highlights of recent history, a very different set of concerns are raised when one considers today's Hong Kong, 15 years after its handover to China. This chapter focuses on the case of Ma Shi Po, a soon-to-be demolished village in northeastern Hong Kong, and the social activism of its residents and advocates in order to examine how global environmental and agricultural concerns have brought about new understandings of farming, urban planning and community in Hong Kong today.

This chapter contributes to ongoing debates about global environmental struggles and communal garden movements as they relate to food security, food safety, and alternative food networks (Armstrong 2000; Evers and Hodgson 2011; Firth, Maye, and Pearson 2011); ecological citizenship (Baker 2004; Seyfang 2006); and food democracy in global urban contexts (Hassanein 2003). The article argues that rural activism in Hong Kong is part of a global environmental movement to support and sustain community gardens and motivates critical reflection on issues such as food production and consumption, urban planning, and development. But I will also highlight how this case has been crucial in the last few years in shaping new public debates and new meanings of social and environmental activisms in Hong Kong.

In the last few decades, local environmental groups in Hong Kong have largely been focused on the technical and lifestyle aspects of environmental issues, such as advocacy for using fewer plastic bags and eating vegetarian food, and conducting professional environmental assessments for government projects. Green groups, some of them funded by major real estate corporations in Hong Kong, have cut off their campaigns from critique of developmentalism and from engaging with major socio-political issues in the city. The result is that the green movement has focused on concerns of middle-class lifestyle consumption, sometimes even running the risk of providing technical knowledge for the justification of more development (Man 2014). The Ma Shi Po rural activism has radically redefined the meaning of local green activism by linking environmental concerns directly to the city's major developmental contradictions, namely the dominance of land developing interests in the making of Hong Kong's political economy and the everyday lives of citizens. This chapter shows how the case of rurally based Ma Shi Po activism has made it possible for a very different kind of Hong Kong to be imagined—from a colonial space solely occupied with land developer–led economic growth to one that stresses family roots, community development, and urban agriculture. This chapter draws on my visits, from 2011 onward, to the Ma Shi Po community and on interviews with the activists and participants in its farming course, baking class, and farm tours. It also draws on extensive media reports on Ma Shi Po from 2012 to 2014 to examine the way the movement is represented and evaluated.

Ma Shi Po: A remaining germ of farming in the city

The city of Hong Kong is mainly composed of three major areas: the Hong Kong Island, the Kowloon Peninsula, and the New Territories, which include many outlying islands. Ma Shi Po village is located in Fanling, the northeastern part of the New Territories, close to the Hong Kong–China border. The existing literature on the New Territories is largely anthropological and investigates its ancient village traditions, rites and rituals, and lineage politics (Watson and Watson 2004). However, the New Territories is no longer simply an area of rural villages and quiet farmland as, in the last two decades, the urban sprawl of Hong Kong Island and the Kowloon Peninsula has spread northward. New towns, big malls, and a booming population are becoming common features of some parts of the New Territories. Farmlands still remain, but these are also undergoing radical changes. Big land developers have been buying up thousands of hectares of farmlands in the New Territories from the families of early settlers who came to the region a few hundred years ago. These early settlers' indigenous identity and landownership, however, need to be understood in the historical context of Britain's wars with China over trading ports in the South China Sea. The British seized Hong Kong Island in the first Opium war in 1842 and the Kowloon Peninsula in 1860 and "leased" the New Territories in 1898. In order to pacify the Chinese, the British government acknowledged the traditional rights and customs of those inhabitants who settled in "the New Territories" before 1898 but not those who came later and those outside of it. "Indigenous inhabitants" of Hong Kong is, therefore, a special category of British colonialism in the region as it endorses land rights for only a limited group of people with ancestors in the New Territories and only before 1898. This British legacy not only creates much conflict among local inhabitants who settle in Hong Kong at different times and places; it also becomes a major source of contention as it complicates the plans of real estate developers. Indeed, real estate developers began buying farmlands directly from "indigenous landowners" when it was cheap in the 1990s and before the government was able to implement planning regulations. In the process, developers turned the farmland they bought into car parks and dump sites or simply fenced up areas in order to change the land use from agricultural to non-agricultural.

The experience of Ma Shi Po village is representative of the broader trend of vanishing farmland in the New Territories. As a result of aggressive acquisitions by real estate developers, 80 per cent of farmland in Ma Shi Po has been sold. Henderson Real Estate, one of the four major land developers in Hong Kong, is now the largest landowner in Ma Shi Po village. About half of Ma Shi Po's total area was turned into a middle-class residential area 16 years ago. Today, one enters Ma Shi Po via a newly constructed road for vehicles. South of this road are two middle-class residential developments that each have 20 blocks of apartment buildings that are 30 stories high, and are associated with club houses, swimming pools, shopping malls, and so on. North of this road one sees another world: a vast expanse of green farmland.

In July 2013, the Hong Kong government announced the "Northeastern Development Plan," which is a blueprint for a new satellite city in the New Territories. The plan claims to provide many apartments that would help to meet a serious housing shortage and would notably supply public housing that could accommodate 1,700 members of the lower working class. The plan covers 28 hectares of farmland and six villages, including Ma Shi Po village, which would affect about 1,000 residents. Like many of the remaining farming villages in the New Territories, Ma Shi Po's farmlands are not worked by "indigenous inhabitants" but by non-indigenous inhabitants who came to Hong Kong in the 1950s after World War II and could only rent farmland to survive. The government has promised to move the affected residents, mostly non-indigenous and elderly inhabitants, to public housing, with some compensation for demolishing their housing structures. Indigenous inhabitants who are landowners enthusiastically support the plan as they will benefit through the land compensation deal (948 HKD/sq ft for farmland and 1,878 HKD/sq ft for residential areas). By contrast, non-indigenous residents, although offered public housing as compensation, did not want to see their farmland and spacious housing structures demolished. Many also did not want to move to a public housing estate, which would mean living in a small apartment in a high rise with no green environment and little opportunity of maintaining their crops and agricultural income. And since most affected residents were tenants, the government did not include them in the consultation process and notified them only recently of the demolition plan. Many of them were unhappy with the fact that the government plan did not take tenants' rights and interests into consideration.

Land developers, who have acquired much of the unused farmland in the area, have waited for years for this official development blueprint. Inside Ma Shi Po, they have fenced up the acquired land with plastic ribbons and erected signs warning off trespassers. The few patches of still-active farmland can be found only alongside abandoned pastures and empty houses. While the village once had a population of about 700 people, the majority of the original Ma Shi Po residents have moved out, and only 10 households now remain. Among these 10 households, only five are professional farmers who continue to struggle to grow and sell vegetables. In short, without a campaign against the development plan, Ma Shi Po would have disappeared from the map with little fuss.

In 2010, a small group of activists decided to do something, and they founded the "Ma Shi Po Community Farm" (also called the Ma Po Po Community Farm). With a stated goal of "No Moving and No Demolition," they initiated a series of campaigns to galvanize social and media attention for tenant farmers who want to keep their farmland and farming livelihoods. One major activist, Becky Au, whose parents are tenant farmers of Ma Shi Po, and Choi Kai Kai, a college graduate with a geography degree, are the foremost spokespersons of the campaign. In the following sections, I delineate three major strategies that have been adopted by the rural activists of Ma Shi Po: special farm tours, rights-based nature workshops, and a permaculture farming workshop. I show how these strategies have successfully engaged citizens, captured media attention, and changed public opinions. Using media reports of the Ma Shi Po Community Farm along with interviews conducted with activists and participants, I show how this new form of rural activism has challenged the established values of developmentalism and the almost exclusively urban orientation of Hong Kong. I argue that the campaign has for the first time made visible the importance of urban farming in the city and linked the issue to real estate dominance, regional autonomy, local history, and community building and the identity politics of post-1997 Hong Kong.

Special Farm Tours: Learning about the withering of agriculture in Hong Kong

The barb wire is done by Henderson. The land developer is acquiring land in the area. They send farmers away and demolish many housing structures. They turn farmland into land that is full of weeds. Uncle J thinks it is a waste of land and uses it for sheep grazing. The land developer, however, would come and check the land and drive the sheep away. The forceful removal of villagers happens here every day. [said Choi Kai Kai, tour guide of Ma Po Po Community Farm]

(Law On Kei 2013)

The struggle for preserving Ma Shi Po village did not start with the angry pitching of farmers against land developers or the government. Quite the opposite: The Ma Shi Po activists have from the very beginning framed their campaign with a much broader purpose—to promote the importance of having farmland in the city. In this section, I show how the Ma Shi Po campaign was initially introduced to the general public through farm tours and a farmer's market. First, the Ma Po Po activists persuaded Becky Au's parents (who are tenant farmers), to switch to farming without using chemical fertilizers and to sell directly to retail customers rather than to a wholesale vegetable market. Becky's brother quit his job as an office worker and began work on the farm in order to increase crop production. Their understanding of organic farming does not include a plan to achieve full organic certification but is rather more practically about replacing chemical fertilizer with organic fertilizer and using netting against pests.[1] The idea of switching to organic farming is related to their concern for farming as a community—and an environmentally friendly practice, a point that I will more fully develop in later sections. In addition to Becky's parents, the activists also recruited full-time farmers to work on land they rented from neighboring tenants. Starting from 2010, they have held a regular weekend farmer's market, which first catered to local middle-class families in the New Territories but now also attracts all kinds of visitors. The Ma Shi Po campaign also allied with nearby farmers in order to promote locally grown vegetables even though those farmers do not grow organically.

The Ma Shi Po farm tour is unconventional in the sense that visitors see not only nice green farms and fruit trees but also find out about how major land developers have acquired land in northeastern New Territories and how they have turned productive farmland into abandoned spaces. During the tour, the tour guide shows visitors the many patches of abandoned land filled with weeds alongside still active farmland that is teeming with colorful vegetables. The quotation that opened this section is part of a regular narrative in the guided farm tour of Ma Po Po, which highlights the deteriorating farming conditions and the brutal evictions happening in the region. At the same time, the tour guide emphasizes the benefits of having a farm next to urban neighborhoods, noting that such proximity helps recycle food waste such as soy bean curb residue and fish intestine from the nearby wet market, enables the transformation of food waste into useful fertilizer, provides urban households easy access to the producers of their vegetables, and rejuvenates traditional market spaces. At the conclusion of the tour, visitors are reminded of cases of unsafe food imported from across the China border, such as vegetables with harmful pesticide residue and chickens with flu virus, and hence the importance of having community-supported agriculture both in urban neighborhoods and within the larger Hong Kong area.

Today, the Ma Shi Po farm tours regularly attract around 50 people every other weekend. Urbanites are fascinated to see a farm right next to an urban neighborhood and just a short distance from the train station. But perhaps the biggest impression one gets at the end of the tour is that farming is now seriously threatened by real estate development in Hong Kong. Mrs. Chan, a first-time visitor who went with her family said,

> We love the countryside a lot. It is much better than going to a shopping mall. We learned about this tour activity through Facebook. We have never been to a rural village and farming fields. We really want our kids to see how a farmer works and to know where our food is from.

She felt very regretful, however, when told that the farm would soon disappear with the implementation of the Northeastern Development Plan (Law Wai Yee 2013).

With increasing numbers of visitors and customers, the Ma Shi Po campaign has achieved massive success in attracting public attention. Middle-class families have started to spend weekend holidays there, and schools organize educational tours to the farm. Middle-class housewives concerned with food safety drive to Ma Shi Po to buy organic vegetables. The farmer's market in Fanling, the New Territories, has also begun to attract interest. In 2013, a major Hong Kong newspaper, *Ming Pao*, promoted the farm with the following editorial:

On Sunday morning, the Ma Shi Po Community farm is already crowded with visitors. There are homemade jams, fresh vegetables, handmade bread fresh from the oven, free film screenings and free herbal tea. The vendors and the local customers have lots of chitchats. Ma Shi Po Community Farm is a small place but full of the scent of people. It meets here on the second and the forth Sunday every month

(Lee Pui Man 2013)

Positive media coverage of the community farm such as the above is ubiquitous and usually appears in the leisure/travel sections of newspapers or magazines in Hong Kong. During the summer holidays of 2013, a lifestyle magazine even recommended the Ma Shi Po Community farm as a top outdoor choice for kids.

Cultivating lifestyle consumers' civic engagement: Bread-making workshop

Today Ma Shi Po village shares the same fate the Convent Institute had ten years ago. Both are threatened by the forces of urban development.

(Chan Chun Kit 2010).

The Ma Shi Po campaign is not only good at attracting visitors, it is also good at engaging them and making them understand the goals of rural activism. Shortly after the farm's opening, the activists organized several key workshops: bread making, soap making, and ecological night walks. These workshops have in the last few years attracted hundreds of people who initially had no interest in matters related to farming in the New Territories. Through their fondness for handmade or natural products and associated lifestyles, they are pulled into the campaign and get to learn about social issues such as food safety, alternative food networks, and the concept of rural-urban coexistence. I joined one of the farm's bread-baking workshops in 2011, together with 30 people who learned about it through Facebook and paid 200 HKD per person for the class. That day, the class members ranged from middle-class families and high school girls to housewives. First, the organizer put four to five of us at a table and provided each table with a basin, roller, and sifter. Next, the instructor, Bella Yip, another leading Ma Shi Po activist, started the class by introducing the uniqueness of wild yeast, its fermentation process, and how it adds an authentic and natural flavor to bread. We also learned of the fact that most commercially made bread is made with artificial flavors, chemical catalysts, and preservatives for a longer shelf life. Then the class started the steps of sifting, mixing, rolling, and the rest. While the dough was baking in the six big ovens, the activists gave the class a free tour of the Ma Shi Po Community Farm. At the end of the workshop, the participants not only got to taste the freshly baked bread but we also got a small gift: a small piece of wild yeast. Bella Yip told the class the unique history of the wild yeast, a story later covered by many magazines in Hong Kong.

Farming against real estate dominance 175

I [Bella Yip] went to Melbourne, Australia to take a short course on environmental protection and ran into a baking institute called The Convent. The Convent was built in 1805 and has been using an ancient oven for a hundred years. Ten years ago, the institute became a target of urban redevelopment. Local residents joined hands to petition against the plan and started a court case, which lasted for seven years. The residents eventually won [the case] at court and were able to keep the ancient architecture. The wild yeast used in this baking course was originally from the Convent
(Chan Chun Kit 2010, pp. 108–11)

The class was thrilled to keep this special gift—the 10-year-old wild yeast from the successfully preserved Convent and now kept in Ma Shi Po. Bella taught us how to "feed" the wild yeast by adding flour and water every week, suggesting that we pass it on to more people when it grows too big. She said before saying goodbye, "The wild yeast is like a seed. I hope you can spread it around as much as you can."

The story of the yeast, the handmade bread, and the free farm tour together make an unconventional baking class. It is not so much about bread making. Instead, it highlights the benefits of and the intersections between natural food, a healthy lifestyle, and the need to fight for them as rights. The class goes beyond satisfying the tastes of middle-class organic food lovers. It critiques urban, processed food products and the modern consumer lifestyle more broadly. Indeed, what many take away from the workshop is the feeling that they did not just finish a baking class but rather had a day of learning about local farming in Hong Kong and developing an understanding of the importance that everyone have access to affordable natural food. I quote the following from an interview with a Ma Shi Po frequent visitor that appeared in a newspaper:

I know that the land developers are acquiring their land. My kid Elaine is too young to understand what is happening. The way out is to take her to the farm more often and take more pictures. I will show her the pictures when she is grown up and let her understand the rural changes
(Ng Wing Sheung 2013)

Farm tours, organic markets, natural workshops, cooking classes, and insect watching sessions are not new attractions in the New Territories. Commercial farms and business entities have similar activities to cater to local, well-off, and educated customers as a cultural experience or leisure activity. The Ma Shi Po farmer's market and the workshop strategy similarly fit into the global middle-class demand for "cultural consumption," in which the consumption of natural products or organic food is now attached with new ethics and values of social responsibility and green lifestyle. Critics might see cultural or ethical consumption as purely a more intensive commodification and smart marketing in global capitalist modernity that finds its niche among a growing urban class of "bourgeois bohemians." Žižek, for instance, criticizes cultural and ethical consumption as providing alternative "social distinctions" for the urban middle class, enabling them to gain pleasure from the feeling of belonging to an "inequality-reducing" movement of some kind (Žižek 2014). Ethical consumption might also reinforce an apolitical doctrine of personal responsibility, an ethos that fits well with neoliberal trends of displacing responsibility from governments to individuals (Miller 2007; Lewis 2008).

But the Ma Shi Po campaign goes beyond trying to simply get visitors and customers to feel good through consuming cool organic products. Its tours and classes, rather, enjoin people to reflect on existing modes of urban development and, more particularly, real estate dominance in Hong Kong. Real estate dominance is a prominent political and economic issue in the city as there was no law against monopoly until 2014. Four big developer conglomerates dominate not only in the real estate sector (such as middle-class housing estates, shopping malls, and office buildings) but also in trade and finance as well as in local retail businesses (such as supermarkets, pharmacies, restaurants, and food and drinks businesses) in Hong Kong. These developer conglomerates also control major utility and public service companies in the city, including buses and ferries, telecommunications, power and gas, and cargo logistics. The acquisition of these utility and public service companies has allowed the developer conglomerates to take over an incredible amount of land resource and land holdings at cheap prices without having to compete with other developers in land auctions (Poon 2010, pp. 20–1, and 76–7).[2] No wonder there is a popular saying in Hong Kong that the city is not ruled by the Hong Kong government but by a few business tycoons. Such political economic arrangements have made the few developer conglomerates in the city become the richest companies and families in the world at the expense of a fairer and more equitable Hong Kong society. The monopolized economy also breeds collusion between political and business actors, and public and social policies tilted toward corporate interests (Poon 2010; Goodstadt 2005, 2013).

In the context of such serious real estate dominance, Ma Shi Po's advocacy to preserve urban farming in the New Territories is therefore more than just about supplying organic produce and natural food; it is also about resisting the corporate power that is eating up every inch of life in the city. The Ma Shi Po campaign deploys popular consumption practices to help participants reflect on the political economy of Hong Kong and explore the potential of a "consumer-based mode of political action" (Barnett et al 2005; Lewis 2008). They invite customers to think about the value of having local farms in Hong Kong and connect their love for natural lifestyle to both family needs as well as public interests. In short, one major success of the Ma Shi Po campaign is its ability to combine consumption practices with a citizen concern for the issue of land planning in Hong Kong, thus bringing local politics into the picture. Consuming locally grown produce is, therefore, not just part of an alternative lifestyle; it also helps to revive traditional farming neighborhoods and to generate new forms of social activism and engagement (Lewis 2008).

Permaculture workshop: Cultivating a new Hong Kong community

The Ma Shi Po campaign has a third level of sophistication: the permaculture workshop. If the farmer's market and baking workshop appeal to middle-class lifestyle consumers and natural food lovers, the permaculture workshop targets more hardy learners who are willing to endure sun, sweat, and labor-intensive work. Composed of nine classes, each lasting for 3 hours, the permaculture workshop is different from conventional weekend farmers' courses. Ma Shi Po's permaculture workshop is an in-depth engagement with the concept and methods of permanent agriculture beyond growing organic produce on the weekends. The concept of permaculture stresses the philosophy of working with the natural landscape and existing ecosystem while providing food for humans. It advocates the preservation of biodiversity, picking instead of killing bugs, practicing natural composting, and adopting alternate farming (or leaving land fallow) in order to enrich the nutrients in productive land and utilize the least amount of resources for crop production. In Ma Shi Po, permaculture is further emphasized as a practice that connects urban communities to the rural while also reducing municipal waste. Most important, the course aims to equip participants to become professional farmers by linking them to market demands. The instructor, "T.V.", a veteran farmer with an English literature degree and a leading Ma Shi Po activist, reaches out to the food network on behalf of his students so that they can eventually farm to supply for restaurants. In short, the permaculture workshop is serious about nurturing committed individuals to become full-time and part-time farmers.

In my several encounters with T.V., however, it was clear his goal was to do more than convert a small number of people into professional farmers. In public lectures, T.V. has presented his view that farming is a political matter in Hong Kong because it involves negotiating with key stakeholders on issues of land planning, including the government, land developers, and indigenous residents. In the New Territories, these powerful stakeholders are more interested in turning farmland into sites of development and profit. Ma Shi Po's campaign for preserving farmland is, therefore, highly political because it would adversely affect these stakeholders' interests. But T.V. believes it crucial for all global cities to have urban farming for the purposes of long-term sustainable development. In a newspaper interview, he articulated his thoughts clearly:

> The success of cities in mainland China is not just evaluated by their real estate development, but also by their self-sufficiency rate in terms of food provision. Why does Hong Kong not need it? It is true that Hong Kong is small but Singapore is even smaller and still keeps a higher self-sufficiency rate on food supply. How important is agriculture in Hong Kong? The Hong Kong government does not have the guts to face the issue! Hong Kong is now losing the resourceful New Territories without thinking about agriculture, rural villages, farmers and their relationships with Hong Kong's sustainable development
>
> (Lui Yek 2013)

My interviews with four students of T.V's permaculture workshop also reveal their broader concern with political and social matters that go beyond leisurely weekend farming. One of them, Ah Tak, told me,

I am a member of the 'Northeastern New Territories Concern Group' and I joined this course to improve my understanding of the region's future development.[3] I grew up in the area and know that flooding has become more frequent in the area as the amount of available farmland gradually decreases. This farming course gathers a group of people who are both interested in farming as a weekend activity and in the region's long term development. We all think that expanding farmland is in the best interests of the region.

Another student, Evelyn, is a graphic designer. She told me that the class has taught her how urban life has become segregated from farming. In the beginning, she just wanted to have some fun on the weekend, but she was quickly affected by the activism of the Ma Shi Po farm. Having completed both the preliminary and intermediate courses, Evelyn wanted to integrate farming practices into part of her daily urban work life. She told me how she fought with her office building management to allow her to put large foam boxes of soil on the building rooftop and eventually won the right to practice organic farming in her everyday work life. In recent years, rooftop farming has become a more popular communal activity and an emerging business in Hong Kong.

Similarly, Mr. Tsang, a university professor, also one of the Ma Shi Po trained farmers, believes that it is important to think about farming not as a hobby in post-industrial society but a crucial part of contemporary urban life. In a magazine interview, he told the reporter,

> Farming is not just about growing crops, but it is about how one lives. Many young people today have never experienced cooking, not to say growing crops. The better-offs have domestic helpers serving food for them at home. Those in lower class families have a lot of fast food or do take away. If you can cook something you grow, it will take you to a new level of life satisfaction
> (Lui Yek 2013)

After 2 years of taking Ma Po Po's permaculture workshop, Mr. Tsang set up another organic farm in the New Territories to promote sustainable agriculture.

The social impact of Ma Shi Po continues to grow. In 2014, Mr. Chu, a high school teacher, set up what he calls the "Rural Soil Society" after taking the permaculture course and has since recruited members ranging from school teachers to artists. The society not only offers organic farming classes but also organizes students to gather oral histories from elderly villagers in the New Territories in order to put together a folk record of rural change in the area. Mr. Chu noted in a magazine interview,

> Our members help collect tea leaves and coffee residue from cafes in Shek Wu market every week and put them into our farm. Our farm helps reduce community waste and provide people with fresh organic produce. It is a win-win situation. Think about this: How can a community without farms stay healthy and beautiful?
> (Green Life 2013)

While Ma Shi Po has encouraged a few young people to become professional farmers, to date not many have persisted long term. I met the first professional farmer, Ah Yin, while he was working in the fields in 2011. He told me how he successfully grew a kind of tomato, which he later sold at a very good price to a restaurant serving European cuisine. Ah Yin, however, dropped out from farming after a year because the income was too low and there was too much climate uncertainty and market risk involved. Another university graduate, Gar Son, joined Ma Shi Po as a professional farmer in 2012 after farming infrastructure such as the anti-pest nets had been installed. With an improved harvest, Gar Son told me in a short conversation in 2014 summer that he could now earn an average monthly income of 10,000 HKD (approximately $1,200), but even that is subject to seasonal fluctuation. Gar Son's decision to become a farmer has attracted some media attention (Slivia 2013; Lee Pui Man 2013), however, farming as a career is not yet an attractive option for most young people.

To conclude this section briefly, Ma Shi Po farmers are committed to bringing a global community-based urban agriculture movement to Hong Kong. More than that, however, they have worked to strategically highlight the ecological, social, and political aspects of practicing farming in the context of Hong Kong's real estate dominance. They propose that not only should farming be vigorously defended for the purposes of local food provision; it should also be expanded so as to improve community well-being and to create a more sustainable urban lifestyle. In many ways, the Ma Shi Po campaign points to a brand new understanding of environmental movement, farming practice, and the sustainability of urban community by highlighting their interdependence. The permaculture workshops have made members become reflexively aware of everyday life practices and their role as potential agents of change (Lewis 2015, p. 354). Many gain not only a sense of empowerment but also a new sense of civic engagement and social activism that highlight the roles of bodily skills, working with new tools, and the natural environment (Lewis 2015).

The permaculture workshop thus sets out to define new norms, alternative ways of consuming, and living at the individual level. At the social level, it shakes up the deep-rooted belief that the decline of the farming sector is part of an inevitable and irreversible trend. It also ardently questions the popular opinion that Hong Kong does not need farming at all because it can easily rely on imported food from mainland China. Through its advocacy for urban-rural coexistence, Ma Shi Po activism successfully emerges as an urban farming alternative in the New Territories, which for the first time in Hong Kong history articulates problems and issues regarding real estate dominance and food security and advocates community gardens as an alternative food source.

New nodal points of politics and identity in Hong Kong

As the demolition plan approached, the Ma Shi Po community farm gradually extended their campaign beyond Fanling in order to gather more social support. The activists collaborated with major universities by holding seminars and cultural festivals and establishing exhibits that highlighted the importance of preserving farmland and village communities in the New Territories (Yuen Hau Yan 2014). In response, university students have set up groups on agricultural development and concerned artists went to make art and documentaries at Ma Shi Po (Yuen Hau Yan 2013; Ng Sai Ling 2014). Inspired by the Ma Shi Po campaign, a group of artists designed a program called "Art Travel Learning on Urban Rural Co-existence" in 2014 and put together an exhibition of agricultural and household tools combined with an oral history documentary of villagers and farmers in the New Territories. Theatre artists have also made the Ma Shi Po story into a staged performance (Kafka 2014). In other words, the Ma Shi Po campaign has actively engaged with the educated classes, art communities, and other social organizations so as to popularize their message. In the process, many young people have become keen supporters of this cause.

Indeed, Ma Shi Po activism speaks directly to a younger generation of citizens who were born and grew up in Hong Kong after 1997. The Ma Shi Po campaign is attractive because it helps to imagine a different kind of community and development in Hong Kong by enabling a very different narrative and understanding of the city. The history of Hong Kong is often narrated as follows: It developed from a small fishing village to today's global financial center under the reign of benign British colonialism, and its legacy is the rule of law and the value of economic liberalism. This narrative is taught in schools, reiterated in travel books and tightly integrated into the politics of place identity. Such a narrative, however, often works most favorably for global business elites, advocates for unending economic development, and easily neglects peoples' interests at the grassroots as well as their many micro- and local histories of place.

Agriculture in the New Territories (by indigenous and later by non-indigenous tenants) is a major "micro"-history of Hong Kong that is rarely mentioned in the "official" or mainstream discourse. But the Ma Shi Po campaign has nicely articulated a micro-history of the New Territories and woven it into a major development debate that concerns today's Hong Kong. The campaign reminds us that agriculture has been central to the region for at least 300 years, well before the commencement of British colonialism. Agricultural development also had a significant renaissance after World War Two when many migrated from southern Chinese towns such as Nanhai, Panyu, and Shunde and brought to Hong Kong new vegetable species, farming methods, and associated communities and local cultures (Janice 2014). For many young people in Hong Kong, Ma Shi Po's rural activism is therefore about rescuing and/or re-valuing a major part of Hong Kong's history, culture, and identity that has been largely forgotten in the hegemonic narrative of Hong Kong as a global financial center. It helps the younger generation to think about how Hong Kong can chart a path that is different from the past and that promotes a new sense of sustainable community.

Ma Shi Po's opposition to the development of the northeastern New Territories, just across the mainland border, also makes it central to recent debates about the position of Hong Kong as a special administrative district of China after 1997. Hong Kong relies heavily on China for all kinds of resources (such as food, power, and

Farming against real estate dominance 181

water) but also, in recent years, economic growth and jobs through tourism from the mainland. Many citizens consider that this increasing dependence on China threatens the autonomy that Hong Kong enjoys under the Sino-British agreement of "One country Two systems". They hence believe that Hong Kong is becoming more vulnerable to interventions from Beijing in its public sphere—in such areas as its press, and freedom of speech more generally, and in determining candidates for local government elections. There is a growing local movement that aims to reestablish a sense of Hong Kong's cultural distinctiveness and unique colonial identity in order to resist increasing influence from China. In this context, even though the Ma Shi Po campaign is mainly about preserving urban farm communities, it is inevitably part of broader social debates about Hong Kong politics, local identity and the future of development. It also raises many questions about whether Hong Kong should integrate more with mainland China through urban growth or maintain a certain distance through reviving traditional farming communities.

Conclusion

On June 6, 2014, several hundred protesters, composed mainly of tenant farmers and university students, had a large-scale sit-in outside of the Legislative Council (Legco) Building when the finance committee met to approve the budget for the initial engineering works of the northeastern New Territories Development Plan. The rally successfully interrupted the meeting after protesters stormed into the building, breached security lines, and forced the government to schedule a second finance committee meeting. Knowing that the Ma Shi Po campaign would mobilize even more supporters against the second meeting, the Legco and the Hong Kong police responded by raising the security level and zoning away the protest area from the main building (Chong and Cheung 2014). The event drew more attention to the new social activism and provoked heated debate about the conventional economic growth model, the city's housing shortage, and changing young people's aspirations.

The Ma Shi Po campaign may have originally intended to defend a small group of tenants' resident rights and forge a grassroots response to government land planning in the New Territories, but the movement has grown to become a major local movement in post-1997 politics and has provoked reflection on the identity and direction of Hong Kong society. In this chapter, I have argued that the efforts of Ma Shi Po rural activists to preserve farmland in the New Territories have formed a major site of "counter-hegemonic democratic politics" (Dirlik and Prazniak 2001, p. 3) in Hong Kong in the last few years by mounting a critique of the prevailing models of real estate development and urban planning and the loss of local rural communities. Through petitioning against the demolition of a small farming village, the movement has staged a lifestyle-based and yet highly political environmental campaign that touches on global environmental concerns, lifestyle consumption practices, local community development, and the socioeconomic problems that are specific to Hong Kong.

I argue that the rural activism in Ma Shi Po has been successful in sparking new public debate about farming by casting it as a political concern that has several dimensions. First, the Ma Shi Po campaign has made it possible for marginalized farmers to defend their way of life, their homes, and their livelihoods against the increasing urban sprawl of Hong Kong. Second, the campaign is the first to raise the possibility of having farmland coexist with urban neighborhoods in Hong Kong. Third, through promoting ethical consumption practices and lifestyles and art, cultural, and communal projects, the activities of Ma Shi Po activists contribute to a new micro-political, lifestyle-based as well as place-based identity politics and social activism in post-colonial Hong Kong.

I discussed how the rural activism of Ma Shi Po has created a unique space that speaks to global environmental concerns and local political, economic, and environmental problems. In many ways, this case of rural activism is one instantiation of the global community gardens movement that provide opportunities for urbanites to dirty their hands, grow their own organic food, develop stronger neighborhood relations, and improve community health and well-being (Armstrong 2000; Firth, Maye, and Pearson 2011). And even though the size of Ma Po Po's community farm is comparatively small, its activists consistently address concerns about food security and the importance of Hong Kong having its own food production (Green Local Trend 2013). Through its farmers' market and various workshops, the campaign links its struggle to global critiques of modern industrial agricultural systems, which are producing unhealthy, processed food and harming both the environment and the people. Although the Hong Kong activists seldom use the term "alternative food network", which is one of the major concerns of community garden advocates in the Euro-American context (Anderson and Cook 1999; Evers and Hodgson 2011), they are expressing similar aims when they speak about the necessity of having urban neighborhood farms instead of relying entirely on imported food from China.

The case of rural activism in Ma Shi Po both resonates with community gardens movements in many parts of the world (Baker 2004) and makes unique interventions in the local context as it addresses the problem of real estate dominance and questions the conventional growth model and the colonial narrative of Hong Kong history and society. This activism has differed from that of conventional party politics, which is often protest-based and relies on a few elite spokesmen. Instead, it extends the meanings of civic engagement to include lifestyle consumption practices and patterns of everyday life in late modernity (Lewis 2015). This has won much support, especially from the younger generation for its ability to connect a green transformational politics with a new form of community making. The rural activism of Ma Shi Po offers a glimpse into the changing sociocultural and geopolitical landscape of post-colonial Hong Kong, in which government policy, land planning, place-based cultural identity, food security of the special administrative region, and lifestyle practices and micro-political activism have become tightly intertwined.

Notes

1 See http://mapopo.wordpress.com/about/
2 These four land developer conglomerates are (1) Cheung Kong Holdings, (2) Sun Hung Kei Properties, (3) Henderson Land Development Companies Limited, and (4) Hong Kong Landholdings Limited.
3 The Northeastern New Territories Concern Group is a grassroots organization initiated by some of the Ma Shi Po activists. It is based in Ma Shi Po but extends its activists' concern to other areas of the New Territories. The group's objectives are to advocate residents' rights, implement democratic planning, defend local agriculture, resume village life, and protect natural ecology. See http://www.northeastntconcern.blogspot.hk

References

Anderson, Molly D., and John T. Cook. 1999. "Community Food Security: Practice in Need of Theory?" *Agriculture and Human Values* 16 (2): 141–50.
Armstrong, Donna. 2000. "A Survey of Community Gardens in Upstate New York: Implications for Health Promotion and Community Development." *Health & Place* 6 (4): 319–27.
Baker, Lauren E. 2004. "Tending Cultural Landscapes and Food Citizenship in Toronto's Community Gardens." *Geographical Review* 94 (3): 305–25.
Barnett, Clive, Nick Clarke, Paul Cloke, and Alice Malpass. 2005. "The Political Ethics of Consumerism." *Consumer Policy Review* 15 (2): 45–51.
Chan Chun Kit. 2010. "That Day, I Made a Bread that Breaths." *Next Magazine, Food Lovers,* November 19.
Chong, Tanna, and Gary Cheung. 2014. "Protestors Storm Legco over Northeastern New Territories Plan." *South China Morning Post,* June 7.
Dirlik, Arif, and Roxann Prazniak. 2001. "Introduction: Cultural Identity and the Politics of Place." In *Places and Politics in an Age of Globalization,* edited by Roxann Pranzniak and Arif Dirlik, 3–13. Oxford and New York: Rowman & Littlefield Publishers.
Evers, Anna, and Nicole Louise Hodgson. 2011. "Food Choices and Local Food Access among Perth's Community Gardeners." *Local Environment: The International Journal of Justice and Sustainability* 16 (6): 585–602.
Firth, Chris, Damian Maye, and David Pearson. 2011. "Developing 'Community' in Community Gardens." *Local Environment: The International Journal of Justice and Sustainability* 16 (6): 555–68.
Goodstadt, Leo F. 2005. *Uneasy Partners: The Conflict between Public Interests and Private Profits in Hong Kong.* Hong Kong: Hong Kong University Press.
Goodstadt, Leo F. 2013. *Poverty in the Midst of Affluence: How Hong Kong Mismanaged its Prosperity.* Hong Kong: Hong Kong University Press.
Green Life. 2013. "From the Past to Present, Old Market Now and Then." *Next Magazine, Food Lovers,* April 12.
Green Local Trend. 2013. "How Much, How Good? Self-Reliance!" *Weekend Weekly,* G025, June 10.
Hassanein, Neva. 2003. "Practicing Food Democracy: A Pragmatic Politics of Transformation." *Journal of Rural Studies* 19 (1): 77–86.
Janice. 2014. "Living museum, Ma Po Po, Community farm." *Hong Kong Daily News,* Q18–19, February 26.

Kafka. 2014. "Ignorance of the Nostalgic, Recklessness of the Demonstrator: Love for the Urban and Rural." *Hong Kong Economic Journal*, C01, January 30.

Law, On Kei. 2013. "Ma Shi Po Perspective: Photo Tour." *Sing Tao Daily*, E02, October 18.

Law, Wai Yee. 2013. "Go to Countryside, Look at the Farms and Appreciate the Ecology." *Hong Kong Economic Times*, C09, September 11.

Lee, Pui Man. 2013. "Weekend Market, Rural Urban Linkage." *Ming Pao*, S03, January 20.

Lewis, Tania. 2008. "Transforming Citizens? Green Politics and Ethical Consumption on Lifestyle Television." *Continuum: Journal of Media and Cultural Studies* 22 (20): 227–40.

Lewis, Tania. 2015. "'One City Block at a Time': Researching and Cultivating Green Transformations." *International Journal of Cultural Studies* 18 (3): 347–63.

Lui Yek. 2013. "Local Organic Revolution." *Cup Magazine*, February 1, 66–77.

Man, Si Wai. 2014. "Hong Kong Style Environmental Protection. Who Does it Serve?" *Inmedia*, February 27. Accessed September 13, 2015. http://www.inmediahk.net/1021176

Miller, Toby. *Cultural Citizenship: Cosmopolitanism, Consumerism, and Television in a Neoliberal Age*. Philadelphia, PA: Temple University Press.

Ng, Sai Ling. 2014. "Exhibits of 'countryside' in the Heart of City, Power of Art for Northeastern Style." *Ming Pao Daily*, D02, January 24.

Ng, Wing Sheung. 2013. "Summer Holiday DIY." *Next Magazine, Food Lovers*, July 4.

Poon, Alice. 2010. *Land and the Ruling Class in Hong Kong*. 2nd ed. Singapore: Enrich Professional Publishing.

Seyfang, Gill. 2006. "Ecological Citizenship and Sustainable Consumption: Examining Local Organic Food Networks." *Journal of Rural Studies* 22 (4): 383–95.

Slivia. 2013. "Ma Po Po: Farming dreams of the post-80 generation." *The Sun Daily*, E02 and E03, June 8.

Watson, James L., and Rubie Sharon Watson. 2004. *Village Life in Hong Kong: Politics, Gender, and Rituals in the New Territories*. Hong Kong: Chinese University Press.

Yuen Hau Yan. 2013. "Back to Agriculture Fun in Chinese University Life Festival." *Sing Dao Daily*, F02, March 6..

Yuen Hau Yan. 2014. "Cultural Festival for the Thirty Anniversary of City University of Hong Kong." *Sing Tao Daily*, F02, February 12.

Žižek, Slavoj. 2014. "Fat-Free Chocolate and Absolutely No Smoking: Why Our Guilt about Consumption is All-Consuming." *The Guardian*, May 21. Accessed September 13, 3015. http://www.theguardian.com/artanddesign/2014/may/21/prix-pictet-photography-prize-consumption-slavoj-zizek.

Index

Bold page numbers indicate figures, *italic* numbers indicate tables.

advertising, responses to green messages in 108
agency of non-humans 52–3
agriculture. *See* community farming in Hong Kong; urban farming; natural farming in Taiwan
Agyeman, J. 144, 145
air-conditioning: history 23–4; increased usage 21, **22**; and indoor/outdoor spaces 22; lack of environmental attention given to 21; science of indoor comfort 23–4; Singapore 21, **22**; and social practice theory 29–33; and societal trends 26–7. *See also* thermal comfort
air quality monitoring in China: citizen-initiated 114–15; citizen/official 119–21; communication channels 125; Community Air Monitoring network 126; community-based 115–16, 119, 126; complaints system 117; concerns over air quality 114–15; environmental NGOs 119–25, 126; grassroots monitoring 116–18, 126; Internet-based 118, 121–3, 125; local knowledge and capacity for 115–16; microblogging 118, 121–3; NGO organized 115; public reporting 117; relationship-building 125
Amin, A. 69
Amine, L.S. 39
Antil, J.H. 38
architecture: and thermal comfort 27–8; thermal comfort as domain of 24–6, **25**
architecture, green 24–6, **25**
Asia, focus on, need for 2–3

Bailey, O.G. 147
Barr, M. 5
Barrett, B.F.D. 144
Bawa, G. 28
Beck, U, 11
Berkhout, F. 9
Berlant, L. 131
Berque, A. 161
bird sanctuaries in Singapore 75–6, 78
Brand, U. 2, 7
Broadbent, J. 144
Brundtland Report 37
Bryman, A. 73, 77
Bullard, R.D. 145

Calhoun, C. 11, 12, 99, 101, 104, 107
camera phone practices 130–3; *Shibuya: Underground Streams* project 136, **136**, **137**, **138**, 138–9
Cammaerts, B. 147
Carpentier, N. 147
cartographies of Tokyo 129
cause-related marketing 40; India 45–6, *46*
celebrity endorsement 41–2
Chakrabarty, D. 46
Chan Chun Kit 174
Changi Airport, Singapore **71**, 71–3, **72**, **73**
Charter, M. 39
China: achievements, environmental 100, 102; awareness of environmental issues 100; capacity to enforce environmental policies 100; censorship 102–3; commodification of 'green' 107–10; consumer-oriented television 105; consumption practices 107–10; diversity as media policy 103–4; economy and stability as government focus 102; environmental NGOs 103; event-driven environmentalism 102; governance,

environmental 4–5; green economy 108; as green modernizer 10–11; green public sphere 99–100, 107; greenspeak discourse 99, 107; health risks and environmental issues 106–7; impact of non-official monitoring 123–5; lifestyle television programmes 104–7; *Low Carbon Everyday* TV programme 109–10; politization of environmental issues 101; responses to green messages 108; stability maintenance 101; state media 101–7, 108–9; television programmes 104–7, 108–10; Travel TV 108–9. *See also* air quality monitoring in China
Chua Beng Huat 8
cities. *See* urban farming
City in a Garden, Singapore as 68–9
civil society in South East Asia 4, 5
clothing practices 30
comfort practices. *See* thermal comfort
commodification: of 'green' in China 107–10; of nature and eco-tourism in the Philippines 92–3
communities: of actors 12; revitalization of 148, 150
community farming in Hong Kong: bread making workshop 174–5; campaign of 172–4; civic engagement of consumers 174–6; extended campaign 179–80; farm tours 173–4; farming as political concern 181–2; founding of Ma Shi Po 172; growth of movement 181; impact of 178–9; increasing Chinese influence in area 180–1; indigenous inhabitants of Hong Kong 170; and local identity 180–1; media coverage 174; New Territories of Hong Kong 170; permaculture workshop 176–9; political and social concerns of 177–9; real estate dominance 170–1, 176; as redefining local activism 169–70; resistance to corporate power 176; vanishing farmlands 170–1. *See also* natural farming in Taiwan; urban farming
consumption: Asian middle classes 7–8; China, practices in 107–10; consumer-oriented television in China 105; ethical consumption, temporal/spatial ramifications of 38; green and ethical consumer markets 5; hybrid 77, 78
cooperative living associations in Korea: alternative food supply chain 142; alternative media, use of 146–8; civil/state power 146; *dure* (cooperative labor) 143, 148–9; *Dure* living co-op 148; encouragement of 142; equality and sustainability 144, 151; food production communities 149–50; *Hansalim* 149–50; Hope Institute 142; key issues 146; lack of research into 143; local food production 149–50; *ma-eul* 148, 150; 'moving back to the village' phenomenon 142–3, 150–1; neoliberalism in Korea 145; podcasts 147–8; revitalization of communities 150; Seongmisan *ma-eul* 148; social enterprise 144–5; socio-political climate 142–3; sustainability and economic development 143
cosmopolitian perspective 11
culinary experiences in Singapore 74–7
culture as capitalist strategy in Singapore 66

Disneyization 73
domestic eco-tourism. *See* Philippines, eco-tourism in
dure (cooperative labor) 143, 148–9
Dussel, E.D. 8–9

eating. *See* food and eating
eco-culture, Singapore as 68–9; air-conditioning usage 21, **22**; Changi Airport **71**, 71–3, **72**, **73**; as City in a Garden 68–9; culture/nature/affect combination 68–9; as eco-culture 68–9; experience economy 70–3, **71**, **72**, **73**; food and eating 74–7, 77–8; Gardens by the Bay project 69; as Global City of Buzz 67; greening of 67–8; hybrid consumption 78; memory and food 77–8; senses, exploitation of 69–73, **71**, **72**, **73**, 77–8; synaesthesia 77; themed environments 73, 77; urban wilds 68–9; wildlife encounters 75–6; zoos and bird sanctuaries 75–6, 78
eco-tourism. *See* eco-culture, Singapore as; Philippines, eco-tourism in
economic development: real estate development in Hong Kong 170–1, 176; and sustainability 143
Edo 165
education and moblogs 131
engineering, thermal comfort as domain of 24–6, **25**
environmental movement in South East Asia 4–6

equality and sustainability 144, 151
Esty, D.C. 38
ethical consumption, temporal/spatial ramifications of 38
Evans, B. 145
event-driven environmentalism in China 102
everyday environmentalisms: communities of actors 12; focus on 1; importance of 1–3
experience economy 70–3

Fanger, O. 23–4
fans 30–1, **31**
Farman, J. 130
farming. *See* community farming in Hong Kong; natural farming in Taiwan; urban farming
Fergus, N. 32
Fletcher, R. 81–2
food and eating: and memory 77–8; production communities 149–50; in Singapore 74–7. *See also* community farming in Hong Kong; natural farming in Taiwan; urban farming
Frow, J. 75
Fujii, M. 165
furniture design and thermal comfort **31,** 31–2

games, mobile 135
Geall, S. 5
Global City of Buzz, Singapore as 67
governance, environmental 4–6
grassroots movements: air quality monitoring in China 116–18, 126; South East Asia 4, 5. *See also* community farming in Hong Kong; urban farming
green architecture 24–6, **25**
green consumerism: cause-related marketing 40; emergence and definition of 38–9
green credentials, success of 27
green economy in China 108
green issues, market impact of 38
green marketing: cause-related marketing 40, 45–6, *46*; celebrity endorsement 41–2; challenges of 39, 42; definition 39; as double-edged sword 47; India 40–4, *43, 44*; paradoxes 46–7
green modernities 8–11
green public sphere in China 99–100, 107
greenspeak discourse 99, 107
greenwash 107

half-farmer-half-X 158–9
Hansalim 149–50
Hawkins, R. 46
health risks and environmental issues in China 106–7
Ho, P. 101
Hoffman, L. 10
Hope Institute 142
Howes, D. 70
Hseuh, Y.-F. 60
Hsiao, H.-H.M. 117
Huang, R. 118
Humphreys, H. 32
hybrid consumption 77, 78

India: cause-related marketing 40, 45–6, 46; celebrity endorsement 41–2; green marketing 40–4, 43, 44; legislation 40; Mission Swachh Bharat (Clean India) campaign 41–2
indigenous people: Hong Kong 170; marginalization of in the Philippines 85–6, 94
indoor/outdoor spaces and air-conditioning 22
insect-damaged tea leaves 53–4
Internet: air quality monitoring in China 118, 121–3, 125; cooperative living associations in Korea 146–8; food production communities 149; podcasts 147–8. *See also* mobile media

Japan: 3/11 Earthquake 132–3; camera phone practices 130–3; cartographies of Tokyo 129; environmentalism in 133–4; governance, environmental: 4; intimate-public blurring 131–2; keitai mizu 136, **136, 137, 138,** 138–9; sense of place 130–3; Shibuya: Underground Streams project 136, **136, 137, 138,** 138–9. See also Shibuya: Underground Streams project; urban farming
Jay, M. 70
Joo, K.-H. 150

Kashiwa City, Chiba Prefecture 163–4
keitai mizu 136, **136, 137, 138,** 138–9
Keogh, B. 135
Kito, S. 158
Korea: governance, environmental 4. *See also* cooperative living associations in Korea
Koskinen, I. 130

labor, cooperative (dure) 143, 148–9
land development in Hong Kong 170–1
Law On Kei 172
Lewis, T. 117
life-work balance in Japan 157–9
lifestyle(s): Asian middle classes 7–8; green and ethical consumer markets 5; shifting norms around 6–7
living co-ops. *See* cooperative living associations in Korea
local food production 149–50
Low Carbon Everyday TV programme 109–10
Lubin, D.A. 38

ma-eul 148, 150
Ma Shi Po community farm in Hong Kong: bread making workshop 174–5; campaign of 172–4; civic engagement of consumers 174–6; extended campaign 179–80; farm tours 173–4; farming as political concern 181–2; founding of 172; growth of movement 181; impact of 178–9; increasing Chinese influence in area 180–1; indigenous inhabitants of Hong Kong 170; media coverage 174; New Territories of Hong Kong 170; permaculture workshop 176–9; political and social concerns of 177–9; real estate dominance 170–1, 176; as redefining local activism 169–70; resistance to corporate power 176; vanishing farmlands 170–1
Ma Tianjie 102–3
Macnaghten, P. 67, 76
marketing, responses to green messages in 108
Martens, S. 118
materiality 53
May, S. 10
media: air quality monitoring in China 125; cooperative living associations in Korea 146–8; state media in China 101–7; television programmes in China 104–7, 108–9
microblogging of air quality monitoring in China 118, 121–3, 125
middle classes 7–8
Mission Swachh Bharat (Clean India) campaign 41–2
mobile media: 3/11 Earthquake 132–3; camera phone practices 130–3; and environmental concerns 132–3; environmentalism in Japan 133–4; games 135; intimate-public blurring 131–2; *keitai mizu* 136, **136, 137, 138**, 138–9; location-based services 130; qualitative research using 132; and sense of place 130–3; *Shibuya: Underground Streams* project 136, **136, 137, 138**, 138–9; in traumatic times 134–5. *See also* Internet; social media
moblogs 131
modernity: multiple modernities 8–11; tropical modernism 27–8
Molyvann, V. 27–8
multiple modernities 8–11

national eco-tourism. See Philippines, eco-tourism in
natural farming in Taiwan: agency of non-humans 52–3; constraints on practitioners 54; ecosystem, tea fields as 53–6; experience of tea makers 59–60; insect-damaged tea leaves 53–4; local environment and tea processing 58–9; materiality of tea 53, 60; plants and animals surrounding 51; processing of tea 56–60; producer/non-human world relationship 54–6; quality of tea 57; 'relying on heaven' notion 52, 55–6; small green leaf hoppers 53–4; style of tea making and the market 61–2; tea produced 52. *See also* community farming in Hong Kong; urban farming
neoliberalism in Korea 145
New Territories of Hong Kong 170
Ng, C. 76
non-humans, agency of 52–3

Ong, A. 8
Ortolano, L. 117
Ottman, J. 39
outdoor/indoor spaces and air-conditioning 22

Pantzar, M. 24, 29, 33
Peattie, K. 39
Petersen, S.M. 130
Philippines, eco-tourism in: Central Palawan Island 83–6, *84,* **85**; commodification of nature 92–3; day trip to PPUR 90–3; domestic eco-tourism 83–4, *84,* 95; increased visitors to PPUR, impact of 88–90; indigenous people, marginalization of 85–6, 94; methodology for case study 83; national support for 81–3; privatization of nature 94; Puerto

Princesa Subterranean River National Park (PPSRNP) 84–6; Puerto Princesa Underground River (PPUR) 84; transformation of spaces 93–4; travel 84; voting campaign for PPUR-N7WN 86, **87, 88**
Pink, S. 130
play-work 158–9
podcasts 147–8
pollution. *See* air quality monitoring in China
Polonsky, M. 39
Postrel, V. 70
Potter, E. 117
privatization of nature 92–3, 94
Puerto Princesa Subterranean River National Park (PPSRNP) 84–6, 88–90, 93–4
Puerto Princesa Underground River (PPUR) 84, 90–3, 93–4
punkah fans 30–1

real estate development in Hong Kong 170–1, 176
'relying on heaven' notion 52, 55–6
rental garden program 163
Roaf, R. 32

Schatzki, T.R. 29
science of indoor comfort 23–4
Seksan, N. 28
senses, exploitation of 69–73, **71, 72, 73**, 77–8
Seongmisan *ma-eul* 148
Shah, P. 39
Shibuya: Underground Streams project 129, 136, **136, 137, 138**, 138–9
Shove, E. 6–7, 24, 29, 33
Singapore: air-conditioning usage 21, **22**; Changi Airport **71**, 71–3, **72, 73**; as City in a Garden 68–9; culture as capitalist strategy 66; culture/nature/affect combination 68–9; as eco-culture 68–9; experience economy 70–3, **71, 72, 73**; food and eating 74–7, 77–8; Gardens by the Bay project 69; as Global City of Buzz 67; greening of 67–8; hybrid consumption 77, 78; memory and food 77–8; senses, exploitation of 69–73, **71, 72, 73**, 77–8; societal trends and thermal comfort 26–7; synaesthesia 77; themed environments 73, 77; urban wilds 68–9; wildlife encounters 75–6, 78; zoos and bird sanctuaries 75–6, 78

Skillington, T. 11
Slater, D.H. 133–4
small green leaf hoppers 53–4
social activism in South East Asia 4, 5
social enterprise in Korea 144–5
social media: 3/11 Earthquake 132–3; air quality monitoring in China 118, 121–3, 125; cooperative living associations in Korea 146–8; food production communities 149; intimate-public blurring 131–2; sense of place 130–3. *See also* mobile media
social practice theory 6–7; and thermal comfort 29–33
socio-technical regimes 9
South East Asia: environmental movement 4–6; focus on, need for 2–3; governance, environmental: 4-6
state media: air quality monitoring in China 125; China 101–7, 108–9
Strengers, Y. 26, 29
sustainability: and economic development 143; and human equality 144, 151; market impact 38
Sutton, D. 77–8
synaesthesia 77

Taiwan: governance, environmental 4. See also tea farming in Taiwan
Taylor, J. 133
tea farming in Taiwan: agency of non-humans 52–3; constraints on natural farming practitioners 54; ecosystem, tea fields as 53–6; experience of tea makers 59–60; insect-damaged tea leaves 53–4; local environment and tea processing 58–9; materiality of tea 53, 60; plants and animals surrounding 51; processing of tea 56–60; producer/non-human world relationship 54–6; quality of tea 57; 'relying on heaven' notion 52, 55–6; small green leaf hoppers 53–4; style of tea making and the market 61–2; tea produced 52
technology, thermal comfort as domain of 24–6, **25**
television programmes in China 104–7, 108–10
textiles and clothing practices 30
themed environments 73, 77
thermal comfort: as accomplishment 30; architecture based approaches 27–8; colonial practices 32–3; as engineering/technology/architecture domain 24–6, **25**; fans 30–1, **31**; furniture design **31**, 31–2;

individual control 27; outdoor/indoor spaces 22; persistance/disappearance of practices 32–3; science of indoor comfort 23–4; social practice theory 29–33; and societal trends 26–7; textiles and clothing practices 30; tradition based approaches 27–8; tropical modernism 27–8. *See also* air-conditioning

Thrift, N. 67, 69

Tokyo: cartographies of 129. *See also Shibuya: Underground Streams* project; urban farming

tourism: increased attention to environmental issues 20–1. *See also* eco-culture, Singapore as; Philippines, eco-tourism in

transformation of spaces 93–4

tropical modernism 27–8

Understanding Alternative Media (Bailey, Cammaerts and Carpentier) 147

urban farming: amount of food produced 163; benefits of urban farming 155–6; development of 159–62, **160**; Edo 165; half-farmer-half-X 158–9; Kashiwa City, Chiba Prefecture 163–4; life-work balance in Japan 157–9; opportunities for 163–5, **164**; planning, urban, rethinking of 161–2; play-work 158–9; rental garden program 163; revitalization of cities through 162–5, **164**; universality/uniqueness 156, **157**; vacant lots 162–3; work culture, changes in 156–9; worldwide interest in urban farming 155. *See also* community farming in Hong Kong; natural farming in Taiwan

urban wilds in Singapore 68–9

Urry, J. 7, 67, 76

Warwick, M. 117

Watanabe, T. 165

Watson, M. 24, 29, 33

wildlife encounters in Singapore 75–6, 78

Wissen, M. 2, 7

work culture, changes in Japan 156–9

Yang, G. 99, 101, 104, 107

Yip, N. 118

Yokohari, M. 165

Zhang, J.Y. 5

Žižek, S. 175

zoos and bird sanctuaries in Singapore 75–6, 78